"Exhaustive, inclusive, and innovative, *Reimagining Mobilities across the Humanities* is a treat for both professionals and newcomers to this discipline and capable of generating new ideas and perspectives. I wholeheartedly recommend it to a broad audience, confident that it will pique their interest in the ever-expanding field of mobility studies."

Hager Ben Driss, Associate Professor of English,
University of Tunis, Tunisia

"Mobilities of ideas and concepts, of material things and images – are just some of the cases considered in theoretically sophisticated and geographically diverse chapters. *Reimagining Mobilities* is a foundational work as it provides a unique tool to understand mobilities in history, from ancient times to the present."

Giorgio Riello, Chair of Early Modern Global History,
European University Institute, Italy

Reimagining Mobilities across the Humanities

Volume 1: Theories, Methods and Ideas explores the mobility of ideas through time and space and how interdisciplinary theories and methodological approaches used in mobilities studies can be profitably utilised within the humanities and social sciences. Through a series of short chapters, mobility is employed as an elastic, inclusive and multifaceted concept across various disciplines to shed light on a geographically and chronologically broad range of issues and case studies. In doing so, the concept of mobility is positioned as a powerful catalyst for historical change and as a fruitful approach to research in the humanities and social sciences.

Like its sister volume, this volume is edited and written by members of the Centre for Advanced Studies in Mobility and the Humanities (MoHu) at the Department of Historical and Geographical Sciences and The Ancient World (DiSSGeA) of the University of Padua, Italy. The structure of the book mirrors the Theories and Methods, and Ideas thematic research clusters of the Centre. Afterwords from leading scholars from other institutions synthesise and reflect upon the findings of each section.

This volume, together with *Volume 2: Objects, People and Texts*, makes a compelling case for the use of mobility studies as a research framework in the humanities and social sciences. As such, it will be of interest to students and researchers in various disciplines.

Lucio Biasiori is associate professor of early modern history at the University of Padua, Italy. He was previously a fellow of the Harvard Center for Italian Renaissance Studies in Florence, Italy, and assistant professor in early modern history at the Scuola Normale Superiore di Pisa, Italy. His research encompasses the early modern period, with particular reference to the cultural, religious and political history of 16th-century Europe, studied in an interdisciplinary and cross-cultural framework.

Federico Mazzini is associate professor of digital history and history of media and communication at the University of Padua, Italy. His previous work has focused on the sociocultural history of the First World War, particularly the peasant experience of the trenches and the popularisation of technoscience.

He is currently working on various aspects of digital history, including web archiving, metadata and historical communication online, and 'technical cultures', such as radio hams, phreaks and hackers, in the 20th century.

Chiara Rabbiosi is associate professor of economic and political geography at the University of Padua, Italy. Her previous research has dealt with the social and spatial dimensions of urban studies and consumer culture, including the critical geographies of shopping tourism, cultural heritage and place branding. She is currently working on tourist spatial imaginations of Europe, and on the transit of tourism (including walking and multi-modal transport), approaching tourism mobilities in an embodied and performative way.

Changing Mobilities

This series explores the transformations of society, politics and everyday experiences wrought by changing mobilities, and the power of mobilities research to inform constructive responses to these transformations. As a new mobile century is taking shape, international scholars explore motivations, experiences, insecurities, implications and limitations of mobile living, and opportunities and challenges for design in the broadest sense, from policy to urban planning, new media and technology design. With world citizens expected to travel 105 billion kilometres per year in 2050, it is critical to make mobilities research and design inform each other.

Series Editors: Monika Büscher, Peter Adey

Alternative (Im)Mobilities
Edited by Maria Alice de Faria Nogueira

Reimagining Mobilities across the Humanities
Two volume set
Edited by Lucio Biasiori, Federico Mazzini and Chiara Rabbiosi

Reimagining Mobilities across the Humanities
Volume 1: Theories, Methods and Ideas
Edited by Lucio Biasiori, Federico Mazzini and Chiara Rabbiosi

Reimagining Mobilities across the Humanities
Volume 2: Objects, People and Texts
Edited by Lucio Biasiori, Federico Mazzini and Chiara Rabbiosi

For a full list of titles in this series, please visit www.routledge.com/Changing-Mobilities/book-series/CHGMOB

DiSSGeA

DIPARTIMENTO DI SCIENZE STORICHE GEOGRAFICHE E DELL'ANTICHITÀ

MOHU

MOBILITY & HUMANITIES
Centre for Advanced Studies

Reimagining Mobilities across the Humanities

Volume 1: Theories, Methods and Ideas

Edited by Lucio Biasiori, Federico Mazzini and Chiara Rabbiosi

LONDON AND NEW YORK

First published 2023
by Routledge
4 Park Square, Milton Park, Abingdon, Oxon OX14 4RN

and by Routledge
605 Third Avenue, New York, NY 10158

Routledge is an imprint of the Taylor & Francis Group, an informa business

© 2023 selection and editorial matter, Lucio Biasiori, Federico Mazzini and Chiara Rabbiosi; individual chapters, the contributors

The right of Lucio Biasiori, Federico Mazzini and Chiara Rabbiosi to be identified as the authors of the editorial material, and of the authors of their individual chapters, has been asserted in accordance with sections 77 and 78 of the Copyright, Designs and Patents Act 1988.

All rights reserved. No part of this book may be reprinted or reproduced or utilised in any form or by any electronic, mechanical, or other means, now known or hereafter invented, including photocopying and recording, or in any information storage or retrieval system, without permission in writing from the publishers.

Trademark notice: Product or corporate names may be trademarks or registered trademarks, and are used only for identification and explanation without intent to infringe.

British Library Cataloguing-in-Publication Data
A catalogue record for this book is available from the British Library

ISBN: 978-1-032-24454-9 (hbk)
ISBN: 978-1-032-24448-8 (pbk)
ISBN: 978-1-003-27866-5 (ebk)

DOI: 10.4324/9781003278665

Typeset in Times New Roman
by Newgen Publishing UK

Printed in the United Kingdom
by Henry Ling Limited

Contents

List of figures xi
List of tables xii

Introduction to Volume 1: Theories, methods and ideas 1
LUCIO BIASIORI, FEDERICO MAZZINI AND CHIARA RABBIOSI

SECTION 1
Theories and methods 5

1 "Moving textuality" in early modern Europe 7
   PAOLA MOLINO

2 The challenge of mobility for commodity chains: time, actors, and value from an historical perspective 22
   MARCO BERTILORENZI, ANDREA CARACAUSI, CARLO FUMIAN AND BENOÎT MARÉCHAUX

3 Mobilizing pictures: the history of science through the lens of mobility 38
   ELENA CANADELLI

4 Gendered mobilities: spaces, images, and power across the Mediterranean (16th–20th centuries) 53
   TERESA BERNARDI AND SILVIA BRUZZI

5 Handling distances as a key factor in social power dynamics 73
   MARINA BERTONCIN AND ANDREA PASE

x Contents

6   Map-mobilities: expanding the field   88
    LAURA LO PRESTI AND TANIA ROSSETTO

7   Narrative mobilities: moving texts from representation to
    practice   102
    GIADA PETERLE

    Afterword   117
    PETER MERRIMAN

SECTION 2
Ideas   125

8   Mobility: the word and the thing   127
    LUCIO BIASIORI

9   Tyrannical mobility, dictatorial mobility   142
    FRANCESCA CAVAGGIONI, LUCA FEZZI AND FLAVIO RAVIOLA

10 The Anglo-Venetian moment: political and legal
    representations between the Republic of Venice and
    England in the early modern age   159
    MICHELE BASSO, MARIO PICCININI AND ALFREDO VIGGIANO

11 Mechanics, scholars and objects: the spread of Aristotle's
    philosophy and its exponents in early modern Europe   175
    FERDINANDO FAVA AND ANDREA SAVIO

12 Synchronic development or diffusion? The temporal
    mobility of violent practices before and after WWI   187
    GIULIA ALBANESE AND MATTEO MILLAN

    Afterword   201
    ARISTOTLE KALLIS

    Index   209

Figures

4.1 Postcard. *In Italian Libya*. Publisher: G. Cometto, Turin, from a picture by Lehnert & Landrock, Tunis. Courtesy Collection Celso Braglia (Modena) — 58
4.2 *Young Jewish Woman in French Tunisia*, from Mauresques: femmes orientales dans la photographie coloniale, 1860–1910 / texte de Christelle Taraud; photographie des collections Roger-Viollet, p. 26 — 59
5.1 Relational distance and power dynamics — 83
8.1 F. Del Cossa, Palio di San Giorgio, fresco, Ferrara, Palazzo Schifanoia — 128
8.2 *An Excellent New Hymne to the Mobile, exhorting them to Loyalty*. Cover page. Courtesy of Huntington Library — 133
11.1 Filippo Pigafetta, *Le meccaniche*, detail. Courtesy of the Biblioteca Civica Bertoliana, Vicenza — 181
11.2 Filippo Pigafetta, *Le meccaniche*, detail. Courtesy of the Biblioteca Civica Bertoliana, Vicenza — 182

Tables

5.1 Distance: active/imposed, reduced/increased. Some examples 76
5.2 Actions on distance 76
5.3 Types of space and distance (Bertoncin and Pase, 2022) 77
5.4 Types of distance and dynamics of power 79

Introduction to Volume 1
Theories, methods and ideas

Lucio Biasiori, Federico Mazzini and Chiara Rabbiosi

Technological and societal advancement have moved toward an increased interest in mobility—or rather, mobilities—and their complexity. While this phenomenon has seen major involvement of the 'hard' and social sciences, these two volumes argue that the humanities can play an equally important role in understanding mobility from a diachronic and spatial perspective. This conviction led to the need to reimagine mobilities through a humanistic lens, finding new analytical momentum in the cross-fertilisation of studies in past and present mobility phenomena, practices and meanings. The books apply this approach to a range of historical and present questions, developing new insights that will shape this nascent humanistic take on mobilities.

Drawing on the recent theorisation of a humanistic turn in mobilities studies (Merriman and Pearce, 2017), this two-volume book investigates the potential of an emerging 'mobilities and humanities' perspective by showcasing several exemplary reflections, research subjects and case studies focused on mobilities in past and present times, connecting antiquity to contemporaneity and humanities to social sciences, design research and the interdisciplinary mobilities paradigm.

Through a series of short chapters, this edited collection gives the sense of how mobilities are employed (and should be even more so) as a very elastic and inclusive concept that allows for the emergence of unexpected research variations resulting from the proximity of different disciplines, thus positioning the concept of mobilities as a powerful catalyst for inventive research insights and claims.

While including contributions from key figures who have in different ways committed their research to mobilities, both volumes are edited and written by members of the Centre for Advanced Studies in Mobility & Humanities (MoHu) established in the Department of Historical and Geographic Sciences and the Ancient World (DiSSGeA) of the University of Padova. DiSSGeA was selected by ANVUR, the Italian National Agency for the Evaluation of the University and Research Systems, as Department of Excellence for the period 2018–2022. Thanks to this achievement, the department has strengthened research activities, developing excellent teaching methods and enhancing its international profile. The department combines mobilities

DOI: 10.4324/9781003278665-1

studies and research in the humanities, and has become a research hub for the humanistic study of mobilities thanks to the research commitment of its staff, who are active in the fields of history, human geography, anthropology, the antiquities and other humanities, as well as the development of two new research infrastructures: the aforementioned MoHu and the Digital Laboratory for Mobility Research in the Humanities (MobiLab). The project has also included a series of initiatives fostering excellence in education: a new curriculum in Mobility Studies within the already existing Historical Sciences master's programme, scholarships and study prizes for students with an outstanding academic record, additional funding for Erasmus+ outgoing mobility, PhD and post-doc research grants supporting research on mobilities and an invitation to world-renowned visiting scholars. Such initiatives are contributing to the training of a new generation of humanists who know how to manage mobility-related topics with a high degree of awareness of their complexities.

The structure of this two-volume book mirrors the thematic research clusters of the Centre: Theories, Methods and Ideas; and Objects, People and Texts. Taking advantage of a rich and unique mix of disciplines, with a distinctive reference to the connections between past and present times (from antiquity to contemporaneity), both volumes contribute to the emerging area of mobilities studies through the humanities, which is increasingly pursued by other research hubs worldwide. This inclusive and pluralistic approach helps in overcoming the traditional paradigm that reads past and present as static entities developing independently one from the other. The combination of historiographical, philological, geographic and anthropological methods, with a reference also to economic and legal aspects, allows better understanding of the dynamism of human societies and nonhuman entities, and to reconstruct in critical ways the related contexts, practices and experiences at different scales.

At the same time, the volumes seek a dialogue with renowned international scholars in the field of mobilities studies. These scholars had closely interacted with authors and editors and have critically discussed the research outcomes of the books by writing an Afterword for each section, with a critical reflection on its main themes. Readers who may feel disoriented by the multiplicity of themes explored and the diversity of approaches followed in the volume can start from the Afterwords to each section to find an Ariadne's thread to help them find their way through the book.

Let us now turn from the spirit of the project behind this publication to the content of this first volume, which is organised in two sections: Theories and Methods, and Ideas.

As Hannam, Sheller and Urry (2006, p. 15) have noted, the new mobilities paradigm was conceived as "an approach that offers both theoretical and methodological purchase on a wide range of urgent contemporary issues, as well as new perspectives on certain historical questions". Based on this premise, the Theories and Methods section promotes a theoretical and methodological reflection on the most innovative component of the book, namely the combination of mobilities studies and the humanities. The main purpose of this section is to feed a broad theoretical vision on the topic (e.g., varied conceptions of mobilities; development of innovative interpretations; terminological experimentations), on the one hand, and to think in a comparative and transversal way about quantitative, qualitative and creative methodologies, on the other.

This section also aims to explore theories and methods as a basis for stimulating an interdisciplinary dialogue between mobilities studies and the humanities. Hence, there is a need to investigate the implications of this innovative formulation from an epistemological point of view, and through a discussion of methodological possibilities which have already been implemented or are to be experimented. Maintaining the ability to constantly reimagine the relations between mobilities and the humanities, this section also intends to provide theoretical and application tools that are productive for more specific research areas, such as the mobilities of people, objects, ideas and texts.

As highlighted by Peter Merriman in his Afterword, the chapters of this section "demonstrate how a broad range of arts and humanities approaches and methods can be useful for understanding movement and mobility, from archival research to experimental Geohumanities approaches to narratives and texts" (p. 120). Furthermore, they cover a very broad time period (from the 15th to the 21st century), which is rather unusual for transport and mobility history, which mainly focuses on 19th and 20th century transport technologies.

The Ideas section reflects on the processes related to the mobilities of ideas through time and space. It also aims at understanding the forms and reasons for the affirmation and development of some ideas in a context in which they are not the only ones available, as well as how ideas change in time and space. In this context, ideas have been thought jointly with the practices they convey, researching the conditions for their affirmation, reproduction and appropriation in geographical and historical contexts, even very distant.

In his Afterword to the section, Aristotle Kallis has observed that the field of ideas has so far remained the perennial child prodigy in the realm of mobilities studies: "Full of potential yet young and disobliging, it remains somewhat ill-fitting and thus peripheral to the mainstream of mobilities research" (p. 201). This happens because the mobilities of ideas are mostly discussed either through a diffusionist scheme or without making any distinction between mobility and circulation. In this section, however, the mobility of ideas has been interpreted in a sense that is closer to reception rather than circulation. The process of reception always involves one subject emitting and another receiving, but both are changed by this exchange. Treating mobility as reception, and vice versa, helps us overcome a view according to which ideas move in a purely abstract way, i.e. without moving on the legs of the human subjects who create them and the support of the means that allow them to proliferate. From this point of view, the ideas section can be considered as a sort of bridge between the first and second volume, which instead deals with the mobilities of objects, people and texts, guaranteeing the profound unity of the project that animated this book and of which the pages you will read are the final product.

References

Hannam K., Sheller M., and Urry J. (2006). *Mobilities*, Editorial: Mobilities, Immobilities and Moorings, 1(1), pp. 1–22.

Merriman P. and Pierce L. (2017). Mobility and the humanities. *Mobilities*, 12(4), pp. 493–508.

Section 1
Theories and methods

1 "Moving textuality" in early modern Europe

Paola Molino

Historians and sociologists have often conceptualized modernity in terms of increasing connection, universalization, and standardization through the circulation of ideas, people, and goods, so that mobility seems to have been a driving force in the foundation of modern societies. At the same time, such increased connectivity has coexisted with the establishment of a social order that marginalizes other forms of movement on the edge, such as nomads and migrants, for religious or ethnical reasons (Bayly, 2004; Castells, 1996; Cresswell, 2006). However, when looking back in time, particularly to the world prior to 1800, such a view might seem overwhelming, as it intrinsically implies accepting a vision of the pre-modern world as a preparation for the present and requires primarily focusing on those processes that are considered relevant because they have led societies to be where they are today. This attitude is visible in some of the studies carried out by early modern historians in the first decade of the 21th century that have placed mobility at the core of their analysis. There are many scientific books and articles dealing with the circulation of people, ideas, and goods through courts, cities, continents, across known infrastructures or "constructed" networks. However, pressures from today, associated with the idea of mobility as mainly related to individuals on far-away trajectories and cross-cultural encounters typical of the age of globalization, are still perceptible.[1]

As Luca Zenobi (2021: 2) has recently pointed out, since its beginnings, the mobility turn in human geography and sociology has emphasized that, beyond specific (infra)structures (such as high-speed highways) or phenomena (mass migration, tourism, long-distance commuting, or the rise of the Anthropocene) typical of the modern world, "mobility lies at the heart" of all human activity, and thus provides not only an object of study but also a methodological tool for analyzing societies as a whole, in the past and in the present. Methodologically, looking at the early modern world from a mobility perspective requires an almost unnatural gesture for historians. To begin with, it entails accepting different notions of spatiality, scales, and temporality, no longer based on the presumption that "actors are able to do only one thing at a time, and that events follow each other in a linear order" (Sheller and Urry, 2006: 214; Greenblatt, 2010; Revel, 1996). In order to do so, it has been shown

DOI: 10.4324/9781003278665-3

that seriously interrogating pre-modern sources with specific sets of questions, such as those proposed by Tim Cresswell in his piece "Towards a Politics of Mobility" in the modern world, on the reasons for moving, the speed and rhythm of movement, the trajectories and hindrances, and the moments and spaces in which movement actually stops is particularly fruitful (Cresswell, 2010). In their forthcoming book on "the mechanics" of mobility, Rosa Salzberg and Paul Nelles collectively attempt to reconstruct these practices for the 1500–1700 time period almost on an everyday basis, with the help of sources such as account books, court trials, travel diaries, guidebooks, and maps (Salzberg and Nelles, forthcoming). Another option is to consider these mechanics in delimited contexts, such as urban perimeters, and to look at how forms of mobility and immobility have been performed and conceptualized, finally contributing to shaping early modern cities and how, in turn, these dynamics have shaped the lives of men and women who frequented cities in the past (Romano and De Munck, 2019). A recent special issue of the *Journal of Early Modern History*, edited by Luca Zenobi, takes this approach and elaborates further on the entanglement between mobility and spatiality. Religious processions, pilgrimages, rebellions, political performances, inn stays, or transporting wares in a victual market are all examples of practices that highlight the "transforming effect" of mobility for actors and cities. The collection also demonstrates that we do not need to look away from today's societal questions in order to recapture the normalcy of mobility and immobility in the past. These recent works all share the goal of overcoming the idea of movement across geographical space as the only contemplated form of movement, and instead reconstruct *constellations of mobility* emerging from cultural meaning and embodied practices of movement (Cresswell, 2010: 18). As practitioners of a discipline that studies connections in the past and across times, historians are driven not only to study these constellations, but also to discover intrinsic connections among them.

My chapter elaborates on some of these recent suggestions from a specific angle, namely that of the history of pre-modern information, media, and, more specifically, handwritten cultures. The history of information and that of mobility are interconnected in any historical period but they seem even more intertwined in the centuries 1500–1800, when it was not possible to communicate a message—orally, handwritten, or printed—without the short or long-distance movement of a woman, a man, a horse, a carriage, a book, or a letter (Behringer, 2003). Reflections on the presence or absence of the carrier or the media as material objects in order to enact communication, along with those on the changing coordinates of time and space, lay at the core of any investigation of mobility and information in pre-modern Europe. For instance, the German historian and sociologist Rudolf Schlögl dates back to the end of the 15th century the slow transition from a society of present subjects to one in which, with the support of media such as letters, the press, but also money, the actual presence of people to communicate or exchange goods was no longer necessary. This was a society that was becoming increasingly complex and self-reflective, one that did not require bodies to be used as a medium of communication and instead replaced interaction with organization (Schlögl, 2014). My chapter takes a different approach, examining books, information, and the media in the early modern period as embodied practices. It attempts to reflect on the ramifications of documenting the history of information by looking in particular at catalog entries and pieces of news as "moving texts", rather than just as texts bridled into specific media that were eventually put on the move. Books and manuscripts were exchanged, translated, and modified. As such, they had different effects on different groups of recipients. Historians are well aware of this. They have reflected on topics such as translation, the transnational and global exchange of letters and books, the adaptation of contents, and the adjustment of specific texts in different media contexts (Burke, 2007; McDermott and Burke, 2015). What remains undertheorized is how this "moving textuality" can inform and change the past's historical reconstruction and interpretation. In a recent article, Kristin Asdal and Helge Jordheim stress how a mobility turn in the history of textuality is first and foremost a process of liberation from context, regarded as the box in which historians close their objects of study. As such, the turn also implies a liberation from the linguistic representation of texts, which allows one to re-trace and follow texts written in different characters and languages (Asdal and Jordheim, 2018: 59). Their theoretical insights are important insofar as they point out that the mobility of information and media embraces a broader reflection on the power of written texts for the reconstruction of historical realities, a debate that has to consider the material supports through which "words from the past" are handed down.

In early modern Europe the introduction of printing with movable letters brought about a change in the realm of media, knowledge, and information. Historians of the book—after a fascination for the apparently revolutionary and extraordinary character of printing for Europe—consider now the printed book as strongly embedded in the intricate media landscape of the pre-modern world. However, outside the realm of the history of the book and knowledge, the question remains recurring of whether the invention of printing has made the book more mobile in spatial and social terms because it has become cheaper and easier to carry and transport, or less mobile because corrections were more difficult to be enacted and also more visible than in manuscripts. This tension is evoked in Bruno Latour's definition of printed media as *immutable mobiles*, objects that have "properties of being mobile but [are] also immutable, presentable, readable, and combinable with one another" (Latour, 1986: 7, and 10–13). In terms of their mobile nature, Latour sees it as intrinsically linked to the object-book because printing allows the creation of new formats (for instance, the quartos or the octavos) that can be moved more easily, as well as the *fixation* of inscriptions such as notes, maps, and drawings, allowing them to be compared and corrected more quickly. This *fixation* has also enabled and enacted the concentration of knowledge, and thus power, in the hands of a distant reader or collector. As Latour states, "The accuracy shifts from the medium to the message, from the printed book to the context with which it establishes a two-way connection," conveying "a new interest in 'Truth' that does not come from a new vision, but from the same old vision applying itself to new visible objects that mobilize space and time differently" (Latour, 1986: 11).

In the last four decades, the material history of written cultures, analytical bibliography, the sociology of the book, history of reading and communication have all contributed not only to a more nuanced picture, beyond the dichotomy of print-manuscript cultures, but also to a more sophisticated reflection on the implication of putting the book (in its various material manifestations) on the move. In the introduction of the recent volume *Books in Motion in Early Modern Europe*, Daniel Bellingradt and Jeroen Salman look at the mobility of the book from three perspectives: that of spatiality, namely the existing and constructed spaces of its circulation; of materiality, which goes beyond the physical appearance of texts/images and includes all material aspects intrinsic to the movement of books; and sociality, "the actions and motives" of the users (Bellingradt, Nelles, and Salman, 2018: 2 and ff.). In this collective endeavor, similar to that of the most recent works on the history of the book, prints are regarded as media that very quickly revolutionized the organization of labor in the printing shop and the book market, the systematization of libraries, and the organization of topics in scholarly communication. However, from a technical and intellectual viewpoint, including the possibilities of "fixing the inscriptions," of standardization, the multiplication of copies, access to knowledge, and the enlargement of alphabetization, prints joined other existing media and supported and "awaited" social and political change. Even if one seriously contemplates the idea of the concentration of knowledge and power in the same place by the 16th century, be it the center of the Republic of Venice or the court in Madrid, one must acknowledge that most of this "knowledge" converged on the center in handwritten and oral form (De Vivo, 2007). In many respects, this all makes Europe's print culture comparable to other cultures in the pre-modern world. Even in Europe, the early modern period is no longer regarded as the age of printing only. It is, therefore, heuristically beneficial to reflect on the mobility of textuality by considering two media that privileged the handwritten form throughout the early modern era—the library catalog and handwritten news—and to see how their very nature as moving texts has shaped knowledge and information.

If printing did not change early modern European society as a whole, inside the library walls, it contributed to displaying how the world was changing. In the library, the coming of the book was an important trigger for the reorganization of spaces, and indeed of the sciences, for rethinking the function and social role of the librarian and the public (Molino, 2016a). Nonetheless, for a variety of reasons, the same librarians who were so keen to collect printed books, maps, and engravings, and who were so immersed in the new print culture, often preferred to keep the catalogs in handwritten form (Walsby, 2013;

Taylor, 1957).[2] First, this was a question of intellectual and medial continuity. As has been convincingly demonstrated, the visual-spatial conceptualization of knowledge typical of early modern library catalogs was embedded in the manuscript culture, particularly in the "Art of Memory" tradition, and was then transferred to the printed realm (Carruthers, 2008: 151–152; Garberson, 2006: 116). Until the 15th century, catalogs reflected the idea of the library as a systematized mirror of a unified world, a closed theatre, or a living encyclopedia, a visualized field in which all sciences and disciplines were displayed in a specific order. More concretely, the catalog looked like a manuscript book, whose pages had many blank spaces in order to contain small corrections and adaptations to guarantee that specific order over time. This tradition is still visible in the first catalogs drawn up under the impact of printing, starting from the middle of the 16th century. At this time, the growing administration of states and empires, the improved circulation of political and military news in a time of war, the development of denser networks of scholarly communication, innovations in geography and in the sciences, and a boom in commercial overseas travel contributed to the perception of an overabundance of written documents and the increasing importance of this written documentation that led to the reorganization of large institutional libraries and archives (Blair, 2010).[3] As a result of this impact, many book collections associated with political power were spatialized in new ways, and the library became increasingly associated with a specific room—which was still not a reading room, and could be a beautiful *salone librario*, such as the *Salone Sistino* of the Vatican Library, or an ugly, dark, and dusty deposit, such as the Imperial Library of Vienna. As we shall see, this spatialization was the first trigger for the mobility of catalogs and that of books in the time to come. Catalogs continued to be conceived as pictures of the rooms, but slowly these pictures became less and less reliable and needed to be constantly updated. By the end of the 16th century, most European institutional libraries were in the process of conceiving new cataloging criteria for the two main goals that the library had meanwhile assumed. First, the old function of preservation and display; second, as an instrument of power for politicians and information for the members of a scholarly community, who were often elsewhere and, especially in times of war or epidemics, needed manuscripts and books to consult from a distance. In particular, fields of studies, such as oriental languages, whose flourishing was only laterally related to printing, required catalogs to be detailed and with reliable, updated descriptions, and librarians had to be quick to find and share their unique samples (Çelik-Petrolini, 2021). In this context, the decision to keep handwritten catalogs stemmed from centuries of scholarly practices inherited and deployed in libraries for updating catalogs in the most efficient and effective way possible, and to keep track of loans and movements among shelves. This entailed, for instance, copying the same title-entry onto different slips of paper on the same page, using alphabetic-cases to avoid confusion, then cutting and pasting it onto the *folio* page of different catalogs (Krajewski, 2002 and Krämer, 2014). The typologies of catalogs multiplied starting from the middle of the 16th century. As opposed to previous centuries, manuscripts began to be separated from prints, images from geographical maps, and there were also linguistic, shelf, alphabetic catalogs, etc. The handwritten form and use of these specific techniques gave catalog books a stratified temporality, since entries could be added at any time when librarians wanted to update a subject or shelf number, and even over a long span of time. It also supported a method that allowed for changes in book containers but not in library organization, and eventually inspired the transformation of the catalog from a book of memory, a closed encyclopedia, into a massive hypertext scattered across different book volumes, with cross-references and quotations that extended beyond the limits of the library as a physical space (Zedelmaier, 2016).

In consequence, the handwritten catalog allowed for many typologies of mobility to be considered: the first, and most studied, is the mobility of the book inside or outside the library through loans or confiscation, and the possibility of virtually re-creating a library, even if a specific edition or the entire collection was destroyed. Another, less studied, form of mobility is more related to the handwritten form and concerns the textual mobility of titles copied directly into the book or glued onto pieces of paper. This could be a constant movement within the book/catalog or beyond the margins of the book and the walls of the library. The archives of European libraries are full of beautiful examples of this latter typology of textual mobility, which reminds us that each small operation of moving the string of a title from a position associated with a specific category or subject to another had an impact on how canons and disciplines were handed over. At the *Kurfurstliche Bibliothek* in Berlin, the 1660 handwritten subject catalog of medicine was corrected in 1685, with the addition of several titles and authors. What is most relevant, however, is that somebody systematically added slips of paper with descriptions of books on alchemy and chemistry, making *de facto* space for these topics in the field of medicine.

At Munich's Ducal Library between 1570 and 1650, librarians produced more than forty different typologies of catalog (Kellner and Spethmann, 1996: 4 and ff). The library was founded in 1558 through the acquisition of the private collection of the Orientalist Johann Albrecht Widmannstetter (Hartig, 1917: 9–55) and was enlarged in 1571 after the purchase of the rich merchant Johann Jakob Fugger's collection. During the first period, the books (printed and manuscripts) were divided into Latin and non-Latin, and the former subsequently into ten topics: theology, jurisprudence, medicine, history, philosophy, mathematics, poetics, rhetoric, dialectic, and grammar, each with more than one typology of catalog. "Non-Latin" books were simply cataloged by language (Hebrew, German, French, Spanish, and Italian). Latin and German manuscripts were separated from the others. During the same period, librarians also drew up catalogs of geographical maps, genealogical tables, architecture, and unbound books. From 1582–1583, librarians also created a special index of forbidden books dealing with the *Neoterici*, in which they manually extracted titles about new confessions listed in the Roman Index of Forbidden Books from other catalogs and shelves, in order to place them out of reach.

This first activity of cataloging was strictly related to encyclopedic projects of the 16th century such as Samuel Quiccheberg's *Inscriptions, or Main Divisions of a Museum*. Quiccheberg, who was already dead when the Fugger collection arrived in Munich, had been its curator in the preceding decade. In his work, he suggested that the library be organized according to both subjects and languages, and the disposition of the books followed geographical denomination in "Regions" (entire walls devoted to a subject), "Stations" (single shelves), and "Colonies *et* Appendixes" (supplements to the regions). This suggestion was followed in Munich, and the shelf-marks reported a subject followed by "regions, stations, and colonies." However, it was impossible to observe another of Quiccheberg's instructions, namely, using different colours to identify each group of ten books in order to improve their visibility from a distance (Hartig, 1917: 72). This suggestion was appropriate for a library that was not susceptible to movement and growth, that is, a library as a closed collection. One reason for constantly reviewing the catalogs in the 1580s was cross-references between different typologies of catalog (for instance, an alphabetic and a subject one) and the general weeding out of forbidden books undertaken in 1583. Later, in 1632, during the Thirty Years' War—a war in which the confiscation of collections from enemies played a vital role—some 1,700 volumes were removed from the Munich library by the Swedish army. Two years later, as compensation, Maximilian, Prince Elector since 1623, managed to acquire the Württemberg "Fürstliche Liberei" preserved in the Hohentübingen Castle, containing some 732 volumes. The librarian, Claudius Belchamps, first had to manage the transportation of the rarest and most valuable volumes and almost all Latin, Greek, and German manuscripts to a safe place during the Swedish army's occupation. On their return, he embarked on the re-organization of the catalogs, which was continued after his death in 1645 by the new librarian.[4] A brief overview of how the catalogs on the subject "History" were updated is helpful to understand this mobility of texts.

First, we find a shelf catalog of printed books on history, in which all the books—both with and without a known author—are described in full.[5] From the shelf-marks, we gather that, in the new location, the books were now placed on the shelves according to their formats and that the original Quiccheberg system was partly abandoned for practical reasons. One or more shelves were still assigned to a specific subject, but the books were then marked with an ascending serial number (*numerus currens*) according to their accession to the library and placement on that shelf, which allowed for constant enlargements and re-locations. Thus, the new shelf-mark was a combination of the format and this serial number and was now disentangled from a specific location. From the correspondence among librarians at the time, we learn that the "forced mobility" during the war "inspired" new ways of marking books, at least as much as the problem of space in the everyday practice of library management.

However, it was not only this change that provoked many movements within the "History" catalog. Among the pages of the catalog, we can detect a set of small operations in order to apply a new canon that aimed at "polishing" not only theology, but also history (and many other subjects) by non-Catholic authors and books that could be moved into other subjects. For instance, Abraham Ortelius's *Synonymia Geographica*, which was published in Antwerp in 1578 and cataloged in the first alphabetical index with the shelf-mark "Histori 4. 77/75",[6] bears the number 40/93 in the new catalog and is then crossed out and moved into the "Grammar" group, after its inclusion in the latest index of all works by this author, if not expurgated.[7] The same applies to Conrad Gessner's *Bibliotheca Universalis*, at the same time one of the most important encyclopedias and a guide for the organization of libraries. Tellingly, the book was moved to Rhetorics.[8]

The mobility of catalog descriptions written on small slips of paper could also spread errors around Europe for years. In 1665, the Imperial Librarian in Vienna, Peter Lambeck, was the first to notice that a mistake made by one of his predecessors' *amanuensis* in the library's handwritten catalog, resulting from the wrong interpretation of an abbreviation (*Greg. Nyss. Ep.* referring to *Gregorius Nyssenus Episcopus*), gave birth to a completely new person, *Georgius Nicetas*, author of a phantom collection of letters (*epistolae* for *episcopus*) (Lambeck, 1665: 43). Another amanuensis in the library, Adrian Frisius, who happened to be the brother of a later editor of the *Bibliotheca Universalis*, transmitted the string of the handwritten catalog to be inserted into the new printed edition of 1583. From there, the same string was integrated into other repertories, such as that made by Leone Allacci for the Vatican Library, so that in the second half of the 17th century an author and a book circulated that "never exist(ed) in nature but were simply born from the pen of the writer," as Lambeck lamented. This case would disappoint both Bruno Latour and Elisabeth Eisenstein because of printing's capacity to more rapidly display and enact corrections of mistakes, in particular when printed books are put on the move. In Europe, intermediality and mobility both contributed to the (intentional or accidental) reiteration of many mistakes (Daston, 2005).

Information from library catalogs circulated in pre-modern Europe as a sort of hypertext and movements from catalog books to letters, and to other books, could be printed or remained handwritten according to the different fortunes or trajectories of their circulation. Something similar can be said for sheets of paper reporting the freshest news.[9] In Europe, between the 16th and the 17th century, the account of an event, which was made up of the names of people, places, dates, and origins of the news, could actually materialize in various textual contexts, such as a report by a *nuncio* or an ambassador in handwritten or printed gazettes, sometimes literally using the same words and sometimes with paraphrases containing the main words as a sort of algorithm.[10] The handwritten newsletter—*avviso* in Italian, *geschriebene Zeitung* in German, *carta de aviso* in Spanish, and *nouvelle à la main* in French—was one of these textual forms. It was a commodity, a rather expensive one, typical of late Renaissance Italian cities. It originated in the middle of the 15th century in diplomatic correspondence and merchant letters and developed into a more anonymous form in the second half of the 16th century, primarily (but not exclusively) as a consequence of religious wars and those against the Ottoman Empire.[11] They were sold on subscription to wealthy readers, but circulated among the lower strata of society through court or public readings, street and workshop discussions, and—at least in Italy—by posting them on walls in public places.[12] As such, they slowly developed from personal letters into general newsletters, and in this new format, they teased the curiosity of a larger audience. In the aftermath of the Reformation, in a continent divided by religious war and confessional strifes, the news' handwritten form remained an advantage for a long period of time because it avoided the longer process of print privileges and censorship, and used the stable network of the postal system that guaranteed the highest possible speed of time: five days from Rome to Venice, ten days from Venice to Vienna, and fifteen days from Venice to Istanbul (Schobesberger et al., 2016).

If the postal network assured the physical mobility of newsletters, the "paper technology" developed by newswriters facilitated their mobility and remediation in different languages and contexts.

Mechanically, the work of the newswriter involved managing the pieces of different news that converged on his workshop from different directions. That from abroad was brought by post or other channels and, as soon as it reached the workshop, was copied onto one or more sheets. The space for the news was this sheet of paper onto which it was cut and pasted in order to form a *gazzetta* made up of single newsletters written in different localities, four or five days earlier if the city was close, or even a month before if coming from afar. Under pressure to meet the next courier, different pieces of news were copied in haste and sent to subscribers at the very last moment. Such briskness imposed a basic narrative with almost no deeper reflections. Handwritten newsletters generally followed the simple and dry style also suggested in treatises for secretaries and chancelleries, although writers tended to overuse expressions that conveyed a sense of distance between the writer and his sources by using special formulas that connected senses, media, places, and the actors involved: "it was heard," or "it was said," or "through *avvisi* from....," or "news came through the Ambassador from Spain" (Infelise, 2002).

Whereas, in the early years, newsletters were often copied as a continuous flow of text, over time a sort of division into paragraphs arose according to the different directions or sources from which the news reached the workshops. In the 18th century, when news was printed, this "mobile paragraph" developed as "the basic unit of political and military news" (Slauter, 2012: 365). In the handwritten news of the 16th and 17th centuries, the mobile paragraph signaled the different human or geographical directions from which the news reached the workshop. It was a unit of meaning crafted by the newswriter and visible to the reader that allowed the same piece of news to be used and re-used in different geographical contexts and media at the same time. The very existence of the paragraph facilitated the choice of other newswriters to omit a paragraph (or not to give it to be copied) in two otherwise identical newsletters addressed to different subscribers.

The careful cutting and pasting of a specific paragraph was particularly useful and used when news was translated because there were topics that teased the curiosity of the public in certain contexts, but not at all in others. For instance, Italian *avvisi* were very generous when they told stories about weddings and murders in Rome, which were eventually left aside or shortened in their German translation (Molino, 2016b). The result was the proliferation of similar, but non-identical, pieces of news across Europe. Today, it is also possible to find more copies of the same newsletter in different collections diverging by only one sentence or paragraph, or identical paragraphs scattered in different newsletters (Molino, 2019: 125–127). Such a composition of the news has had important consequences for the relationship between textuality and the reliability of information in early modern Europe.

A good opportunity to reflect on these implications between the mobility of texts and the construction of truth are all those cases in which entire sentences lose their meaning as a consequence of copying, recycling, and selecting in haste. There were certain *avvisi* in which the writer tells a story with such zeal, reporting on a variety of people, gestures, and images, and then overlooked the actual news he wanted to convey due to an omission of copying one line.[13] These omissions indicate that the colorful account is unlikely to be based on direct experience, but that the writer was simply copying from another written source. Other instances include those cases where newswriters transmitted an opinion expressed by someone else earlier in another piece of news as mostly certain, or state that a "proven source" has confirmed an unprovable story of a child born with two heads or of a goblin following a noble woman. It is evident that the newswriter, who did not move from his workshop, had to tailor the best product as a result of a dense, reliable, and influential network of authoritative sources from different social strata and locations. This system did not require the newswriter to be physically present in the place where something happened, was quick, and allowed the combination of single pieces of news to meet individual curiosity. In order to perform this complex informative role, the newswriter had to take the question of intermediality very seriously and precisely report the steps in the process through which a piece of news "reached" his eyes, ears, and pen, and mention the social actors who provided confirmation, where possible. Citing the news' original source was a guarantee, not of the accuracy of a fact, but of the news' very existence as a reputable source of information.

The delicate relationship between the immediacy and truthfulness of news, so important for us today, seems to have been equally crucial in the context of the late Renaissance information landscape and was apparently facilitated by the handwritten form and the ways in which a *gazette* was composed and spread. Reading different versions of the same news and events made up of eye-witness accounts and reports, letters and pamphlets contributed to the formation of a new conception of impartiality as a result of textual comparison (Raymond, 2014: 162–163). The receivers of slightly different versions of the same news, conveyed by different media, developed philological methods to find out the truth through textual comparison (Molino, forthcoming, 2022b). From the receiver side—and we have to consider that he or she was often a member of the elite—reaching a "complete" fact in several "textual" stages was considered a way to be fully informed (Brendecke, 2016). In 1588, at the height of the French confessional strifes and the tension between England and Spain, the Duke of Urbino assured his agent in Rome, Grazioso Graziosi, that what he referred to as "variety of texts" was difficult to avoid and should not be avoided because news "came from far away and moved different passions." Nevertheless, he asked Graziosi to highlight untrustworthy messages with a few words in the margin.[14] Graziosi was an agent, not a newswriter, and had nothing to gain from writing more. However, for a newswriter, alluding to different content to be included in subsequent newsletters or possible updates was a way to survive, as it kept readers curious about the next episodes, a feature then taken from handwritten to printed newspapers.

With regard to the oral and printed forms of news, the advantages of these much more flexible "handcrafted" products—if well-made, of course—were immense. Well before Bruno Latour's definition of the *immutable mobiles*, journalism's traditional history considered the textual mobility of handwritten news, especially as a consequence of the newswriter's immobility, to be detrimental to the informative role. More specifically, the idea that a medium's content can be modified on the move, or even deliberately manipulated to cater to the preferences of a specific audience in a different geographical or confessional context, could not be associated with a professional service to the public. The textual mobility of handwritten (let alone oral) forms has been seen as a sign of their informal, private, and contextual function (Schröder, 1995: 4–35; De Vivo, 2019: 185–186).They certainly report fragments of the truth, but only rarely the whole truth. This concept went hand in hand with a view of the media as representations of reality, rather than what they actually were and are today, namely producers of interpretations and, hence, triggers of actions, both of which are entirely intrinsic to the society historians would like to study. When early modern Venetians rushed to the harbor to collect the latest news arriving from Dalmatia, they would most likely have regarded handwritten newsletters, particularly *avvisi*, as "disordered" interpretations of certain events, part of a landscape of interwoven media—printed, written, engraved, shouted, and whispered—in which writers picked what they needed in order to arrive at the most reliable pictures of events in the shortest time possible. Reconstructing this movable aspect of the news also provides a reflection on the origins of our expectations towards the press and the relationship between information and media, along with the need that historians have to reconstruct an ordered past that will assist them in answering the questions that arise from our confused present.

Notes

1 An overview of the recent scholarship on mobility in the pre-modern world in Zenobi (2021: 3–4).
2 A longer and more detailed version of this section on handwritten catalogs will be published in Molino, forthcoming 2022a.
3 These phenomena are not typical of Europe only. For more on the Ottoman Empire and the re-fashioning of early modern libraries, see Sezer, 2016: 25–27 and Erünsal, 2008: 29–30. On China, see Brokaw and Chow, 2005: 3–54. More generally, see McDermott and Burke, 2015: 1–64.
4 The new librarian was Marx Peutinger, author of an "Elenchus Librorum, qui desiderantur in Bibliotheca Serenissimi Ferdinandi Mariae B. V. Ducis Electoris etc." in 1654, now in Munich, Bayerische Staatsbibliothek (BSB), Cbm Cat. 172, encompassing both those taken during the war and those simply lost. On this, see also Hacker, 2000: 69–71.
5 BSB, Cbm. Cat. 140.
6 BSB, Cbm. Cat. 107, f. 1v.
7 BSB, Cbm. Cat. 140, f. 114r.
8 BSB, Cbm. Cat. 143, f. 37r.
9 A longer and more detailed version of this section on handwritten news will be published in Molino, forthcoming 2022b.
10 Colavizza, Infelise, and Kaplan, 2014; Raymond and Moxham, 2016: 4.
11 On this, see Infelise, 2007.
12 Interesting examples for a larger audience of *avvisi* can be read in Infelise, 2002: 42, and 154 and ff.
13 See Öesterreichische Nationalbibliothek, Cod, 8949, f. 358r (Venice, 03.10.1572) for an example.
14 Archivio di Stato di Firenze, Ducato di Urbino, Classe I, fi lza 163, fol. 1533v.

References

Asdal K, Jordheim (2018) Texts on the move: textuality and historicity revisited. *History and Theory* 57 (1): 56–74.
Bayly C (2004) *The birth of the modern world, 1780–1914: global connections and comparisons*. Oxford: Blackwell.
Behringer W (2003) *Im Zeichen des Merkur: Reichspost und Kommunikationsrevolution in der Frühen Neuzeit*. Veröffentlichungen des Max-Planck-Instituts für Geschichte. Bd. 189. Göttingen: Vandenhoeck & Ruprecht.
Bellingradt D, Nelles P, Salman J (eds) (2018) *Books in motion in early modern Europe: beyond production, circulation and consumption*. London: Palgrave Macmillan.
Blair A (2010) *Too much to know: managing scholarly information before the modern age*. New Haven: Yale University Press.
Brendecke A (2016) *The empirical empire: Spanish colonial rule and the politics of knowledge*. Berlin: de Gruyter.

Brokaw CJ, Chow K-W (eds) (2005) *Printing and book culture in late Imperial China*. Los Angeles, London: University of California Press.
Burke P (2007) Cultures of translation in Early Modern Europe. In: *Cultural translation in early modern Europe*. Cambridge: Cambridge University Press, pp. 7–38.
Castells M (1996) *The rise of the network society, the information age: economy, society and culture*. Cambridge, MA; Oxford: Blackwell.
Carruthers M (2008) *The book of memory: a study of memory in medieval culture*. Cambridge: Cambridge University Press.
Çelik H, Petrolini C (2021) Establishing an "Orientalium linguarum Bibliotheca" in 17th century Vienna: Sebastian Tengnagel and the trajectories of his manuscripts. *Bibliothecae.it* 10 (1): 175–231.
Colavizza G, Infelise M, Kaplan F (2014) Mapping the Early Modern news flow: an enquiry by robust text reuse detection. *Social Informatics* 8852 (2014): 244–253.
Cresswell T (2006) *On the move: mobility in the modern Western world*. London: Routledge.
Cresswell T (2010) Towards a politics of mobility. *Environment and Planning D: Society and Space* 28(1): 17–31.
Daston L (2005) Scientific error and the ethos of belief. *Social Research* 72 (1): 1–28.
De Vivo F (2007) *Information and communication in Venice: rethinking early modern politics*. Oxford: Oxford University Press.
De Vivo F (2019) Microhistories of long-distance information: space, movement and agency in the early modern news. *Past & Present* 242 (Issue Supplement 14): 179–214.
Erünsal I (2008) *Ottoman libraries: a survey of the history development and organization of Ottoman foundation libraries*. Cambridge, MA: Department of Near Eastern Languages and Literatures Harvard University.
Garberson E (2006) Libraries, memory and the space of knowledge. *Journal of the History of Collections* 18 (2): 105–136.
Greenblatt S (ed) (2010) *Cultural mobility: a manifesto*. Cambridge: Cambridge University Press.
Hacker R (2000) Die Münchner Hofbibliothek unter Maximilian I. In: *Beiträge zur Geschichte der Bayerischen Staatsbibliothek*. München: Saur, pp. 53–72.
Hartig O (1917) *Die Gründung der Münchener Hofbibliothek durch Albrecht V. und Johann Jacob Fugger*. München: Franz.
Infelise M (2002) *Prima dei giornali. Alle origini della pubblica informazione*. Rome-Bari: Laterza.
Infelise M (2007) From merchant's letters to handwritten political Avvisi: notes on the origins of public information. In: *Cultural exchange in early modern Europe*. Vol. 3: *Correspondence and cultural exchange in Europe, 1400–1700*. Cambridge: Cambridge University Press, pp. 33–52.
Kellner S, Spethmann A (eds) (1996) *Historische Kataloge der Bayerischen Staatsbibliothek*. München, Wiesbaden: Harrassowitz.
Krämer F (2014) Ulisse Aldrovandi's *Pandechion Epistemonicon* and the use of paper technology in Renaissance natural history. *Early Science and Medicine* 19 (2014): 398–423.
Krajewski M (2002) *Zettelwirtschaft. Die Geburt der Kartei aus dem Geiste der Bibliothek*. Berlin: Kulturverlag Kadmos.
Lambeck P (1665) *Commentariorum de Augustissima Bibliotheca Caesarea Vindobonensis, liber primus*. Vindobonae: Typis Matthaei Cosmerovii.

Latour B (1986) Visualization and cognition: drawing things together. In: *Knowledge and society studies in the sociology of culture past and present*. London: Jai Press, pp. 1–40.
McDermott J, Burke P (2015) Introduction. In: *The book worlds in East Asia and Europe, 1450–1850: Connections and comparisons*. Baltimore, MD: Project Muse, pp. 1–64.
Molino P (2016a) World bibliographies: libraries and the reorganization of knowledge in late Renaissance Europe. In: Grafton A, Glenn M (eds) *Canonical texts and scholarly practices: a global comparative approach*. Cambridge: Cambridge University Press, pp. 299–322.
Molino P (2016b) Connected news: German Zeitungen and Italian Avvisi in the Fugger collection (1568–1604). *Media History* 22 (3–4): 267–296.
Molino P (2019) Beyond the language divide. the endless chain of the news between Italian 'Avvisi' and German 'Zeitungen'. *Annali dell'Istituto storico italo-germanico in Trento* 45 (2): 107–128.
Molino P (forthcoming 2022a) When knowledge "squared" was knowledge shared: strategies for coping with an excess of data in early modern library catalogues. In: Krämer F, Sapir I (ed) *Coping with copia. Epistemological excess in Early Modern art and science*. Amsterdam: Amsterdam University Press.
Molino P (forthcoming 2022b) News on the road: the mobility of handwritten newsletters in Early Modern Europe. In: Salzberg R, Nelles P (eds) (forthcoming) *Connected mobilities: the practice and experience of movement in the Early Modern World*. Amsterdam: Amsterdam University Press.
Raymond J (2014) Exporting impartiality. In: *The emergence of impartiality: towards a prehistory of objectivity*. Leiden: Brill, pp. 141–167.
Raymond J, Moxham N (2016) News networks in Early Modern Europe. In: *News networks in Early Modern Europe*. Leiden: Brill, pp. 1–16.
Revel J (ed) (1996) *Jeux d'échelles. La micro-analyse à l'expérience*. Paris: Gallimard et Le Seuil.
Romano A, De Munck B (eds) (2019) *Knowledge and the early modern city: a history of entanglements*. London: Routledge.
Salzberg R, Nelles P (forthcoming) Introduction: the mechanics of early modern mobility. In: *Connected mobilities: the practice and experience of movement in the Early Modern world*. Amsterdam: Amsterdam University Press.
Schlögl R (2014) *Anwesende und Abwesende. Grundriss für eine Gesellschaftsgeschichte der Frühen Neuzeit*. Konstanz: Konstanz University Press.
Schobesberger N et al. (2016) European postal networks. In: *News networks in Early Modern Europe*. Leiden: Brill, pp. 19–63.
Schröder T (1995) *Die ersten Zeitungen. Textgestaltung und Nachrichtenauswahl*. Tübingen: Gunter Narr Verlag.
Sezer Y (2016) *The architecture of bibliophilia: Eighteenth-century Ottoman libraries*. Ph. D. in History and Theory of Architecture, Massachusetts Institute of Technology, Department of Architecture.
Sheller M, Urry J (2006) The new mobilities paradigm. *Environment and Planning A: Economy and Space* 38 (2): 207–226.
Slauter W (2012) Le paragraphe mobile: circulation et transformation des informations dans le monde atlantique du XVIIIe siècle. *Annales: Histoire, sciences sociales* 67 (2): 363–389.

Taylor A (1957) *Book catalogues: their varieties and uses.* Chicago, IL: The Newberry Library.

Walsby M (2013) Book lists and their meanings. In: *Documenting the early modern book world: inventories and catalogues in manuscript and print.* Leiden: Brill, pp. 1–24.

Zedelmaier H (2016) Viel zu viele Bücher. Bibliotheken im Spiegel des Nachdenkens über Glaubenssicherung und Wissensbewahrung im 16. Jahrhundert. In: *Wissensspeicher der Reformation. Die Marienbibliothek und die Bibliothek des Waisenhauses in Halle.* Halle: Verlag der Franckeschen Stiftungen, pp. 19–33.

Zenobi L (2021) Mobility and urban space in early modern Europe: An introduction. *The Journal of Early Modern History* 25 (1–2): 1–10.

2 The challenge of mobility for commodity chains

Time, actors, and value from an historical perspective

Marco Bertilorenzi, Andrea Caracausi, Carlo Fumian and Benoît Maréchaux

2.1 Introduction

Since the dawn of the 12th century, the progressive construction of a "commercial capitalism" (Banaji, 2020) has given rise to complex systems of procurement, processing, and the marketing of raw materials and finished products, supported by increasingly complex and interconnected financial networks. Over the decades, numerous "commodity frontiers" have redefined hierarchies, divisions of labor, geographies, and interdependencies between different parts of the world at the intersection of society and nature (Beckert, 2015 and Patel and Moore, 2017). From one wave of globalization to the next, the timing and volume of exchange has varied depending on available technologies, trade policies, and geopolitical balances (Arrighi, 2010 and Wallerstein, 1980). The operation of today's complex global mobility of goods poses problems that historical research can help identify by analyzing its formation over the long term. What questions, therefore, can mobility studies raise for the study of commodities in an historical perspective? (Adey et al., 2014, section 4, especially pp. 265–7). And, on the other hand, how can an historical approach contribute to a study on the mobility of commodities?

Starting from the extensive existing literature, we decided to focus on four commodities that have driven global trade in different historical periods: Spanish silver between the 16th and 17th centuries, silk ribbons in the 18th century, wheat between the 19th and 20th centuries, and aluminium in the 20th century. Rather than following traditional chronological partitions (modern/contemporary age, pre-industrial/industrial age), or dividing the topic by individual commodities, we have decided to approach the topic by posing some key issues to each commodity, either related to time, actors or value. This approach will allow us to highlight differences or analogies and, beyond the inevitable diversities and ruptures due to the processes of historical change, will allow us to better underline each commodity's uniqueness and the heuristic potential of the method used.

DOI: 10.4324/9781003278665-4

The first section will, therefore, present commodities in their context: their main qualities, their mobile nature, and the role they played in the period under observation. The second section will address the issue of time, investigating the importance of synchronizing the movement and transport of commodities (from the technological, organizational, and political perspective) in order to have goods in the right place at the right time. The third section will address the private and public agents who helped form the markets within which commodities moved in defiance of supply needs, whether alimentary or voluptuary, as well as the financial and environmental risks. The fourth section deals with the relationship between mobility and the value of commodities, investigating the economic choices, speculative practices, and arbitrage affecting the value of a commodity as it moved from one place to another. The last paragraph highlights the main points that emerged and the aspects that still need to be addressed. The purpose of this essay is to show how mobility study approaches can help rethink the history of global commodities through their link with mobility. To do this, we have decided to summarize the main points, also with a view to an interdisciplinary dialogue, and to leave the necessary in-depth studies to the extensive bibliography.

2.2 Global commodities

Silver mined in the American mines of the Spanish empire is often counted among the first commodity chains to develop at a global level (Flynn and Giráldez, 2004; Marichal, 2006). From 1540 onwards, the white metal became a global raw material, commodity, and means of payment. From Peru to the European and then Chinese markets, the precious metal burst onto world markets by riding the western and eastern routes ever since the Manila Galleons connected America and Asia through the Pacific. Silver became a strategic resource desired by all, including governments, due to its dual nature as a commodity and an international means of payment. This contributed to the creation of logistical and arbitrage systems linked to the temporal and spatial coordination between physical mobility and the information related to its value. But the worldwide circulation of what would become a currency par excellence of international trade also had remarkable and asymmetrical effects (even if debated) on hierarchies and the division of labor between territories, on the purchasing power of different social strata, on the competitiveness of local industries, and on the development of financial markets. In this context, the multiplicity of actors involved produced institutional responses and organizational practices destined to play a role in the management of a commodity whose mobility or immobility, often associated with the creation of value, was always the subject of major conflicts of interest and power.

Simple and essential in appearance, the silk ribbon may perhaps be overshadowed by the substance of other raw materials that bound the world together (as with silver) or the finished fabrics that they "manufactured", such as cotton (Riello, 2013). However, a simple ribbon can speak volumes, starting with the "topological complexity" it embodied. Silk, which originated in Persia and China before Europeans began cultivating it at the end of the 15th century; dyeing materials, such as indigo and cochineal, which originated in the Americas or the East Indies; and silver and gold, which first originated in Africa and Central Europe and then the Americas (Cavaciocchi, 1993). To this were added the various techniques, which included thread twisting, also imported from the Orient during the 13th century; the mechanical loom, invented in Holland and then propagated, opposed, and implemented from the late-16th century throughout Europe; and the *miniature* and *picoting* techniques, conceived in France and which then spread to different parts of Europe (Poni, 2009). And finally, as a finished product, originating from the Arab world in the late-14th century, it spread to European and American markets, transforming itself through its movement and associated usage practices. In particular, in the 18th century, as a "fashionable" object, the ribbon became an independent object that conveyed its own meaning, linked to the spheres of honour, love, and sexuality (Caracausi, 2019).

As far as wheat is concerned, the structure of its trade changed radically in the most developed areas in the 19th century—primarily in the United States—especially due to elevator technology and the integration of rail and port systems (the most paradigmatic example is Chicago, which is undoubtedly the principal model of this development, commencing with the setting up, in the 1840s, of the first Board of Trade in the world). We take these transformations for granted, but they were established in a non-linear manner, through fierce competition and conflicts in the legal, economic, technological, and political-diplomatic fields). Here, the transformation of goods into commodities is ensured by two parallel processes: the development of grading procedures for different types of wheat (overseen by internationally recognized agencies—see Hoffman and Hill, 1976) and the market for futures contracts (Williams, 1982, Santos, n.d.), that is, the botanical-commercial alphabet and the financial one of the new (or rather "contemporary") grain trade. It is a process that fully developed in the second half of the 19th century, giving rise to specific professional profiles active in both private and public spheres and which appears to have been dominated by a few "players" capable of acting on a global scale, some of whom are still active today in the worldwide trading of any type of agricultural produce: the leading ones include Cargill-MacMillan, Bunge y Born, Louis Dreyfus, and Continental Grain belonging to the Fribourg family (Mazzamauro, 2016; Broehl, 1992, et al.).

Aluminium has often been referred to as the metal of modernity, lightness, and even mobility (Grinberg, 2003). Although 8% of the earth's crust is made up of aluminium, this metal is not present in nature in a pure state and an industrial process for its separation (electrolysis) was only introduced at the end of the 19th century. In the 20th century, this metal emerged in a series of applications that are part of our everyday life: from soft drink cans to airplanes, from chocolate wrapping to laptops, from bicycles to chairs, and from electric cables to flasks. Its use by the military is substantial: both in the strictest sense, for the manufacture of explosives, ammunition, and warplanes, and in a broader sense, as a material suitable for the production of flasks, helmets, and field accessories that make military equipment lighter. Mimi Sheller (2015) dedicated a volume specifically to the role of aluminium as a material of mobility: if, on the one hand, it has found specific application in the transport of goods or people, on the other, it is able to represent the quintessence of the modern "dream" of transportability, lightness, and, in part, also a certain "take-away" culture. Nevertheless, aluminium also has large implications for mobility from an economic point of view: the governance of this metal's value chains implies a synchronized management of the mobility of several other products and the immobility of others; the processing of waste, for example, or of energy sources, which, as we will see, both have various spatial issues (Bertilorenzi, 2016). Secondly, the production of aluminium on a global scale meant the involvement of multinational companies from a very early stage, which in turn stimulated a transfer of capital, technologies, and organizational forms (Holloway, 1988).

2.3 Commodities and synchronicity

From the time that new forms of production and consumption contributed to making logistics a determining factor in international trade, particularly since the end of the 20th century, moving the right goods at the right time, to the right place, and at the right price has become vital at the level of both business-to-business and business-to-consumer transactions. The focus on logistics is now shaping new distribution modes, labor relations, and forms of business (Sacchi Landriani and De Vito, 2020). One of the key issues is the synchronization of the flow of goods, capital, and people along the supply chain. While there is no shortage of historical work on logistics (military, entrepreneurial, or technological, most recently analyzed by Levinson, 2016), historicizing the issue of synchronization over the long term can help us to better understand the extent to which recent changes toward the global mobility of goods have taken a true quantitative and qualitative leap, and how this issue has been addressed in the past.

The study of American silver in the 16th and 17th centuries allows us to take a step back by observing the synchronization dynamics that integrated mining production, coinage, fleet mobilization, and exchange fairs. From the 1560s onwards, the monetary chain between Spanish America and the metropolis was based on the organization of annual naval convoys. Convoys were effective in terms of security, but they were very expensive and their ports of call and frequency were, therefore, very limited. This had important consequences for the spatio-temporal distribution of value chains: goods from very distant places had to converge in a given place and in a limited space of time. The central node was the Isthmus of Panama (at Nombre de Dios and then Portobelo), which is still one of the major hubs of world trade to this day. There, it was necessary to coordinate the arrival of the

Tierra Firme fleet from Seville (between 40 and 60 ships in the 1580s) and that of precious metal that was loaded from Potosí on the back of a llama to Arrica, from where it was transported by sea and then taken on board the Mar del Sur fleet. Synchronization depended on human factors, but also on technological and environmental factors. Production depended on the importation of mercury from Huancavelica, while, due to the technological limitations of navigation, weather had a major impact on navigation. The entire supply chain also depended on the timing of the rains that pushed the mills needed for production (Álvarez Nogal, 2011; Suárez Espinosa, 2016, et al.). On the other hand, the lack of synchronization could mean the ruin of the *cargadores a Indias*: without the promised silver, in fact, the merchandise coming from Eurasia had no buyers on the Isthmus of Panama, while the king's officials and local merchants had to organize themselves to send the money on time. Delays were frequent, but the *Carrera de Indias* demonstrated a high level of organization (Elliott, 1989: 19–21; Yun-Casalilla, 2019: 58–60). Synchronization was also essential at other global logistics hubs (in Acapulco, but also in Seville, Madrid, Barcelona, and Genoa) for the transportation of silver and capital remittances in exchange fairs (Álvarez Nogal, Lo Basso and Marsilio, 2007, et al.).

Implemented through a complex and spatially multi-situated supply chain, encompassing as many as 20–25 operations and multiple continents, even a silk ribbon required the synchronicity of interconnected movements of raw materials, labor, and finished products, linked in turn to other production sectors (particularly because of the mobility and pluri-activity of labor in agriculture), as well as the marketing of other products. The production cycle began with the financing of the production of raw materials, their hoarding in local markets and/or their arrival and purchase in the major international hubs, their dispatch to the different actors involved (processors, spinners, weavers, and finishers), who had to work on them in a predetermined time frame, the packaging of the products, and their departure to other ports. Even in its simplicity, therefore, a product like a ribbon was tied to a chain of goods that required movement, rapidity, and immediacy. In fact, ribbons were sold through long-distance trade outside Europe at least as early as the second half of the 17th century, if not earlier. Ribbons produced in 17th-century Naples, for example, were particularly popular in Mexico, Brazil, and Peru, where they were exchanged for dyeing raw materials (indigo and cochineal) needed to produce them. On the other hand, in Venice at the end of the 18th century, merchants from Padua produced ribbons for the Atlantic markets using the ports of Cadiz and Lisbon, importing colonial products such as coffee, tobacco, sugar, and pepper. New goods arriving on the market were eagerly awaited, as reported in the correspondences of numerous women in Boston, curious about the new cargoes of English ribbons arriving from London at the end of the 18th century. Missing a shipment could entail great risks, not only because the cargo risked remaining empty with no goods to return, but also because the annual fashion cycle imposed adherence to delivery schedules and the need to stay ahead of new designers who were always ready to change the styles (Caracausi, 2019; Poni, 2009).

By the mid-19th century, but already starting in the 1830s (Brunt and Cannon, 2013; Federico, 2011, 2012), the grain trade began to become increasingly fluid as huge long-distance "grain torrents" emerged (as a result of the planting of massive areas on different continents; Malenbaum, 1953; Milone, 1929), characterized by increasingly regular supplies, greater price stability, and eventually the abatement of acute shortage/scarcity risks. In this framework, railways played a fundamental role on a planetary scale. Japan provides a contrasting example: a famine struck the north-east of the archipelago in 1869, not for lack of food—in this case, rice, abundant in the north-west of the country—but "merely because of the lack of land transportation" (Nobtaro, 1914). This phase coincided with the cultivation of enormous continental or subcontinental spaces and the creation of communication tools (first and foremost, the telegraph) that coordinated the complex movement of goods and information and now acted on an increasingly wide and virtually planetary geographical scale. In addition, towards the end of the century (1880s), there was the "end of seasonality", with the arrival of grains from the southern hemisphere (above all, Argentina and Australia), without forgetting the fundamental contribution offered by Russian grain and the port of Odessa; the (relative) stability of prices and the mobility of goods were reinforced towards the 1890s by the consolidation of the world cereal market and an unprecedented "price harmony" between grain and rice (not parallel but synchronous: rice tends to cost more than grain). As Pomeranz and Topik (2018) suggest, the Indian case was absolutely paradigmatic of this consolidation; paradigmatic also because, in addition to the synchronicity, it calls for reflection upon the actors at this juncture where millions of impoverished farmers were being "prompted" to change their eating habits by the new large markets.

Aluminium presents one more element in the landscape of commodity synchronization. Today, producing one ton of aluminium requires about 8 tons of raw materials (4 of bauxite, which is transformed into 2 of alumina and 2 of scrap—the so-called red mud—and about 4 of coal for the Bayer alumina process and in the form of anodes) and at least 14,000 kwh of electricity. From a logistical point of view, this mass of materials in mobility has resulted in different organizational stances and locations. For many decades, the preferred location for primary aluminium plants was in the Alpine region, in areas close to hydroelectric power plants, while alumina plants were located near bauxite mines. Such locations led to flows of goods arriving and departing from areas that were often difficult to access, resulting in infrastructural and logistical solutions that were not always efficient. As economies of scale in production grew (while in 1900 the minimum efficient size of a factory was about 1,000 tons/year, it was at least 6,000 in the 1920s, 20,000 in the run-up to World War II, and 100,000 in the 1950s), the problem of synchronizing the inbound flow of raw materials and the outbound flow of finished products was combined with that of location. At the same time, the possibility of transporting electricity for hundreds of kilometers as a result of the spread of new technologies and the reduction in shipping costs played an important role in moving production from the Alpine areas (close to the energy) to the sea, where inbound and outbound mobility was much easier. The case of the alumina and aluminium factories in Porto Marghera, built between 1924 and 1928, is the first historical example of this transition, which later became the norm (Stuckey, 1983).

2.4 Actors of mobility

Who controlled the different segments of the silver value chain? The State played a central role in shaping global markets. In 1503, the Spanish Crown established a monopoly in Seville, but did not directly manage it except for the minority portion of silver, essentially the revenues from the *quinto real* (the 20% tax levied on mining production). However, it strived to promote, regulate, and protect the exploitation and private trade of money. Its involvement in the forced migration of miners, the minting of coins, the coordination of transport (the Atlantic, Pacific, and Mediterranean), the regulation of exports and seizures of metal, all helped to shape silver markets and labor relations along the commodity chain (Álvarez Nogal, 2003; García Guerra, 2006). Despite playing a key role in accessing loans from international bankers, crown-owned money flows were a very minor part of the total transported to Seville (Álvarez Nogal, 1997 and Suárez Espinosa, 2016: 186). Most of it was privately owned. In Peru and Mexico, metallurgical mining was carried out by private concessionaires who reinvested the money in commercial or financial activities. By the end of the 16th century, about 13,000 forced laborers were employed in Potosí (Tandeter, 1981). The money was then bought and distributed by merchants and individuals who marketed it and used it as a means of payment throughout the continent. However, much of it ended up in the hands of those large merchant-bankers in Lima, Panama, or Mexico, who used it to purchase goods shipped from Seville or Manila (Serrano Hernández, 2019). As a result, money was used to finance American imports and, in particular, the consumption of local *élites*. By the time it arrived in Seville, the metal would have changed form (if monetized), but mostly hands: the bulk of the royal money passed to the Crown's creditors, while that from trade was seized by the *cargadores a Indias* and other agents who had sold their goods on credit a few months earlier. Behind the apparent homogeneity of its flows, the global monetary chain was highly segmented and socially constructed. It was composed of several intermediaries whose functions responded to the imperfect nature of the markets, but also to the logic of power. Significant to this trend were the *peruleros*, who constantly traveled in fleets between Spain and Peru, bypassing the Panama fairs, and selling the money directly in Seville, where they vied with members of the powerful *Consulado*. The largely fraudulent trade depended heavily on consolidated social ties, and information on the value of the goods elsewhere in the chain was highly flawed (Álvarez Nogal, 2011; Vila Vilar, 1982).

Merchants, milliners, peddlers, *marchandes de mode*, and, of course, the consumers themselves (women, in particular) were the key players in the mobility of ribbons. Between the late 17th and early 18th centuries, ribbons increasingly dominated women's fashions and, thanks to their lightness, became more and more widespread at fairs and rural markets. Peddlers played an important role in this process. In late-17th-century England, groups of petty chapmen sold several kinds of "colored ribbons, plain ribbons, and cheap tobacco," as well as chevrons, lace, and combs. These peddlers travelled extensively and attracted people, especially from the countryside, if, as the master ribbon-makers of Turin said in the mid-18th century, "[country people] love its bright appearance and low price." In 18th-century Paris, the *marchandes de mode* and *revendeuses à la toilette* made the daily rounds of the city's wealthiest neighborhoods with baskets full of ribbons and other items of fashionable accessories that women needed to complete their wardrobes (Sargentson, 1996). The masters who wove ribbons were totally subject to the whims of the *marchandes de mode*, who decided on the type and quality of the ribbon, the quality of the yarn to be used, the supply, and the arrangements on dresses and hats. The merchants, on the other hand, used to lure women to the front of their store windows by displaying classic baby dolls, such as the famous *piavola de Franza*. The women themselves were agents of this mobility, being attracted by the arrival of these products and showing them off once purchased or after receiving them as gifts. So did the merchants, as we will see in the following section (Ribeiro, 2002).

In the case of the global grain market, the non-exclusive but certainly fundamental formula sees the combination of family businesses and multinationals, whose appearance on the economic scene occurs right around the time of the global cereal market. The major players on the world stage since the mid-19th century are the Dreyfus, Cargill, and Bunge & Born families, and a few others; being "family-owned" companies means not being listed and being able to keep financial statements and documents secret. The secrecy of such companies is legendary, despite their entrepreneurial gigantic size. The Dreyfus case is paradigmatic. Léopold Dreyfus invested heavily in elevators (huge silos moved by motor, first with the help of steam and then electricity) to efficiently store grain, and in the grain trade with Odessa, Ukraine, importing Russian grain to Marseille via Livorno. Léopold Louis Dreyfus also expanded the trade to corn, barley, and other cereals, acquiring important shares of the Canadian, Australian, and US markets. In the 1940s, the company was managed by Jean, François, and Pierre Louis Dreyfus, who expanded into Argentina and London. The company became the first grain exporter in France, the third world exporter of grain, the fourth exporter of grain in the United States, the fifth exporter of Argentine grain (8% of the market), and the world's leading exporter of grain to Russia, thanks to a large fleet of bulk carriers and tankers operating all over the world. Similar trajectories characterize the other "giants" that emerged in the second half of the 19th century (Morgan, 1979): the Continental Grain Company, which transports nearly 75 million tons of grain, oilseeds, rice, cotton, and energy products each year, thanks to a merchant fleet, offices, and plants in 50 countries and 6 continents; or Cargill, which, through its subsidiaries, operates 800 plants, has 500 offices in the United States, 300 offices abroad, and operates in 60 countries; in 125 years of operation—since the 1860s—Cargill has only had five chief executive officers, and the control of the first three spans an entire century, all starting with a small "Frontier" grain merchant who became the owner of two elevator companies along strategic rail lines in Wisconsin and Minnesota.

The impossibility of finding all the three main components of aluminium production (bauxite, coal, and cheap electricity) in one single country—with the exception of the US—contributed to the creation of companies that, by achieving vertical integration of their production activities, gave birth to transnational organizational systems. In fact, all the pioneer companies founded at the end of the 19th century, such as the Swiss Alusuisse, the American Alcoa, or the French Pechiney, developed from the outset as multinational companies. The high capital intensity required by this technologically advanced and energy-intensive production also prompted these companies to adopt internationalization strategies in order to tap distant markets. Alusuisse was already exporting to Japan on a permanent basis at the beginning of the 20th century, while, in many European countries, aluminium was also called *"le métal français"* because of the importance of Pechiney's strategies of penetration into international markets. The great strategic importance that this metal has gradually acquired since the Great War has also contributed to linking companies with rearmament policies, as in the case of the German and British industries in the 1930s (Bertilorenzi, 2014), or those of the Americans and Russians during the Cold War (Frøland and Ingulstad, 2012). In contrast to other commodities, however, the role of merchants appears to be diminished: the high integration of downstream and upstream production of this metal created value chains in the hands of manufacturing companies, which, at the same time, ensured a continuous dissemination of technologies and know-how, standardization of product quality, and a system of feedback on quality from customers. The practice of marking aluminium ingots with the name of the producer emerged in 1901 in order to identify the origin, a practice that still continues to this day (Bertilorenzi, 2016).

2.5 The nexus between value and mobility

American silver was often exchanged as a means of payment. To meet its military expenditures, the Spanish administration transferred it from one region to another; the metal was also used to finance trade deficits (e.g., Europe's vis-à-vis China). Due to its metallic stability, the *real de a ocho* also became the standard currency of international trade (Chaudhuri, 1965; Guerra, 2006). Its mobility was not so much related to its adaptation to the tastes of the local consumer, but to its unchanged material properties from one place to another on the globe. Furthermore, mobility gave value to silver: as with other commodities, large traders (Dutch, Italian, Chinese, etc.) sought to speculate on the value of silver, buying it where it cost less to resell it where it cost more. It is known that, due to the huge demand from China, especially after the paper money crisis, arbitrage practices were gradually channelling money to Asia. At the same time, European mints were large consumers of money, which they transformed into local currencies, creating value through seigniorage (Cipolla, 1989; Spooner, 1962). Bankers' arbitrage also contributed to the formation of the value of silver. Indeed, the practices of Genoese bankers are indicative of sophisticated value-creation mechanisms resulting from the mobility of silver. Between 1575 and 1640, the Genoese exported to Italy the money obtained in the Iberian peninsula to support their loans to the Piacenza exchange fairs. The discontinuous mobility of the galleys carrying silver partly determined the value of the precious metal in Italian markets (Da Silva, 1969). In this context, sending money to Genoa when few were able to do so was profitable. At the same time, bankers tried to sell silver where it was worth the most (a typical place being Venice), counting on the possibility of obtaining bills of exchange (which reduced their debts at the fairs) of higher value. These financial instruments were often payable in Antwerp, where the Genoese financed the Spanish armies as a result of these simultaneous movements of metals and capital (Álvarez Nogal, 2006; Maréchaux, 2017).

In the case of ribbons, a mix of elements related to mobility influenced their value. To attract consumers and create new markets, merchants and merchant-manufacturers experimented with a wide range of marketing strategies. The same ribbons could change value depending on the name they had, based on real branding strategies linked to commercial networks and merchant strategies. The first particularly demonstrates the role of certain "hubs" through which the ribbons passed. In Paris, "*Padoue de Lyon*" ribbons were called "from Lyon" not because they were produced in Lyon, but because Parisian merchants bought ribbons imported from Saint Etienne and Saint Chamond *through* Lyon. Merchant strategies, on the other hand, influenced the name in other ways. On the one hand, merchants sought to sell products that recalled exotic or foreign fashions in order to influence markets. On the other hand, they organized trade and monitored production to increase profits. For example, while ribbons "from London" were popular in Paris, in London it was the ribbons "from Paris" that were the most successful on the market. However, in the 18th century, Milanese merchants preferred to export the finest raw silk to France, importing high-quality fancy ribbons from Lyon, and distributing lower-quality raw silk to local producers to weave lower-quality ribbons. The consequence was that Milanese merchants made greater profits in local markets by selling foreign ribbons at higher prices, while local artisans were unable to compete because of the low-quality silk they received. Mobility transformed not only the value of ribbons, but also their innermost significance. Moving across geographic spaces, ribbons became a *genderized* product linked to the sphere of sexuality. In fact, the consumption of ribbons was particularly linked to eye-catching and pleasurable consumption, female vanity, and changing fashions. Especially in America, ribbons were gifts of love during fairs, at times implying amorous and sexual promises that were not always linked to marriage. Ribbons had multiple uses, some of which "involved the physical placement of ribbons on intimate parts of the body." The metaphor *love ribbon* referred to a specific object used on both sides of the Atlantic that involved "attaching items to undergarments and sleeves-ties to the closest parts of the bodies" (Martin, 2008).

Mobility has always played a central role in the formation of "grain value". However, while in the modern era it was essentially short-haul, characterized by an anarchic and feverish activity profoundly influenced by the timing of harvests, sales, and emergencies, in the second half of the 19th century it progressively freed itself from the tyranny of economic geography. This is a phase that coincides with the creation and institutionalization of new centers that ensure price determination far from the centers of production and, in the commodity value chain, in positions closer to the markets, such as the Chicago Board of Trade, the Baltic House in London, or the Halle du Blé in Paris. The new link between mobility and value gradually moves away from the simple speculation of merchants who buy where grain is plentiful to resell it at a high price where it is scarce, and is linked to the development of complex financial instruments, such as futures contracts. These contracts, in fact, determine the value of wheat by linking it both to "future mobility", now ensured by major logistical innovations (warehouses, major lines of communication, and large-scale sea and rail transport), and to the ability to forecast the size of harvests on a planetary scale. On the one hand, the creation of a regular commodity chain freed the market from seasonal shortages and climatic risks; on the other, it was based on specific hubs, such as commodity exchanges, that negotiated futures contracts, offering outlets for production and assuming the risk of sudden variations in the value of the grain itself.

The value of aluminium has always been linked to its mobility, adopting a distinction typical of classical and then Marxist economics in terms of use value and exchange value. The spread of aluminium applications was linked to its intrinsic properties, such as lightness or the impossibility of developing rust, in a wide variety of cases: increasing the performance of air, land, and sea carriers; cable sections in the transport of electricity; or reducing the dead weight (or tons) of packaging for other goods. Unlike other metals, its exchange value was strongly correlated with the "list price", that is, the producer price set by companies based on production costs. The ability of producers to select factors of production, by size and location, made it possible to stabilize and standardize the price at a global level, an aspect also confirmed by the creation of an international cartel that lasted from the end of the 19th century to 1978. Unlike copper, silver, and wheat, whose prices varied a great deal and were strongly conditioned by metal traders and institutional markets, the ability of producers to control prices guaranteed price stability over the long term. In times of crisis, or for strategic reasons, the value of metal was even linked to its immobility, giving rise to stockpiling activities by companies, banks, or governments (Bertilorenzi, 2016). From 1978 onwards, aluminium began to be listed on the London Metal Exchange, a major commodity exchange in the City of London. The price became unstable and was increasingly influenced not so much by its physical mobility, but rather by the speed at which merchants transmitted information to the market, as in other commodities (Bertilorenzi, 2020). While the value of this commodity had a special link to its mobility, its immobility also had an extensive socio-economic impact, involving political and environmental considerations. Particularly significant was the management of waste from alumina processing, which involved a vast accumulation near the factories themselves or on the sea floor, as this waste was often dumped into the sea. The advantage of the coastal location of the alumina factories, at least for the producers, was therefore given not only by the mobility of materials in and out of the production process, but also by the possibility of dumping waste into the sea, which the producers continued to do for decades in the Venetian Lagoon as well as in other areas (Mioche and Bertilorenzi, 2013).

2.6 Conclusions

This quick journey, undertaken through the analysis of four commodities and through the application of mobility studies, prompts us to some concluding thoughts, albeit in the provisional manner that such a research project may have. Behind the issue of the mobility of these commodities, complex dynamics can be identified that refer back to their topology (Adey et al., 2014: 266; Abrahamsson and Mol, 2014). Each commodity encompasses parts of the world, cultures, and significances that an attentive approach to this mobility can induce us to consider in its main facets: from raw materials to technologies, from labor to the meanings assumed in the different cultures of consumption and production. These worlds are of variable geometry: from the integration of Potosí silver into the world economy to the creation of a Euro-Atlantic circulation of silk ribbons, from the cultivation of wheat on the North American plains to the mobilization of bauxite, we realize that mobility varies over time and follows dynamics linked to specific value chains. The value itself changes with the variation of mobility possibilities that emerge from the complex interaction between markets (understood as encounters between an increasingly global supply and demand), technologies, infrastructures, and logistical elements.

The commodity's topological complexity calls for a reconsideration of the role that certain actors play in mobility. As we have seen, each commodity can have different types of key actors, which, in the case of ribbons, also involves the consumers themselves. The figure of an actor can certainly be related to the type of product. Products such as silver or wheat require the coordination of complex forms of circulation involving States or multinationals, even in the diversity of actors in relation to production (a few thousand miners versus millions of peasants); an item of clothing—in an era in which the personal brand is still remote—sees the use of a complexity of agents even in the smallest folds of the commodity chain. The theme of actors calls us to look at the hierarchies of power that are established along commodity chains. Control over the commodity or information (from the price of the commodity to the conditions of the target market) guarantees competitive advantage. In the case of the role played by the sources of supply (as in the case of silver), control over production or marketing influences the subsequent stages of the commodity chain (from a producer-oriented or trader-oriented perspective), while clothing chains are shown to be strongly buyer-oriented, placing the designers, merchants, or consumers themselves at the end of the chain in the main role, even influencing the very meanings (Gereffi, 2018). It is these hierarchies, after all, that orient commodity markets, whose mobility is anything but anonymous or spontaneous, but constructed, directed, and hierarchical.

Much remains to be done in terms of the analysis of commodities from a mobility perspective. Certainly, for several years now, the global historiographic turn has made it possible to take a new look at the circulation of commodities, also taking up the stimuli of the commodity chains approach (Hopkins and Wallerstein, 1986). However, mobility studies can offer further insights into how to look at products by investigating and framing the commodity in the complexity within each segment of the commodity chain. In fact, the historical economic problem of global markets can no longer be thought of in terms of simple chains or shifts from places of production to places of consumption, but rather as the result of changing topologies, with respect to which the mobility of commodities contributes to altering their forms and dynamics.

References

Abrahamsson C and Mol A (2014) Food. In: Adey P et al. (eds) *The Routledge handbook of mobilities*. London; New York: Routledge, pp. 278–287.

Adey P et al. (eds) (2014) *The Routledge handbook of mobilities*. London: Routledge.

Álvarez Nogal C (1997) *El crédito de la Monarquía Hispánica en el reinado de Felipe IV*. Valladolid: Junta de Castilla y León.

Álvarez Nogal C (2003) Instituciones y desarrollo económico: la Casa de la Contratación y la Carrera de Indias (1503–1790). In: Acosta Rodríguez A, González Rodríguez A and Vila Vilar E (eds) *La Casa de Contratación y la navegación entre España y las Indias*. Seville: Universidad de Sevilla – CSIC – Fundación el Monte, pp. 21–51.

Álvarez Nogal C (2006) La transferencia de dinero a Flandes en el siglo XVII. In: Sanz Ayán C and García García BJ (eds) *Banca, crédito y capital. La Monarquía Hispánica y los antiguos Países Bajos (1500–1700)*. Madrid: Fundación Carlos Amberes, pp. 205–232.

Álvarez Nogal C (2011) Mercados o redes de mercaderes: el funcionamiento de la feria de Portobelo. In: Böttcher N, Hausberger B and Ibarra A (eds) *Redes y negocios globales en el mundo ibérico, siglos XVI-XVIII*. Madrid – Frankfurt: Iberoamericana – Vervuert – El Colegio de México, pp. 53–86.

Álvarez Nogal C, Lo Basso L and Marsilio C (2007) La rete finanziaria della famiglia Spinola: Spagna, Genova e le fiere dei cambi (1610–1656). *Quaderni storici* 124(1): 97–110.

Arrighi G (2010) *The long twentieth century: Money, power, and the origins of our times*. London: Verso.

Atkin M (1995) *The international grain trade*. Cambridge: Woodhead Publishing.

Banaji J (2020) *A brief history of commercial capitalism*. Chicago: Haymarket Books.

Beckert S (2015) *Empire of cotton: A new history of global capitalism*. London: Penguin Books.

Bertilorenzi M (2014) Business, politics, and finance: The rise and fall of international aluminium cartels, 1914–1945. *Business History* 56(2): 236–269.

Bertilorenzi M (2016) *The international aluminium cartel: The business and politics of a cooperative industrial institution, 1886–1978*. London; New York: Routledge.

Bertilorenzi M (2020) From cartels to futures: The aluminium industry, the London metal exchange, and European competition policies, 1960–1980. *Business History* 62(5): 782–814.

Bonialian MA (2012) *El Pacífico hispanoamericano. Política y comercio asiático en el Imperio Español (1680–1784)*. Mexico City: El Colegio de México.

Broehl WG Jr. (1992) *Cargill: Trading the world's grain*. Hanover, NH: University Press of New England.

Brunt L and Cannon E (2013) Integration in the English wheat market 1770–1820. *Discussion Papers* 9504, C.E.P.R. Discussion Papers.

Caracausi A (2019) Fashion, capitalism and ribbon-making in early modern Europe. In: Safley TM (ed.) *Labor before the Industrial Revolution: Work, technology and their ecologies in an age of early capitalism*. London: Routledge, pp. 48–69.

Cavaciocchi S (ed) (1993) *La seta in Europa, sec. 13-20*. Florence: Le Monnier.

Charvet JP (1985) *Les greniers du monde*. Paris: Economica.

Chaudhuri KN (1965) *The English East India Company: The study of an early joint-stock company, 1600–1640*. London: Frank Cass and Co.

Cipolla CM (1989) *Money in sixteenth century Florence*. Berkeley; Los Angeles; London: University of California Press.

Da Silva JG (1969) *Banque et crédit en Italie au XVIIè siècle*, 2 vol. Paris: Klincksieck.

Elliott JH (1989) *Spain and its world 1500–1700*. New Haven; London: Yale University Press.

Federico G (2011) When did European markets integrate? *European Review of Economic History* 15: 93–126.

Federico G (2012) How much do we know about market integration in Europe? *Economic History Review* 65(2): 470–497.

Flynn DO and Giráldez A (2004) Path dependence, time lags and the birth of globalisation: A critique of O'Rourke and Williamson. *European Review of Economic History* 8: 81–108.

Frøland HO and Ingulstad M (2012) 'An age of aluminium': The political economy of the aluminium industry in the 20th century. In: Frøland HO and Ingulstad M (eds) *From warfare to welfare: Business-government relations in the aluminium industry*. Trondheim: Akademika, pp. 15–32.

García Guerra EM (2006) Itinerarios mundiales de una moneda supranacional: el real de a ocho o peso durante la Edad Moderna. *Studia Historica. Historia moderna* 28: 241–257.
Gasch-Tomás JL (2018) *The Atlantic world and the Manila galleons: Circulation, market, and consumption of Asian goods in the Spanish Empire, 1565–1650*. Leiden; Boston: Brill.
Gereffi G (2018) *Global value chains and development: Redefining the contours of 21st century capitalism*. Cambridge: Cambridge University Press.
Grinberg I (2003) *Aluminium. Un si léger métal*. Paris: Gallimard.
Hoffman KJ and Hill LD (1976) Historical review of the U.S. Grades and Standards for Grain. *Illinois Agricultural Economics* 16(1): 1–9.
Holloway SK (1988) *The aluminium multinationals and the bauxite cartel*. New York: St. Martin's Press.
Hopkins TK and Wallerstein I (1986) Commodity chains in the world-economy prior to 1800. *Review (Fernand Braudel Center)* 10(1): 157–170.
Levinson M (2016) *The box: How the shipping container made the world smaller and the world economy bigger*. Princeton: Princeton University Press.
Malenbaum W (1953) *The world wheat economy, 1885–1939*. Cambridge: Harvard University Press.
Maréchaux B (2017) *Instituciones navales y finanzas internacionales en el Mediterráneo de la época moderna. Los asentistas de galeras genoveses al servicio de la Monarquía Hispánica (1500–1650)*. PhD Thesis, Universidad Carlos III de Madrid.
Maréchaux B (2020) Los asentistas de galeras genoveses y la articulación naval de un imperio policéntrico (siglos XVI–XVII). *Hispania* 80(264): 47–77.
Marichal C (2006) The Spanish-American silver peso: Export commodity and global money of the Ancien Regime, 1550–1800. In: Topik S, Marichal C and Frank Z (eds) *From silver to cocaine: Latin American commodity chains and the building of the world economy, 1500–2000*. Durham; London: Duke University Press, pp. 25–52.
Martin AS (2008) *Buying into the world of goods: Early consumers in backcountry Virginia*. Baltimore: Johns Hopkins University Press.
Mazzamauro A (2016) Going global: il mercato mondiale del grano nella seconda metà del diciannovesimo secolo. *Italia contemporanea* 282: 65–89.
Milone F (1929) *Il grano. Le condizioni geografiche della produzione*. Bari: Laterza.
Mioche P and Bertilorenzi M (2013) Les résidus de l'alumine à Portovesme en Italie et à Gardanne/Cassis en France des années 1960 à nos jours. In: Cementeri L and Daumalin X (eds) *Pollutions industrielles et espaces méditerranéens*. Aix-en-Provence: Editions de la MMSH, pp. 275–300.
Morgan D (1979) *Merchants of grain*. New York: Viking Press.
Nobtaro I (1914) *Development of Japanese foreign trade (1868–1913)*. Thesis Submitted in Partial Fulfillment of the Requirements for the Degree of Master of Arts in Economics, Graduate School of the University of Illinois.
Patel R and Moore JW (2017) *A History of the world in seven cheap things: a guide to capitalism, nature, and the future of the planet*. London: Verso.
Pomeranz K and Topik S (2018) *The world that trade created: Society, culture, and the world economy, 1400 to present*. Routledge: New York (4th edition).
Poni C (2009) *La seta in Italia: una grande industria prima della rivoluzione industriale*. Bologna: il Mulino.
Ribeiro A (2002) *Dress in 18th century Europe: 1715–1789*. New Haven: Yale University Press.

Riello G (2013) *Cotton: The fabric that made the modern world*. New York [etc.]: Cambridge University Press.

Rothstein M (1988) Centralizing firms and spreading markets: The world of international grain traders, 1864–1914. *Business and Economic History*, 2nd s., 17: 103–113.

Sacchi Landriani M and De Vito CG (2020) Logistica delle migrazioni. Elaborazione concettuale e prospettive storiche. *Scienza & Politica* 11: 11–30.

Santos J (n.d.) *A history of futures trading in the United States*. Available at: https://eh.net/encyclopedia/a-history-of-futures-trading-in-the-united-states/ (accessed 9 September 2021).

Sardone S (2017) Lo sviluppo del commercio coloniale spagnolo. Il ruolo della *Casa de la Contratación* e del *Consulado* di Siviglia, 1503–1650. *Rises. Ricerche di storia economica e sociale* 3(1–2): 61–93.

Sargentson C (1996) *Merchants and luxury markets: The marchands merciers of 18th century Paris*. London: Victoria and Albert Museum.

Serrano Hernández ST (2019) *La golosina del oro. La producción de metales preciosos en San Luis Minas del Potosí durante el siglo XVII*. San Luis Potosí: El Colegio de San Luis.

Sheller M (2015) *Aluminum dreams: The making of light modernity*. Cambridge, MA; London: The MIT Press.

Spooner FC (1962) Venice and the Levant: An aspect of monetary history (1610–1614). In: *Studi in onore di Amintore Fanfani*, vol. V. Milan: A. Giuffré, pp. 643–667.

Stuckey JA (1983) *Vertical integration and joint ventures in the aluminum industry*. London: Harvard University Press.

Suárez Espinosa M (2016) Metales preciosos, moneda y comercio. La participación del Perú en el mundo ultramarino, siglos XVI–XVIII. In: Contreras Carranza C (ed) *Historia de la moneda en el Perú*. Lima: Banco Central de Reserva del Perú – Instituto de Estudios Peruanos, pp. 155–197.

Tandeter E (1981) Trabajo forzado y trabajo libre en el Potosí colonial tardío. *Desarrollo Económico* 20(80): 511–548.

Vila Vilar E (1982) Las ferias de Portobelo: apariencia y realidad del comercio con Indias. *Anuario de Estudios Americanos* 39: 275–340.

Wallerstein I (1980) *The modern world-system. Vol. 2: Mercantilism and the consolidation of the European world-economy, 1600–1750*. New York: Academic Press.

Williams JC (1982) The origin of futures markets. *Agricultural History* 56: 306–316.

Yun-Casalilla B (2019) *Iberian world empires and the globalization of Europe 1415–1668*. Singapore: Palgrave Macmillan.

3 Mobilizing pictures
The history of science through the lens of mobility

Elena Canadelli

3.1 Intersections

The historian of science, Dagmar Schäfer, wrote in her editorial in *Transfers*, one of the leading journals in the field of mobility studies, that "Mobility is an important theme in the history of science, though it is mainly discussed in terms of the transfer, circulation, travel, or exchange of information, knowledge, objects, and people, and even more in terms of mutable and immutable objects" (2018: viii). "As a historian of science and technology", Schäfer continued,

> I would like to add that the epistemic implications of movement and mobility—its local and global impact on practices and theories of knowledge—and the ontological consequences require attention, too. Mobility not only has a physical and a mental side but, as often as not, is and has been an operative process that becomes apparent in multiple ways. This operative process has historical, scientific, and technological dimensions, as well as one in the humanities and arts.
>
> (2018: viii)

As a result, *Transfers*' first issue of 2019 featured a series of reflections on the role of movement and mobilities in the fields of history of science, technology, and medicine, exploring in four papers the possibilities of cross-disciplinary research, from the movements, or failures to move, of special types of human artefacts such as cropscapes to the impact of individuals' geographic mobility on the spatial dynamics of knowledge in late imperial China, from the movement of knowledge (materials, techniques, and objects) across Eurasia to theoretical reflections on "migrating knowledge" through a short case study concerned with the perception of sunspots through the telescope. As the sociologist Mimi Sheller pointed out in her response to this Special Section, it is the time

> to dispel three myths about mobility studies: The first is the myth that mobility studies are purely about the contemporary world, as a world

DOI: 10.4324/9781003278665-5

of fluidity and flows, and that it is somehow categorically set apart from historical dimensions of mobile processes. The second myth is that the field focuses solely on material phenomenon of physical transport (i.e., of things and people) and ignores the movement of ideas, knowledge, and culture. The third myth is that mobility studies is purely about "flows" and "circulation" and has little to teach us about friction, resistances, blockages, or uneven power relations.

(Sheller, 2019: 88)

In this regard, the history of science seems to be a suitable and flexible field of research to expand the mobility framework in space and time, and to open a conversation about possible exchanges between mobility studies and other disciplinary approaches within a historical perspective, considering a vast array of phenomena on the move, of objects and ideas as well as of people and theories. In fact, from the late 1970s onward, many historians of science have become interested in how scientific knowledge circulated, moved, and was shaped in the process. At the crossroads of history of knowledge, global history, postcolonial studies, gender studies, and sociology of science, to list just a few fields of research, the history of science has in recent years increasingly dealt with concepts such as mobility, circulation, transfer, movement, diffusion, and transit—as well as their opposites, such as place, stasis, and immobility. The historian Pamela H. Smith, in collaboration with a research group at the Max Planck Institute for the History of Science in Berlin, who is working on *Itineraries of materials, recipes, techniques, and knowledge in the early modern world*, has focused, for example, on knowledge and science "in motion", outlining a framework of

(1) "material complex," meaning the constellation of substances, practices, techniques, beliefs, values, and knowledge accreted around materials that endow them with meaning; (2) the "relational field," that is, the social, intellectual, economic, and emotional domain, which is formed by a "node of convergence"—often a hub of trade and exchange—within which a particular material complex crystalizes; and (3) "itineraries," or the routes that materials take into and through nodes of convergence, by which they stabilize and/or transform into new material complexes.

(Smith, 2019a: 76; 2019b)

According to Smith, focusing on these concepts allows historians to follow routes of knowledge-making extending over very long distances and/or great spans of time. Already in 2004, in a seminal essay entitled *Knowledge in transit* and published in *Isis*, the journal of the History of Science Society, James A. Secord recognized the centrality of knowledge in circulation and processes of movement, translation, and transmission in the discipline. Instead of focusing on the traditional concepts of origin, novelty, discovery, and innovation, he argued that working on the categories of circulation and mobility in science would allow a real change of perspective. "Writing a history of knowledge as circulating practices would not be easy"—Secord wrote—"but at least it is possible to see how it might be done" (2004: 667). He encourages his colleagues to address questions such as how and why knowledge circulates, suggesting that all scientific activity should be seen as a form of communication. The transformation of knowledge as it moves between different social strata, media, places, and environments should be at the core of analysis, focusing on the conditions and material aspects of circulation, movement in society at large, and the mediality of these phenomena.

As a result, the shift from production to circulation has allowed historians to focus less on the making and location of scientific knowledge and more on how it circulates in space and time (Östling et al., 2018: 18–23). This is particularly true if we look at the history of science on a global scale, especially in the early modern period. Thus, it has been up to scholars of the modern age, above all, to investigate topics such as science and imperialism, science and colonialism, science and exploration, focusing on a world that was expanding at great speed along trade routes and spatial and intellectual borders, and in which scientific and economic development were increasingly intertwined. Influenced by post-colonial studies, many have focused on the history of science in geographical areas other than Europe, such as India, China, the Ottoman Empire, Southeast Asia, and Oceania, considered in their relations with the European powers of the time, from Great Britain to France, such as in the works of David Arnold and Kapil Raj. The actors, vectors, and places of transmission (or non-transmission) of knowledge are central to these works, as are scientific practices such as cartography or botany, in a mutual interaction, translation, and exchange of knowledge between the local and global dimension. To give just a few examples, in 2010, *Isis* hosted a rich focus entitled *Global histories of science* edited by Sujit Sivasundaram, the aim of which was, among other things, to reread the processes underlying the globalization of science in the modern age, starting from sources, languages, methodologies, and different chronologies. In the same year, the *British Journal for the History of Science* dedicated a monographic issue to the topic *Circulation and locality in early modern science*, edited by Kapil Raj, focusing on the concept of circulation on a global scale of knowledge, instruments, and scientific texts in the modern age, as in the case of entomology in 18th century France or vaccination treatment and prevention against smallpox in Guatemala. Just a year earlier, *Itinerary*, the international journal on the history of European expansion and global interaction, had focused on a similar topic, *Science and global history, 1750–1850. Local encounters and global circulation*, edited by Lissa Roberts. In 2012, Jürgen Renn edited the substantial volume *The globalization of knowledge in history*, dedicated to investigating the role of the circulation of science and, more generally, of knowledge in past globalization processes through a series of comparative cases that go back to the Neolithic, ancient Eurasia, or the Babylonians. In France, works such as *Les savoirs-mondes. Mobilités et circulation des savoirs depuis le Moyen*

Âge, edited in 2015 by Pilar González Bernaldo and Liliane Hilaire-Peréz, identified a new theoretical framework in the mobility and circulation of knowledge. In the same year, in the renowned journal *Annales. Histoire, Sciences Sociales*, historians of science Antonella Romano and Simon Schaffer took stock of what it means to make history of modern science in the era of globalization and how to rethink the world history of science through a specific case study on the standardization of measurement practices (see bibliography in Canadelli, 2019).

As emerges from these examples, an examination of the concept of circulation in the broad sense leads to a rereading of the pivotal concepts of the discipline—including the very ideas of science, modernity, scientific revolution, and progress—whose origins and stratifications are critically discussed. Too often, science has been looked at as an ahistorical phenomenon, detached from the concrete context of its production and diffusion, a priori linked to concepts of universality, objectivity, modernity, and cosmopolitanism. There is no doubt that in recent years, the history of science and global history have increasingly intertwined their paths in search of sources and methodologies capable of shifting the gaze towards the formation and circulation of knowledge and scientific practices on a global scale (Renn and Hyman, 2012). As argued by Francesca Bray, Barbara Hahn, John Bosco Lourdusamy, and Tiago Saraiva, global history and the history of science are now dealing with similar subjects: "Global history likewise follows flows and encounters, knowledge and materials in motion, while history of science and technology are now increasingly interested in the mobility of knowledge systems, focusing on transfers and resulting processes of transformation and appropriation" (2019: 21). This is demonstrated by the works published, especially since the 2000s, by historians of science and knowledge such as James Delbourgo, Jürgen Renn, Simon Schaffer, Sujit Sivasundaram, Kapil Raj, Antonella Romano, and Lissa Roberts, to name just a few (Fan, 2012). These works wonder about the peculiarities of the contribution of science to globalization over the centuries and the complex processes of negotiation, connection, and comparison through which the various scientific disciplines and institutions have taken shape. In this sense, the concepts of circulation and mobility play a very crucial role. But it is not only the history of science that has taken this path. The history of technology is also integrating global themes and approaches within it. In France, for example, the volume *Les techniques et la globalisation au xxe siècle: réseaux, échanges et espionnage industriel*, edited in 2016 by Liliane Hilaire-Peréz and Larissa Zakharova, focused on the role played by techniques in globalization processes. According to the two editors, this perspective is not common in the discipline, traditionally devoted to the theoretical framework of civilizing technological progress. Among the rare attempts to trace a global history of technology, one of the most interesting is that proposed by the English historian of science and technology, David Edgerton. In his book *The shock of the old: technology and global history since 1900*, published for the first time in 2006, Edgerton asks for a historiographic change, necessary to deconstruct and demythologize the categories of invention, innovation, and progress with which, up to that moment, the history of technology had been almost totally identified. Rather than talking about innovation centers, he suggests focusing on the category of use of things, on a global history of techniques purified from the idea of a false universality built by considering only a handful of places around the world.

To break away from this historiographical "machine", while a historian of technology like Edgerton prefers to talk about the use of things, many historians of science look at the formation of the global world in relation to local contexts by working on the concept of mobility and circulation of objects, ideas, people, and practices. Accounting for the mobility of natural knowledge beyond its site of origin has become a major concern. Scholars have thus convincingly demonstrated that "scientific propositions, artefacts, and practices are neither innately universal (because of their epistemological force) nor forcibly imposed on others. Rather, they disseminate only through complex processes of accommodation and negotiation, as contingent as those involved in their production" (Raj, 2007: 9). In this way, science is no longer looked at ahistorically and positivistically as a purely Western and, at the same time, universal phenomenon, but as the result of a dialectic of local encounters and global circulation—where anonymous intermediaries also play an important role (Schaffer et al., 2009)—in an intertwining of spatial dynamics and transfers of ideas, people, texts, practices, tools, and procedures. In Europe, as in China, science therefore appears to be the result of processes of negotiation and dialogue (or non-dialogue) between global knowledge and local traditions and encounters. In this framework, mobility and circulation have become core concepts.

3.2 Circulation, or mobility, that is the question

The majority of historians speak more of "circulation" than of "mobility" when they deal with phenomena variously connected with movement, knowledge transfer, diffusion, and dissemination. In fact, "circulation" is currently one of the most widely employed words in the language of global history and the history of globalization, as argued by the historian Stefanie Gänger in an article recently published in the *Journal of Global History*. Gänger examines uses of the word in a set number of English-language issues appearing in three journals, excluding reviews, front or back matter texts, letters to the editor, editorial introductions, frontispieces, and other similar material from the count: the *Journal of World History*, the *Journal of Global History*, and *Isis,* which is particularly relevant to our examination in connection with the history of science, medicine, and technology. As analysed by Gänger,

> In these journals, "circulation", or the verb "circulate", occurred in 42%, 52%, and 37% of the articles published between 2009 and 2016, respectively: in 63 of 150 articles in the *Journal of World History* in the issues

that came out between March 2009 and December 2016, and in 81 of 155 articles in the *Journal of Global History* in the issues that came out between March 2009 and November 2016. "Circulation", or the verb "circulate", was used somewhat more sparingly in the journal *Isis*, where they occurred in 97 out of 260 articles in the issues that came out between March 2009 and December 2016—or fewer, were we to omit "focus" sections dedicated to a new, global history of science, where "circulation", or the verb "circulate", occurred in as many as 85% of the articles.

(Gänger, 2017: 304)

In *Isis*, Gänger continues, "in 78 out of 97 mentions, authors use the term to refer to the 'circulation' of 'stories', of 'new research findings', of 'a memorandum to federal patent officials', of 'reagents, techniques, and researchers', or of 'metaphors and models'" (Gänger, 2017: 306). These figures clearly demonstrate how interest in these topics has recently grown in the history of science, with a focus on what is happening in the fields of global history and history of knowledge. On the other hand, if we examine the occurrence of terms such as "mobile" or "mobility" in *Isis* with the same parameters used by Gänger, we only find around 40 articles that use these words. But only a small percentage properly deals with issues such as knowledge circulation, global relations, translation, and reuse, such as *Making mobile knowledges: the educational cruises of the Revue Générale des Sciences Pures et Appliquées, 1897–1914* (2010) by the cultural geographer Veronica Della Dora; *Global knowledge on the move: itineraries, Amerindian narratives, and deep histories of science* (2010) by the historian Neil Safier; *Listing People* (2012) by the historian of science James Delbourgo; and *Beyond Postcolonialism ... and Postpositivism: Circulation and the Global History of Science* (2013) by the historian Kapil Raj. Compared to "circulation", "mobility" seems to be a less frequent term for historians of science, even though recent works by scholars such as Dagmar Schäfer and Pamela H. Smith show a new trend in the field.

One may wonder where the difference between "circulation" and "mobility" really lies. Both terms deal with concepts of transmission, transfer, spread, dissemination, and diffusion. Actually, it seems more a question of terminology than of substance, depending on the use and the meaning assigned to movement by different scholars. The first term is traditionally used within the human sciences, whereas the second appears more common in the social sciences. On the one hand, scholars from the history of knowledge and global history usually prefer to speak about "circulation", considering it a process embedded in a social context, continuously formed in cultural processes and shaped by power relations. As Philipp Sarasin and Andreas B. Kilcher put it, since the 1990s, "circulation" has become a "catchword" for all kinds of processualities and transfers (2011: 8). According to historians of colonialism such as Claude Markovits, Jacques Pouchepadass, and Sanjay Subrahmanyam,

Circulation is different from simple mobility, inasmuch as it implies a double movement of going back and forth and coming back, which can be repeated indefinitely. In circulating, things, men and notions often transform themselves. Circulation is therefore a value-loaded term which implies an incremental aspect and not the simple reproduction across space of already formed structures and notions.

(in Östling et al., 2018: 21)

On the other hand, scholars from the social sciences, such as the geographer Tim Cresswell or the three editors of the book *Mobilities of knowledge* (2017), Heike Jöns, Michael Heffernan, and Peter Meusburger, prefer to speak of "mobility", which seems to offer a broader theoretical umbrella. In particular, according to Cresswell, mobility involves a "fragile entanglement of physical movement, representations, and practices" (2010: 18), outlining three aspects of mobility: "the fact of physical movement—getting from one place to another; the representations of movement that give it shared meaning; and, finally, the experienced and embodied practice of movement" (2010: 19). Already in 1987, in his book *Science in action,* Bruno Latour spoke of mobility, together with stability and combinability, among the requirements for scientific knowledge to be accumulated away from the field. Indeed, he asked:

How to act at a distance on unfamiliar events, places and people? Answer: by *somehow* bringing home these events, places and people. How can this be achieved, since they are distant? By inventing means that (a) render them *mobile so* that they can be brought back; (b) keep them *stable so* that they can be moved back and forth without additional distortion, corruption or decay, and (c) are *combinable so* that whatever stuff they are made of, they can be cumulated, aggregated, or shuffled like a pack of cards. If those conditions are met, then a small provincial town, or an obscure laboratory, or a puny little company in a garage, that were at first as weak as any other place, will become centres dominating at a distance many other places.

(Latour, 1987: 223)

"Circulation" and "mobility" both attempt to replace words discredited by their association with Eurocentrism, such as diffusion, which implies a center of innovation and origin in Western countries and their unidirectional dissemination in other contexts. In other words, focusing on "things-in-motion", as the anthropologist Arjun Appadurai wrote in his seminal book *The social life of things: commodities in cultural perspectives* (1986), enables us to construct a history that extends beyond particular instances, and this is particularly true with regard to science and technology, as demonstrated in the first paragraph of my essay. In her article, Gänger extensively discusses the term "circulation". In 2013, according to the global historian of science, Kapil Raj, the value of "circulation" lay precisely in that it served "as a strong counterpoint to the unidirectionality of 'diffusion' or even of 'dissemination' or 'transmission', of binaries such as metropolitan science/colonial science or center/periphery, which all imply a producer and an end user" (in Gänger, 2017: 309). Also, the global historian of science, Lissa Roberts, writes in 2009 that "circulation" ought to describe "a movement without center", without "a clear and privileged point of origin and return", a "continuous path whose formative trajectory is constituted out of multiple points of local contact and exchange" (in Gänger, 2017: 316). In contrast, "circulation" might be a misleading term to other historians. As the historian of science, Fa-ti Fan, phrased it in 2013, circulation suggests that "'people, information, and material objects flowed smoothly along networks and channels', obscuring the efforts that went into transportation, the absence of 'teleology' in these trajectories, and the obstructions, standstills, and delays involved" (in Gänger, 2017: 311). As reported by Gänger,

> Circulation not only makes global processes appear smooth and unimpeded; just as Stuart A. Rockefeller has argued for the term flow, it also bestows an "abstract and disembodied quality" upon the processes it is used to describe. In the vast majority of the articles under consideration, "circulation", or the verb "circulate", are employed without reference to agency. Again, this tendency is less marked in the journal *Isis*, where authors employ the term "circulation", or the verb "circulate", in 48 out of 97 articles that resort to those terms (49%) without reference to agency.
> (Gänger, 2017: 312)

The problem with using "circulation" seems to lie in the tendency to emphasize movement over agency, highlighting "the fact of movement" of goods, people, or ideas rather than the causes, contents, or conditions of movement (Gänger, 2017: 313). That is why, at a time when historical scholarship is preoccupied with uncovering the "agency" of movement, "mobility" might suggest a broader terminological galaxy than "circulation".

3.3 Mobility of pictures: the *Iconoteca dei botanici* at the University of Padova

As argued above, in recent years there has been a greater emphasis placed on the ways in which various groups of individuals, including researchers from different scientific communities, produced knowledge and science through the framework of mobility. As argued by the three editors of the book *Mobilities of knowledge* (2017), the mobility of people, practices, institutions, ideas, technologies, and things has significantly impacted epistemic systems of knowledge. Particularly interesting is the study of the mobility of specimens and museum collections (Cornish and Driver, 2020; Driver, Nesbitt, and Cornish, 2021; Arens, 2015). The pivotal role of such mobilities in the acquisition, exchange, and making of knowledge and science is exemplified in my paper by the case study of the *Iconoteca dei botanici*, a collection of portraits of Italian and foreign botanists at the University of Padova Botanic Garden. The formation of this collection is mediated through the mobility of specific objects: the portraits of botanists, mostly *cartes de visite*, gathered in Padova through a dense network of correspondents by the Italian botanist and mycologist, Pier Andrea Saccardo, who was the director of the Botanic Garden between the 19th and 20th centuries. Today, it consists of around 2,380 portraits of Italian and foreign botanists. Most of them are photographs, but there are also drawings, paintings, engravings, and prints (Canadelli, 2020).

Instead of looking at global and post-colonial studies, this case study demonstrates how fruitful it can be to mix history of science with visual and media studies through the lens of mobility studies. In terms of identity building and symbolic representations, the study of portraits of scientific personas has a long tradition in the history of science, as evidenced by the works of Ludmilla Jordanova (2000), Alessandro Tosi (2007), and Marco Beretta (2020), to mention just a few. In the *Iconoteca*, we find the "fragile entanglement of physical movement, representations, and practices" discussed by Cresswell. This collection of portraits shows how botanists have produced knowledge and agency through the framework of mobility. The circulation of photographic portraits acquires a peculiar meaning in connection with the dynamics of production and dissemination of knowledge, intended as the sociologist Nico Stehr in 1994 called "a capacity for social action" (in Jöns, Heffernan, and Meusburger, 2017: 5) or, as in this case, a capacity for gaining authority from the Italian community of botanists, reinforcing a specific tradition centered on the role played by Italian botanists and flora in the discipline's history. In Saccardo's view, the formation of this collection was ultimately connected to his project of writing the history of botany in Italy. On this subject, he published the two volumes of *La botanica in Italia. Materiali per la storia di questa scienza* in 1895 and 1901. The formation of the *Iconoteca* is tightly related to the mobility of botanists' portraits through the hands of different scholars, collectors, relatives of botanists, and donors by means of photographs such as *cartes de visite* and photographic copies of drawings or other photos. Bringing photographs together into a single collection was an attempt to create a sort of Latourian "immutable mobiles" in order to give authority to a community. This is their agency.

On the one hand, this corpus of portraits elucidates the practice of using images as material objects in specific cultural and social contexts. On the other, it shows us the way in which different groups of individuals, including researchers from different scientific communities such as botanists, have produced knowledge and authority through the framework of mobility.

In the case study of the *Iconoteca*, different ideas of mobility are mingled together thanks to portraits: the mobility of people—what the sociologist John Urry identified in 2007 as the "corporeal travel of people"; the mobility of objects—what he identified as the "physical movement of objects"; and the mobility of representations and visual images—what he called "imaginative travel" (in Jöns, Heffernan, and Meusburger, 2017: 3). Thus, at the center of our analysis there is a network of botanists, local amateurs, their connections, and their pictures on the move, for the purpose of forming what Saccardo imagined to be a "Pantheon of botanists". In a letter published in the journal *Malpighia*, his friend, the botanist Oreste Mattirolo, wrote that:

> It would be a great enterprise to revive the more or less nice faces of our predecessors and to put together a sort of "pantheon", exhorting Italian botanists to embrace Saccardo's "call to arms" and to gather "national memories" in order to "track down and preserve the features of our Italian predecessors in the field of botany".
>
> (1899: 257)

Photographs as material objects were set in motion in specific cultural and social situations, in the context of more or less institutionalized groups, as well as in private exchanges between individuals. According to the historians of photography, Elizabeth Edwards and Christopher Morton, "Photographs were increasingly understood as not only the content of an image and the information therein, but as things that people use and have different effects in different forms and cultural contexts" (2015: 13). Thus, a photograph is not only a visual, aesthetic object, an image with a specific grammar to be analyzed as a textual production of an author or as a social vehicle of power forms and ideologies projected onto it, but also an object which, individually or as a corpus, can tell something about a practice or a specific network of people. Authors like Geoffrey Belknap, Christopher Morton, Caroline Cornish, and Simone Natale are studying the "social use" of photography and the ways in which photographs circulate and change hands in different social and cultural circles, both within organizations and institutionalized groups and in private and informal contexts. And here again, mobility is called into question since mobility is a function of materiality, and photographs are intrinsically mobile. Photography is indeed also a "tool for putting images in movement in order to be carried, marketed, and transported" (Leonardi and Natale, 2018: 6), including by botanists.

The main focus of the *Iconoteca* was on Italian or foreign botanists who studied Italian flora. There are scholars from the past and botanists who were contemporary with Saccardo. Most of the collection consists of Saccardo's colleagues' *cartes de visite*, but there are also several photographic copies of paintings portraying botanists of past centuries preserved in Italian or foreign institutions. Furthermore, there are also reproductions of pictures from books and journals. There are also a few oil paintings, watercolors, drawings, engravings, and prints. Frames of different sizes were hung on the walls of the library, classrooms, and laboratories of the Botanical Institute. In 1922, Saccardo's successor, the botanist Augusto Béguinot, recounted that the collection was first arranged "in a small room in the library together with books and fossils, and thereafter in a special gallery which leads to the classroom. The collection occupies an entire wall 21 meters long and 2.90 high under the name of Iconotheca botanicorum" (1923: 47).

After Saccardo, his associates and successors proceeded to expand the Iconoteca. Beguinot speaks of around 1,400 portraits. The Botanic Garden's picture gallery was thereafter dismantled and removed from the Botanical Institute's walls, probably in the 1930s.

Today, the pictures have been restored, preserved in the library, and are available on the official website of the University of Padova's digital collections (https://phaidra.cab.unipd.it/). What was lacking to date is a detailed understanding and historical analysis of the collection's formation as a whole, considering the subject in the framework of the mobility of distinctive objects such as photographs. Thanks to the accession register, the printed catalogue, Saccardo's publications, and his remarkable correspondence, all preserved in the Botanic Garden's archive in Padova, we can now follow and retrace the movements and channels through which these pictures arrived in Padova and from whom.

As Saccardo recalled, the collection had been started by two of Saccardo's predecessors: first, the botanist Antonio Bonato, whose heirs donated seven paintings in 1843 that were portraits of well-known botanists such as Gabriele Fallopio, Prospero Alpini, and Giulio Pontedera; and secondly, Roberto De Visiani, who added the engravings of some of his predecessors and an album with around 50 photographs of Italian and foreign colleagues to the collection. Once appointed director, Saccardo had these pictures framed and hung in one of the library's rooms. Between 1895 and 1899, he began to add to the collection with watercolors of past Italian botanists, a pastel painting of De Visiani, and around 150 photographs of mycologists from his own private collection. Saccardo began to search for missing portraits in Italy and abroad while writing the history of botany in Italy at the end of the 19th century. In 1899, the Iconoteca consisted of 725 portraits (excluding copies) subdivided into 273 frames of different sizes (most of them were 32x24 centimeters). In less than three years, the Iconoteca had grown to include 1,173 portraits in 427 frames. Saccardo looked back on the collection's expansion in two articles published in 1899 and 1901, in which he also published the complete and detailed lists of the items, without images. He classified the portraits into two categories: in the first, Italian or foreign botanists who had been naturalized at the time; in the second, those foreign botanists who had made a contribution to the study of Italian flora. Botanists were grouped by centuries and listed in alphabetical order. Saccardo also pointed out where the portraits were displayed in the Botanic Garden, as well as their dimensions and origins.

Photography, intended as a reproduction tool useful for documentary acquisition and historical research, helped him to complete his project. In fact, Saccardo embarked on a campaign of photographic reproductions of subjects scattered across several galleries and libraries all around the world, from the Botanical Institute of Bologna's mid-18th century watercolor collection to the collection of De Candolle in Geneva. Students and collaborators assisted him, as did certain photographic studios, such as those of Luigi Caporelli in Padova and Giuseppe Zoboli in Bologna.

For Saccardo, the collection's value lay mostly in its documentary value and not in its uniqueness or originality, since the collection mostly consisted of reproductions. In Saccardo's opinion

> either portraits have to be considered as a pivotal part of biographies, or they have to be taken as a tribute to true talent and industriousness; either way, it is certain that the task of collecting them and preventing their dispersion is not despicable, indeed it is almost a duty.
>
> (1899: 91)

As shown by Saccardo's correspondence, his contacts in Italy and abroad consisted of botanists, local amateurs, friends, colleagues, men of the institutions, family members, and heirs of dead botanists. Often, it was widows and daughters who managed exchanges. Each scholar contacted by Saccardo was, in turn, in contact with other agents in Italy and abroad, further expanding the scientific network and the circulation of portraits. Relationships between official centers of knowledge, such as the University of Padova and local contexts, were also important. If some correspondents donated their photographs, many of them wanted them back once Saccardo had arranged for their reproduction.

Saccardo transformed private souvenirs, such as photographic portraits and *cartes de visite*, into elements of an ambitious documentary project made visible through the frames that hung in his Botanical Institute's rooms. He used photography as a useful medium for reproduction and documentation, as well as an efficient tool to make portraits mobile.

In their paper *Photographs as scientific and social objects in the correspondence of Charles Darwin*, Geoffrey Belknap and Sophie Defrance demonstrated that, at the time, photographic portraits enacted the purpose of identifying a relationship through a portrait exchange (2015). Each *Iconoteca* photograph is bound to other objects inside or outside the portrait collection, ranging from the volumes from which they were copied to the letters that arrived in Padova with the pictures. In the latter case, if the portraits and letters were sent together, they were separated from each other once they reached the Botanic Garden in order to fulfill different functions. After the pictures were removed from the letters, these image-objects were saved, used, and displayed in different ways than the letters themselves. Letters were filed, archived, and organized for later private reference, whereas portraits were removed and placed in frames, assuming a performative and public role—to show the faces of the people involved in Saccardo's network, together with the protagonists of the flourishing and glorious history of botany in Italy, to the Garden's visitors.

In conclusion, the case of the *Iconoteca* highlights the great potential of using the "mobility" category as an effective theoretical tool in the history of science in relation to visual studies. The collection was made possible by negotiations between different agents in various locations: botanists, amateurs, families, and many others. Photography, as a medium that allows the making of copies, plays a major role in this story. Botanists' portraits circulated in a network and converged in Padova to create a celebratory, didactic, and visual history of botany, which gave particular attention and recognition to the Italian tradition. Gathered, exchanged, circulated, and distributed, private souvenirs such as *cartes de visite* became elements of an ambitious documentary project made visible through the frames hanging in his Botanical Institute's rooms, illustrating the entangled epistemic implications of movement and mobility—and their impact on practices and theories of science.

References

Arens EH (2015) Flowerbeds and hothouses: botany, gardens, and the circulation of knowledge in things. *Historical social research/Historische Sozialforschung* 40(1): 265–283.

Béguinot A (1923) *I materiali di archivio del R. Istituto e Orto Botanico di Padova*. Messina: Stab. Tip. dell'Avvenire.

Belknap G, Defrance S (2015) Photographs as scientific and social objects in the correspondence of Charles Darwin. In: Edwards E, Morton C (eds) *Photographs, museums, collections. Between art and information*. London: Bloomsbury Academic, pp. 139–156.

Beretta M (ed) (2020) *Icone di scienza. Autobiografie e ritratti di naturalisti bolognesi della prima età moderna*. Bologna: Bononia University Press.

Bray F, Hahn B, Lourdusamy JB, and Saraiva T (2019) Cropscapes and history. Reflections on rootedness and mobility. *Transfers. Interdisciplinary Journal of Mobility Studies* 9(1): 20–41.

Canadelli E (2019) Scienza e tecnica. Approcci storiografici e dinamiche globali. In: Fumian C and Giuntini A (eds) *Storia economica globale del mondo contemporaneo*. Roma: Carocci, pp. 165–185.

Canadelli E (2020) Documentare e celebrare: Pier Andrea Saccardo e l'Iconoteca dei botanici di Padova tra Otto e Novecento. *Physis. Rivista internazionale di storia della scienza* 55(1–2): 71–86.

Cornish C (2015) Collecting photographs, constructing disciplines: the rationality and rhetoric of photography at the Museum of Economic Botany. In: Edwards E and Morton C (eds) *Photographs, museums, collections. Between art and information*. London: Bloomsbury Academic, pp. 119–137.

Cornish C and Driver F (2020) 'Specimens distributed'. The circulation of objects from Kew's Museum of Economic Botany, 1847–1914. *Journal of the History of Collections* 32(2): 327–340.

Cresswell T (2010) Towards a politics of mobility. *Environment and planning D: Society and space* 28(1): 17–31.

Driver F, Nesbitt M, and Cornish C (2021) Introduction: Mobilising and re-mobilising museum collections. In: Driver F, Nesbitt M, and Cornish C (eds) *Mobile museums. Collections in circulation*. London: UCL Press, pp. 1–20.

Edwards E and Morton C (2015) Between art and information: towards a collecting history of photographs. In: Edwards E and Morton C (eds) *Photographs, museums, collections. Between art and information*. London: Bloomsbury Academic, pp. 3–23.

Fan F (2012) The global turn in the history of science. *East Asian Science, Technology and Society: An International Journal* 6: 249–258.

Gänger S (2017) Circulation: reflections on circularity, entity, and liquidity in the language of global history. *Journal of Global History* 12: 303–318.

Jöns H, Heffernan M, and Meusburger P (2017) Mobilities of knowledge: an introduction. In: Jöns H, Heffernan M, and Meusburger P (eds) *Mobilities of knowledge*. Cham: Springer, pp. 1–19.

Latour B (1987) *Science in action. How to follow scientists and engineers through society*. Cambridge, MA: Harvard University Press.

Leonardi N, Natale S (eds) (2018) *Photography and other media in the nineteenth century*. University Park, PA: Penn State University Press.

Ludmilla J (2000) *Defining features: scientific and medical portraits 1660–2000*. London: Reaktion Books.

Mattirolo O (1900) Come si avrebbe una bibliografia botanica italiana; un bullettino annuale delle novità floristiche e bibliografiche; e come si potrebbe completare la Iconoteca dei botanici italiani. Lettera aperta al Prof. P.A. Saccardo. *Malpighia* 13(7–10): 257–266.

Östling J, Larsson Heidenblad D, Sandmo E, Nilsson Hammar A, and Nordberg K (2018) The history of knowledge and the circulation of knowledge: an introduction. In: Östling J, Larsson Heidenblad D, Sandmo E, Nilsson Hammar A, and Nordberg K (eds) *Circulation of knowledge: explorations in the history of knowledge*. Lund: Nordic Academic Press, pp. 9–33.

Raj K (2007) *Relocating modern science. Circulation and the construction of knowledge in South Asia and Europe, 1650–1900*. New York: Palgrave Macmillan.

Renn J, Hyman MD (2012) The globalization of knowledge in history: an introduction. In: Renn J (ed) *The globalization of knowledge in history*. Berlin: Max Planck Institute, pp. 27–51.

Saccardo PA (1899) *La Iconoteca dei Botanici nel r. Istituto botanico di Padova*. Genova: Tipografia Ciminago.

Saccardo PA (1902) *La Iconoteca dei Botanici nel r. Istituto botanico di Padova*. Genova: Tipografia Ciminago.

Sarasin P, Kilcher A (2011) Editorial. In: Gugerli D, Hagner M, Hirschi C, Kilcher A B, Purtschert P, Sarasin P, and Tanner J (eds) *Nach Feierabend 2011. Zirkulationen*. Zürich: Diaphanes.

Schaffer S, Roberts L, Raj K, Delbourgo J (eds) (2009) *The brokered world: go-betweens and global intelligence, 1770–1820*. Sagamore Beach, MA: Science History Publications.

Schäfer D (2018) Editorial. Mobility studies, a transdisciplinary field. *Transfers. Interdisciplinary Journal of Mobility Studies* 8(1): vii–x.

Secord JA (2004) Knowledge in transit. *Isis. A Journal of the History of Science Society* 95(4): 654–672.

Sheller M (2019) Response. The mobile itineraries of knowledge-scapes. *Transfers. Interdisciplinary Journal of Mobility Studies* 9(1): 87–94.

Smith PH (2019a) Tracing the movement of knowledge across vast distances and long temporal spans. *Transfers. Interdisciplinary Journal of Mobility Studies* 9(1): 75–86.

Smith PH (ed) (2019b) *Entangled itineraries: materials, practices, and knowledges across Eurasia*. Pittsburgh, PA: University of Pittsburgh Press.

Special Section: History of science (2019) *Transfers. Interdisciplinary Journal of Mobility Studies* 9(1): 20–94.

Tosi A (2007) *Portraits of men and ideas. Images of science in Italy from the Renaissance to the 19th Century*. Pisa: Pisa University Press.

4 Gendered mobilities

Spaces, images, and power across the Mediterranean (16th–20th centuries)

Teresa Bernardi and Silvia Bruzzi[1]

4.1 Introduction

Gender and mobility are deeply intertwined. The very concept of gender is intrinsically on the move, as are gendered identities. "Becoming a woman" or "becoming a man" is defined as a process in feminist theories (De Beauvoir, 1973: 301). The idea that even gendered subjectivities are on the move, in between boundaries and across categories, evokes the crucial value of gender in understanding geographic and social mobility. According to Rosi Braidotti's concept of "nomadic subjectivity" (Braidotti, 1994), subjects "are itineraries without fixed targets or destinations, but are punctuated by constant encounters with otherness as a multi-layered and multi-directional landscape" (Braidotti, 2014: 7).

While gender can be understood as "a primary way of signifying relationships of power" (Scott, 1986: 1067), its articulation with mobility reveals differences and inequalities in representing, experiencing, performing, and disciplining male and female mobilities. A challenging history of gender and mobilities, which focuses on how mobility is experienced and represented, should be "men's history, women's history, and gender history at the same time" (Green, 2012: 785). It is from this perspective that we suggest adopting a "gender-sensitive approach" to mobility by taking into account not only the specificities of female and male mobility, but also the role of gender relations in mobility practices (Timmerman et al., 2018; Zucca Micheletto, 2022: 1). This approach involves a critical understanding of gender-linked notions and categories. For instance, it leads one to consider how gender is spatially produced through the contested binary of public and private, or how masculinity tends to be represented as mobile and active while femininity as "stationary" and passive (Cresswell and Uteng, 2008: 2).

For a long time, scholars have described migrant women as subjects who followed their husbands, fathers, and brothers. Alternatively, they have been primarily portrayed as actors who endured forced mobility. However, from the late 20th century, feminist scholars started to consider women's economic and social roles as a crucial part of the migration experience (Phizacklea, 1983; Morokvasic, 1984; Donato, 1992; Gabaccia, 1996). Since then, several

DOI: 10.4324/9781003278665-6

studies have investigated women's involvement in migration trajectories and family projects, demonstrating their agency in using and sharing their own economic resources and multi-local social ties (Sharpe, 2001; Gabaccia and Iacovetta, 2002; Donato et al., 2006).

Moreover, the mobility turn has led us to consider mobility in a more extensive sense, including different forms and scales of mobilities such as corporeal travel, physical movement of objects, and imaginative, virtual, and communicative travel (Hannam et al., 2006; Sheller and Urry, 2006; Adey et al., 2014: 2–20). A further step was to look at gender dynamics in different mobility patterns. By adopting an intersectional approach, which takes into account the interaction between different social categories, historians have provided new insights into understanding how differences in terms of sex, gender, class, race, age, religion, or nationality have impacted mobility's representations and practices over time, and *vice versa* (Hancock, 2016). Although many scholars have studied international migrations from a gender perspective today and in recent historical periods, little has been done with regard to the Mediterranean region prior to the second half of the 20th century (Stabili and Tirabassi, 2014; Martini and Mukherjee, 2019; Guerry and Thébaud, 2020; Zucca Micheletto, 2022).

This chapter will introduce the "gender prism" as a crucial methodological tool for examining mobility, given the compelling role that gender analysis has had in challenging our understanding of mobility processes. To address this question, we take a long-term historical perspective (from the 16th to the 20th centuries) and examine the Mediterranean region through the lens of two different historiographical frames. On the one hand, we consider early modern research on the Italian Peninsula, with a particular emphasis on the city of Venice and its domains; on the other, we examine contemporary (post) Ottoman Mediterranean literature, with a particular emphasis on the city of Tripoli.

Without repeating the well-known debate on the Mediterranean, we refer to this space not as a coherent unity (e.g., Braudel, 1966), nor as an "exception" (Herzfeld, 2005), but rather as a sort of historical laboratory within which to test a comparative approach. The Mediterranean is a helpful but challenging framework within which to explore phenomena relating to mobility from a long-term perspective, especially in our research exploring the two urban centres of Venice and Tripoli. They were both port cities, in which many people, objects, and ideas circulated. In the 16th and 17th centuries, Venice was one of the most populated urban centres in Europe (with about 150,000 inhabitants), being situated at the crossroads between Northern Europe, the Adriatic Sea, and the Ottoman Empire. The 19th century Tripoli, for its part, was both a seaport (turned towards the world of the Mediterranean, at the intersection between the Ottoman and European colonial spaces) and a desert port (namely, for the sub-Saharan diaspora), where Muslim, Jewish, and Christian communities mingled. Besides being places of multiple encounters, they were also cities in which diverse local institutions were involved in controlling mobilities and urban spaces, producing a huge variety of documentation.

Despite these connections between the two cities, there are also major differences between their political and social contexts. Indeed, this chapter attempts to tackle specificities that could seem incomparable. Rather than considering this aspect as a limit, however, we decided to take each of our respective sources as a "nexus of specificities". In fact, this analysis does not start from general assumptions, but from specific texts, languages, and actors, which are embedded and circulated in particular contexts (Cerutti and Grangaud, 2017: 9). Only after a careful practice of contextualization has it been possible to compare these very different historical and political contexts, and to suggest sources, methods, and theoretical questions that historians from diverse backgrounds should consider in order to work on mobility without overlooking the underlying gender dynamics.

The first part of the essay questions the visibility and representation of female and male mobilities in historical records. What emerges is a strong link between female mobility and morality, but also the constant need to ponder why and under what specific circumstances women's mobility was traced and made visible. The second part explores how both institutions and local communities controlled and documented gendered mobilities. The focus on female mobility, combined with the intersectional analysis, brings to light spaces and social actors that mobility studies have often marginalised. At the same time, the fact that women often appeared to be unclassified and their mobility undocumented highlights the need to cross different typologies of documentation, such as official and administrative records, with legal proceedings and literary, visual, and oral sources. The third and final section is dedicated to the theme of (im)mobility, with a particular focus on "distance" and gendered spaces. It examines how gender analysis has contributed to challenging some historiographical assumptions concerning human mobility more broadly, most notably the sharp distinction between long- and short-distance mobility, as well as mobility and immobility practices.

4.2 Representing gendered mobilities in historical records

At the end of the 16th century, the scholar Giovanni Passi published a treatise "I donneschi difetti" that illustrated a series of unforgivable defects ascribed to women. The text is part of a long tradition of literary works that claimed the natural inferiority of women. Along with cruel, lustful, jealous and fragile women, there is also the category of vagrant women and its significant description:

> The vagrant woman does not bring her husband much honor, nor any reputation for herself. For this reason, Cato ordered that no Roman matron should leave her house alone during the day, and that the company with whom she went out during the day should be that of her husband and relatives, such that, just as a dissolute woman is frowned upon today, so too is a woman who is known to leave her house often.[2]

According to Passi's words, female mobility had moral implications and could represent a threat to the honour of both women and their families. Indeed, the author associates the bad reputation of a "dissolute woman" with the image of a woman who used to leave her house alone, without supervision. This suggests that the only movement allowed for women was from one family group to another, namely on the occasion of marriage. Nothing new, if we consider the long tradition of literary works depicting female mobility in negative terms (Biasiori, in this volume). However, Passi's reference to a distant past, to the world in which Catone lived and ruled, may also imply another reflection: that description was likely intended to discourage female mobility and to impose a model of conduct on a society that, in fact, went in the opposite direction; a society in which women regularly found ways to move beyond their prescribed spaces and social roles. In other words, we can envision a gap between crafted narratives on the one hand, and effective mobility practices on the other.

This treatise enables us to introduce some preliminary observations about women's alleged immobility in past Mediterranean societies and the issue of their invisibility in historical documents. As recent studies have pointed out, women's (im)mobility would also depend on the way in which female mobility was represented in the sources, as well as on the way—we would add—in which historians read them (Harzig and Hoerder, 2009: 119–123). Indeed, a new field of research is developing the notion that mobility encompasses not only physical movements but also the narratives and discourses that give movement a cultural meaning (Cresswell and Uteng, 2008: 6). We claim, therefore, that while male and female physical mobility is the same, the meanings and discourses referring to it are often different. This is because their movements always occurred in spaces that are not neutral: "gendered bodies move through gendered social spaces" (Clarsen, 2014: 97). For this reason, it seems relevant to pay particular attention to the narrative construction of these sources (Zemon Davis, 1987), in order to disclose the gendered expectations about who moves, how they move, and where (Cresswell and Uteng, 2008: 5). At the same time, an emic approach may have an impact on their interpretation (Ginzburg, 2012), as it leaves historians wondering which actors produced a particular description of female mobility and for what purposes.

The importance of this methodology is even more evident when we analyse court records, which are more revealing of the crafted nature of the narratives on mobility (Tomas, 2006: 313). This is the case in legal proceedings where the negative connotation of women's mobility was used as part of a rhetorical defence strategy, for example by a Genoese captain, Piero Carpazio, who tried to justify an act of brutal violence as the mere consequence of a woman's mobility. In the late 17th century, Carpazio was brought before the *Esecutori contro la Bestemmia*, a Venetian magistracy in charge of morality and public order, accused of raping a young girl. The man did not deny the fact, but rather justified himself by claiming that the only person responsible for the sexual violence was the girl who was denouncing it. In doing so, he argued that her virginity was in fact incompatible with her marked mobility:

> She converses in every place, she exhibits herself; indeed, she ventures into every danger, mingles with men on ships, noted for many months wandering about before the time of the desired deflowering, of which she accuses me. The case of Dina, daughter of Jacob, is famous: she came out of the house as a virgin, merely moved by curiosity towards the women of Salem, but having been violated and having lost her honor, leaving the house was the same as losing her virginity.[3]

In these words, the moral connotation of women's mobility evokes a similar narrative to the one we have seen in Passi's treatise. However, in this legal context, its negative representation served a different and specific purpose, as it was instrumentally used by the accused to justify his behaviour and shift the blame to the woman. Once again, we note that even when historical sources explicitly refer to women's mobility, it does not necessarily mean that they represent a suitable field of investigation to explore how women likely experienced and practised mobility. They could instead express narratives about gender-linked values and notions such as virginity, honour, shame, and other moral systems that were ostensibly threatened by women's mobility. According to historians, none of these gendered meanings associated with mobility are static, but change over time and differ across diverse locations (Clarsen, 2014: 97).

Indeed, if we pass on to the Mediterranean in the 1920s–1930s, we can see how women's long-distance mobility may not only have been accepted, but also encouraged and promoted. Within the context of national building processes, for instance, it is possible to observe a close link between female international travel and feminist emancipation movements. Both the European women involved in their homeland's imperial building projects in Africa and the African women from the local elites gained access to the political sphere mainly by travelling and crossing international borders within the Mediterranean. Additionally, the press and visual media portrayed these women on the move as national icons, which allowed them to redeem and affirm a new image of the nations and the empires on an international scale (Sorbera, 2006; Bruzzi, 2017). These practices of feminine mobility were, in fact, connected to broader political narratives, social values, and global processes, such as feminist, nationalist, and imperialist projects.

Visual sources such as drawings, portraits and, for modern historians, photography, represent further resources for the examination of gendered mobilities. However, even in this case, where images may seem to look like reality, we can observe a discrepancy between women's visual representations and their effective involvement in the mobility process. For example, if we look at the development of commercial photography at the end of the 19th century, we can see how the global circulation of visual media participated in the spread of gender stereotypes and representations of female (im)mobility.

58 *Bernardi and Bruzzi*

Colonial postcards that circulated across the Mediterranean and beyond became a means of mass communication between the metropolis and the colonies, but were also tourist and collectors' items. The images reproduced on the postcards were definitely influenced by Orientalist iconography, since they portrayed "sensual" and anonymous Arab and African women as fixed subjects in a "waiting" pose. Moreover, commercial photography created and invented human types: the anonymous bodies of colonial female subjects were classified into ethnic types apparently rooted in the colonial landscape, according to the diktat of the captions.

Figure 4.1 Postcard. *In Italian Libya*. Publisher: G. Cometto, Turin, from a picture by Lehnert & Landrock, MOXA-CDMC Archive, Collection Celso Braglia (Modena).

Figure 4.2 Postcard. *Young Jewish Woman in French Tunisia*, from a picture by Lehnert & Landrock (Taraud 2003: 126).

Beyond the construction process of ethnic types, we find clear examples of circulation, reproduction, and manipulation of images, as in these two *clichés* of a young Jewish girl in Tunisia, reproduced for the Italian Libya (Figures 4.1 and 4.2). Throughout the colonial occupation, therefore, photographs and private postcards gave great visibility to female colonial subjects, while their mobility practices are under-documented in colonial archives. Certainly, the (in)visibility of subaltern groups, such as women, is a crucial question that has always concerned women and gender scholars, and mobility studies are definitely not an exception. As we will see, the records typically used to study human mobility and migration, such as official and identification documents and consular and legal records, are mainly concerned with male migrants, while female migrants appear only as anonymous and dependent actors in the mobility process (Sharpe, 2001: 6).

4.3 Documenting and controlling gendered mobilities

While scholars seem to agree that international migration is today almost evenly split between men and women, we cannot say the same for past societies. One explanation may lie in the specific type of documentation that scholars have used until now to study the control of mobility and the identification of migrants. If we consider, for instance, police records and administrative documentation, we can observe that migrant women were often undocumented and unclassified subjects in comparison to migrant men. This may well depend on the very nature of the registration, and on the role of gender relations in a particular social context. For example, in early modern times, only the male heads of households (*paterfamilias*) were usually required to register on behalf of the entire family. Therefore, when migrant women are recorded in registers, they typically appear alongside their husbands, just as children and slaves do (Bertrand, 2017: 10).

Similarly, in the modern Mediterranean, it is also possible to observe that women are seldom present in official registrations. For instance, they usually appear to be associated with a lineage or a male family member (Clancy-Smith, 2005: 70). Even when it came to acquiring national citizenship, their social *status* was contingent upon and subordinate to that of men, fathers, or husbands. Indeed, in accordance with the Latin maxim *uxor statum mariti sequitur*, wives followed the nationality of their husbands during the liberal epoch in Italy and in other Mediterranean countries, such as France. Women had a sort of "dependent nationality" (Donati, 2013: 38), which followed the membership status of the father and then, once married, of the male spouse. This may help to explain, once again, their poor visibility in these types of sources.[4]

Institutional concern with regard to mobility appears to have been largely a gendered process, based on a particular ideology on masculinity and femininity. In comparison to male mobility, female mobility could be traced and documented in different ways, for different reasons, and by different actors. That is why it is important to reflect on the (in)visibility of women (or men) from both a quantitative and qualitative point of view. With regard to the early modern period, particular attention has been paid to the identification practices implemented by public authorities and institutions to control mobility and register migrants (Winter and De Munck, 2012; Greefs and Winter, 2019). However, only current research takes a gender perspective. This is a major turning point, since this approach makes it possible to question the gender ratio of migrants in particular historical contexts. Above all, it enables an examination of how institutions conceptualised male and female mobilities (Harzig and Hoerder, 2009: 126–127; Bernardi and Pompermaier, 2019).

In this perspective, intersectional methodology has proven to be a very challenging approach (Hancock, 2016). Consider, for instance, the city of Venice in the 17th and 18th centuries and legislation governing the registration of foreign inhabitants. It seems that certain categories of "mobile" people drew special attention from public authorities—foreigners who were not subjects of the Republic, Jews, people without a fixed abode, or those who were unemployed. Foreign men were required to register since they were practically unknown at the local level, and primarily for reasons concerning public order and taxation. Otherwise, even if the documentation contains only few references to foreign women, we can still observe that female mobility was monitored, thus becoming visible in the sources, especially when migrant women appeared to be "unsupervised", were prostitutes, or were members of a religious minority (Bernardi, 2022).

An alternative is to observe the interactions of these very categories. In 1642, the magistracy in charge of registering foreigners and verifying their right to reside in the city alluded to the necessity of knowing the names, surnames, origin, and abode of Jewish foreign women who lived in the Ghetto. In their own words, the aim was to avert scandals and, most likely, to avoid sexual intercourse between Jewish women and Christians (Bernardi 2022: 43; Nirenberg, 2002; Caffiero, 2013).[5] Again, the moral dimension and control over female bodies played a crucial role in justifying the need to monitor women's mobility. What appears significant in this regard is that this very dynamic seems to be valid across time and space (Luibheid, 2002; Sinke, 2006).

In the Mediterranean in the mid-19th century, women's mobility was also documented in relation to similar categories of people and for similar purposes. Women travelling alone and crossing international borders were submitted to special regulations to control and restrict their movements. In this way, their honour and sexual conduct was under the careful scrutiny of State authorities and elites from both sides of the Mediterranean (Clancy-Smith, 2005). Consuls and colonial authorities, for instance, used to collect information on Italian single women who worked as teachers or sex workers abroad. On the one hand, Italian authorities maintained a close watch on their private lives in order to "preserve the honour" of their homeland overseas (Di Pasquale, 2014). On the other, police records meticulously registered specific groups of migrant women, such as foreign prostitutes working in licensed brothels, like those in Egypt, Malta and Libya (Biancani, 2018; Schettini, 2019).

According to the literature on gender and contemporary labour migrations, women were often invisible as migrant workers because they were usually involved in low-income and informal work sectors, such as domestic services, care work, and sex work, which were not included in the prevailing definitions of "work" (Rowbotham, 2002: xvi). However, when women workers were alone or unsupervised, they were instead visible in official documents (e.g., consular and colonial reports). In this case, sources attest to the anxiousness of the male authorities and elites to control and monitor the moral conduct of single women workers. This was also noted in relation to thousands of women who crossed the Mediterranean to work in North African port cities, such as Tunis and Alexandria. They used to find work as servants and wet nurses in the households of prominent local residents, eventually exposing themselves to sexual dangers and exploitation (Clancy-Smith, 2005; Biancani, 2019).

Recent studies on mobility and nationality in the modern Mediterranean assert that marriage was another site of administrative anxiety and a "driving force behind nationality litigation and legislation" (Hanley, 2017: 138). Similarly, legal and administrative records shed light on the unique circumstances under which the authorities produced documents and information on women's mobility. One such example is Italian colonial Libya when foreigners married, thus crossing intercommunitarian and national borders. Political and judicial authorities were reluctant to recognize mixed unions, since marriages between Libyans and Italians could undermine colonial order and racial hierarchies. In 1927, for example, the Court of Appeal in Tripoli annulled the marriage of Giulia Hannuna, an Italian-born Jewish woman who converted to Islam, and a Muslim Libyan man. The judge decreed that the woman possessed Italian citizenship due to the fact that her father, a Jewish man born in Livorno, was registered with the Italian consulate in Tripoli. However, prior to the authorities officially defining her identity, local networks had always recognized Giulia as a member of the local community and considered her marriage to be a legitimate union (Bruzzi, 2021).

The comparison of similar typologies of sources in relation to different historical contexts demonstrates that the gender perspective represents a transversal key tool for challenging certain historiographical assumptions about mobility and identification. First of all, it has been demonstrated that authorities were not concerned with foreigners or mobility *per se*, but rather with specific groups of people and, consequently, for reasons that varied between men and women. Moreover, what emerges from the documentation is that institutions usually controlled women's mobility when it threatened the social order and the honour of their families, homelands, and nations. Hence, it was mostly in instances where the local control of their community of belonging (family, neighbours, etc.) failed or threatened to fail that the authorities intervened. With this in mind, the (in)visibility of women in the sources suggests that their mobility could also be traced outside of institutions, and for diverse purposes (Herzog, 2004; Buono, 2014; Bernardi, 2020).

These considerations underline the importance of taking into account other kinds of documents that do not directly deal with the control of mobility or the regulation of urban spaces. With regard to the early modern period, inquisitorial trials are also used to study human mobility, especially in terms of encounters between people of different religious and political backgrounds. Family archives, diaries, and private correspondence—including love letters exchanged between mixed couples in colonial contexts and then censored—have shed new light on the interplay of mobility with intimacy and politics in the modern period (Dieste and Muriel García, 2020). Court records and inheritance or dowry proceedings have also revealed the central role of women as active actors in the migration process. Moreover, current research on early modern premarital inquiries and matrimonial disputes are disclosing the multi-local social ties and resources available to women on the move, even over long distances.[6]

4.4 Gendered (im)mobility between spaces, distances, and networks

The way in which women's mobility is represented and documented in the sources has definitely contributed to the underestimation of their role in migration processes. To overcome this issue, it is necessary to shift the focus from representations to practices, but most of all, to redefine the very concepts of mobility and immobility. A first step forward has been made by those historians who have begun to consider mobility in a broader context, initially focusing their research on the movements (temporal and seasonal) between different cities, urban areas, and the countryside, to then address inter-urban mobility (Arru and Ramella, 2003). Moreover, the use of a micro-analytical approach that focuses on individual experiences may allow us to challenge a number of assumptions about gendered mobilities and spaces, particularly the concept of distance and the assumed distinction between female short-distance mobility and male long-distance migration.

When the geographer E. G. Ravenstein tried to demonstrate that women usually moved more often than men, he also claimed that this occurred only across short distances (Ravenstein, 1885, 1889). The sociological model based on the idea that men were the long-distance movers par excellence has been considered valid for a long time and is trans-disciplinary. For example, there is a substantial body of literature on men's participation in pilgrimages to the holy cities across the Mediterranean and the Red Sea, such as Jerusalem and Mecca, while women are more visible actors within local and regional devotional visits to shrines and monasteries. However, recent research has revealed that traces of female pilgrimages to Jerusalem have existed since late Antiquity (Craig, 2009: 133). Of course, we cannot deny that migrant women may have faced specific constraints and impediments, such as the economic difficulties of participating in the labour markets of their destination cities, the dangers of displacement, and sexual abuse. Nevertheless, both modern and early modern scholars have widely demonstrated how women managed to overcome such constraints and even crossed long distances, eventually changing their marital status, religion, and building new social networks (Siebenhüner, 2008; Colley, 2007; Dursteler, 2011).

Transnational family and diaspora studies have prompted critical reflection on the communitarian dimension of all movements. We can say that the migrant was never alone, and this aspect is even more visible when the migrant was a woman. Their mobility, therefore, seems to be constantly monitored and supervised not only by the authorities, but also through local communities (such as social networks, charitable institutions, national communities, and neighbourhoods). With regard to the Italian Peninsula, Eleonora Canepari demonstrated that many women who migrated to Rome and applied for admission to the charitable institution of San Sisto Hospital could rely on properties and relationships in both their hometown and the new city. She mentioned a "double horizon" that could potentially multiply on the basis of women's trans-local networks and, in fact, it nuanced the distance between localities (Canepari, 2014: 13). The relational approach to mobility has also resulted in the need to focus on intermediaries. Even when women did not move, their mobility could be traced through a series of people and documents that were on the move instead.

As Jonas Larsen has suggested, the "mobilities turn has somewhat exaggerated the significance of corporeal meetings and travel" (Larsen, 2014: 125). Recent literature, which involves geographers, historians, and anthropologists, is demonstrating that proximity was not only related to geographical spaces. On the one hand, migration did not always imply a redefinition of identities and networks; on the other, inter-urban mobility (or even immobility) could mean a change in social ties or conditions. It, therefore, seems necessary to abandon a rigid concept of both mobility and urban spaces in order to pay more attention to the crossing of internal borders and their social and cultural value in specific historical settings. Historical records attest to prohibitions that regulated women's conduct and mobility, even within urban spaces. In Venice, for example, those women who were considered prostitutes were not always permitted to roam freely throughout the city, and in specific periods of time, they were also required to wear a yellow garment to be identifiable (Scarabello, 2006; Ferraro, 2018).

Similar visual stigmas were inscribed on foreign sex workers at the turn of the 20th century in the Red Sea cosmopolitan port city of Massawa. Here, foreign "prostitutes" were required to wear identification tags on their arms and necks to be identified by colonial authorities (Bruzzi, 2018: 44). Historically, dress and body markers have been used to visibly identify not only prostitutes, but other social groups as well (e.g., slaves, nobles, etc.). Indeed, they played a crucial role in marking social boundaries within urban spaces, namely by performing and thus defining gendered, social, and religious identities and hierarchies. However, women themselves could use distinctive garments in order to have access to particular urban spaces. Wearing the hijab, for example, became a "spatial strategy" for some women at the turn of the 20th century in the cities of Istanbul and Cairo, to maintain social respectability while crossing inter-urban borders and moving across new public and "promiscuous" masculine spaces. Indeed, changes in modern city plans and transport, such as with the introduction of steamboats and tramways, reduced the distances between women and men, thereby drafting new spaces where the sexes could meet and mingle (Altınbaş, 2014: 115).

In the early modern period, material and immaterial borders could precisely define and separate urban spaces. If we consider the city of Venice as an example, the Jewish Ghetto comes to mind, which was subjected to strict rules concerning its inhabitants and their interactions with the rest of the city as from 1516; or, alternatively, the Fondaco of Turks, which served as the sole residence and storage facility for Turkish merchants and travellers as from 1621 (Calabi and Lanaro, 1998; Chambers and Pullan, 1992). These places guaranteed the presence and security of ethnic and religious minorities in the city. However, they were also subjected to court inspections that ensured their separation from the rest of the Christian community. Therefore, moving between these places could sometimes produce a series of social and cultural implications. This was also true in less institutionalised and physically defined spaces. Parishes, for instance, could be more than just administrative or religious units; they could also be spaces of social encounter and belonging. Women's mobility from one parish to another on the occasion of a marital union—or the dissolution of family ties—in some cases even resulted in a change of name and a consequent new identity registration in parish registers, as well as in the redefinition of social relations (Bernardi, 2017).

Moreover, the attention paid to women's mobility within urban spaces has allowed us to demonstrate how they could also use institutions to claim local resources, representing themselves in different ways on the basis of the authorities with which they had to deal. This is due to the context of legal pluralism that characterised Mediterranean urban spaces over time. Women's mobility between courts and across different jurisdictional frameworks emerges, for instance, if we study matrimonial disputes. In early modern Venice, both the lay and ecclesiastical authorities were involved in the control of marriage, even if for different reasons. It was not uncommon, therefore, for women especially to turn to one court or another on the basis of their contingent needs (Ferraro, 2001; Hacke, 2004; Bellavitis, Filippini, and Plebani, 2014). This aspect is even more marked in the Ottoman and Islamic Mediterranean, where women could benefit from "forum shopping" by addressing different courts to demand divorce contracts or alimony, report abuses and violence against them, or request maintenance payments from their husbands or ex-husbands, as well as the custody of their children (the pioneering work of Tucker in 1985 and most recently 2020).

Rather than further emphasising the possibility that women could move across diverse spaces, we propose to reflect on the heuristic value of immobility and permanence. In this regard, urban anthropology introduced to other disciplines the idea of the city as a set of multiple spaces of sociability and belonging (Hannerz, 1980). These spaces, in addition to parishes, courts, national communities, and neighbourhoods, could also be specific buildings such as churches, mosques, shrines, and houses. The city of Venice, for example, was characterised by great residential proximity and an outer projection of social life, one that guaranteed social interaction between individuals and the exchange of languages and beliefs (Barbierato, 2006). However, it was not only public spaces (in their traditional sense) that facilitated encounters: even houses—often shared by people from different social classes, origins, and occasionally even religion—served as places for socialising and work.

In this perspective, a gender approach to mobility has brought to light spaces that had not previously been considered in mobility studies, such as internal and domestic ones, where the intimate and subjective experience of transnational mobility took place. The intimate space of the house, from the furniture to the objects and artefacts that inhabit it, becomes the material expression of experiences of dislocation, namely of a "diasporic intimacy" (Boym, 1988). If we consider the history of the Jewish diaspora from Libya, for instance, the analysis of photographs and oral memories concerning images of homes and domestic cultures has disclosed transnational mnemonic processes and the intertwining between gendered mobilities, memory, forgetting, and fantasy (Spadaro, 2018). Finally, the focus on intimacy and mobility leads to a reversal of the dichotomy between public and private spheres, with internal and familial space serving as the privileged site for investigating mobility processes even in their social dimension.

4.5 Conclusions

These last considerations concerning geographical distance and urban sociability bring us back to the beginning of this chapter. How were male and female mobilities documented and represented in the sources? It was within a plurality of urban spaces and communities that mobility was controlled and migrants identified. The gender perspective, indeed, helps to better disclose the communitarian level of every identification process. Women's registration (and non-registration) supports the conclusion that social, moral, and political controls on mobility were exercised not only by urban and national institutions, but also by society as a whole. Furthermore, we can argue that the need for registration especially emerged in cases where female mobility was not exclusively geographical, but also social and cultural. The focus on both gender subjectivities and relations also allows us to consider mobility in a broader sense, including the diverse typologies of mobility: such as long and short-distance movements, or extra and inter-urban mobility, as well as real and imaginative journeys. From this perspective, we can say that the gender approach also demands the interweaving of geographical and social displacements. This refines the centrality of "spatial distance", emphasising the critical role of local and trans-local social ties in establishing proximity, even when women appear to be immobile actors.

Places where men and women from different social and cultural backgrounds meet each other offer a privileged point of observation of the plurality of forms that mobility, and immobility, can incorporate. That emerges if we look at the following description of an African diaspora religious festival in Tripoli. As the Orientalist and Arabist scholar Tommasi Sarnelli observed in the 1920s, meeting the Muslim community of the city's sub-Saharan diaspora was possible even without embarking on a long-distance journey or a caravan trip across the Sahara. Here, only ten or twenty minutes from the "centre" of Tripoli, a caste of African women (*godye*) played a central role as the hub of migration trajectories and urban networks:

> The festive and noisy Mèlaab that takes place outside the city, twice a year, with the participation of almost all the black population of Tripoli [...]. On both occasions, a procession of men and women is formed, in which the godye [*the caste of women officiating the bori cult*] have a place of honor, headed by a banner of multicolored cloths [...]. The procession leaves in the morning from the center of the ancient city, near the house of the "scèkha", and goes to the "regebia", outside the walls, towards the mosque-cemetery of Sidi Mesri. There, they stop and the typical African songs and dances commence, in a clearing near the witch doctor...This is Africa! The real Africa that lives and rumbles, denied and unrecognized, there, just a stone's throw from the modern city.
> (Sarnelli, 1924, 220–221)

Through this testimony, we can glimpse the corporeal travel and physical movement of objects, but also the imaginative travels that were performed during religious festivals. These different forms of mobility can be traced by following the collective journey that led the sub-Saharan African diaspora in Tripoli from the residence of the *shaykha* (the African woman leading the cult) in the city centre, towards the southern neighbourhood, to the shrine of a holy man where music, dances, and evocations nourished the imaginative journey of attendees. We have decided to close with these words because Sarnelli describes a real and imaginative journey that crosses inter-urban spaces, evokes long-distance travels across the Sahara, and stops in spaces of sociability that serve as proper hubs for social networks. Once again, the "gender sensitive approach", which we have applied to different historical and geographical contexts, places the gendered "body"—in both its physical and social dimensions—at the centre of different mobility representations and experiences.

Notes

1 This paper is the result of the collaboration and the constant dialogue between two authors. Teresa Bernardi has written the following paragraphs: 3; 9 (including the quote); 10; 11; 12 (including the quote), 13; 17; 19; 20; 21; 25; 27; 29; 30; 32; 34; 36. Silvia Bruzzi has written the paragraphs: 1; 14; 15 (including images); 16; 18; 22; 23; 24; 31; 35; 37 (including the quote); 38. They wrote together the paragraphs: 2; 4; 5; 6; 7; 8; 13; 26; 28; 33.
2 Giuseppe Passi, "I donneschi difetti", Vincenzo Somasco, Venice: 1618, 126–127, cited in Dialeti and Plakotos (2015).
3 Archivio di Stato di Venezia, *Esecutori contro la Bestemmia (Esecutori)*, b. 1, Processi, fasc. "Carpacio Pietro".

4 For what concerns the acquisition of citizenship and its relative registration in the early modern period, see Costa (1999) and Bellavitis (2001).
5 Archivio di Stato di Venezia, Esecutori contro la Bestemmia (*Esecutori*), b. 58, reg. 2, 28 May 1642, c. 5v.
6 This is the case with the ANR Project (2019–2022) "Processetti. Marriage and Mobility in Venice (16th–18th centuries)", supervised by Professor Jean François Chauvard.

References

Adey P, Bissell D, Hannam K, Merriman P and Sheller M (2014) *The Routledge Handbook of Mobilities*. London–New York: Routledge.

Altınbaş N (2014) Marriage and Divorce in the Late Ottoman Empire: Social Upheaval, Women's Rights, and the Need for New Family Law. *Journal of Family History* 39 (2): 114–25.

Anthias F and Lazaridis G (2020) *Gender and Migration in Southern Europe: Women on the Move*. London–New York: Routledge.

Arru A and Ramella F (2003) *L'Italia delle migrazioni interne*. Rome: Donzelli.

Arru A, Caglioti DL and Ramella F (2008) *Donne e uomini migranti. Storie e geografie tra breve e lunga distanza*. Rome: Donzelli.

Barbierato F (2006) *Politici e ateisti. Percorsi della miscredenza a Venezia fra Sei e Settecento*. Milan: Unicopli.

Bellavitis A (2001) *Identité, mariage, mobilité sociale: Citoyennes et citoyens à Venise au XVIe siècle*. Rome: École Française de Rome.

Bellavitis A, Filippini NM and Plebani T (2014) *Spazi, potere, diritti delle donne a Venezia in età moderna*. Verona: QuiEdit.

Bernardi T (2017) Mobilità e appartenenze multiple a Venezia: il caso di Tarsia *alias* Laura Malipiero (1630–1660). *Genesis* 16 (2): 37–59.

Bernardi T (2020) *Mobilità femminile e pratiche di identificazione a Venezia in età moderna*. PhD diss., Scuola Normale Superiore di Pisa.

Bernardi T (2022) Tracing Migrations Within Urban Spaces: Women's Mobility and Identification Practices in Early Modern Venice. In: Zucca Micheletto B. (ed) *Gender and Migration in Historical Perspective: Institutions, Labour and Social Networks*, 16th to 20th Centuries. London: Palgrave Macmillan, 39–81.

Bernardi T and Pompermaier M (2019) Hospitality and Registration of Foreigners in Early-Modern Venice: The Role of Women Within Inns and Lodging Houses. *Gender & History* 31 (3): 624–45.

Bertrand G (2017) L'administration vénitienne et l'évolution des techniques d'enregistrement des étrangers dans le contexte de la Révolution française (1789–1797). *Diasporas* 29: 105–29.

Biancani F (2018) *Sex Work in Colonial Egypt: Women, Modernity and the Global Economy*. London–New York: I. B. Tauris.

Biancani F (2019) Gender, Mobility and Cosmopolitanism in a Trans-Mediterranean Perspective: Female Migration from Trieste's Littoral to Egypt, 1860–1960. *Gender & History* 31 (3): 699–716.

Bini E (2003) Fonti fotografiche e storia delle donne: la rappresentazione delle donne nere nelle fotografie coloniali italiane. In: *La storia contemporanea in Italia oggi: linee di tendenza e orientamenti di ricerca*, Sissco Congress, Lecce, 25–27 September 2003.

Boym S (1998) On Diasporic Intimacy: Ilya Kabakov's Installations and Immigrant Homes. *Critical Inquiry* 24 (2): 498–524.
Braidotti R (1994) *Nomadic Subjects: Embodiment and Sexual Difference in Contemporary Feminist Theory*. New York: Columbia University Press.
Braidotti R (2014) Metamorphic Others and Nomadic Subjects. Tanya Leighton. Available at: https://rosibraidotti.com/wp-content/uploads/2018/06/Braidotti-Rosi-Writing-as-a-Nomadic-Subject.pdf (accessed on 20 January 2022).
Braudel F (1966) *La Méditerranée et le monde méditerranéen a l'époque de Philippe II*. Malakoff: Librairie Armand Colin.
Brendecke A and Molino P (2018) *The History and Cultures of Vigilance: Historicizing the Role of Private Attention in Society*. Pisa–Rome: Fabrizio Serra.
Bruzzi S (2017) *Islam and Gender in Colonial Northeast Africa: Sittī 'Alawiyya, the Uncrowned Queen*. Leiden: Brill.
Bruzzi S (2021) Pluralismo giuridico e diritto di famiglia nella Libia coloniale italiana. In: Bartoloni S. (ed) *Cittadinanze incompiute. La parabola dell'autorizzazione maritale*. Rome: Viella, 77–95.
Buono A (2014) Le procedure di identificazione come procedure di contestualizzazione. Persone e cose nelle cause per eredità vacanti (Stato di Milano, secc. XVI e XVIII). In: Antonielli L. (ed) *Procedure, metodi, strumenti per l'identificazione delle persone e per il controllo del territorio*. Rubbettino: Soveria Mannelli, 35–65.
Caffiero M (2013) *Legami pericolosi. Ebrei e cristiani tra eresia, libri proibiti e stregoneria*. Turin: Einaudi.
Calabi D and Lanaro P (1998) *La città italiana e i luoghi degli stranieri: XIV-XVIII*. Rome–Bari: Laterza.
Canepari E (2014) "In My Home Town I Have...". Migrant Women and Multi-local Ties (Rome, 17th–18th centuries). *Genesis* 13 (1): 11–30.
Cerutti S and Grangaud I (2017) Sources and Contextualizations: Comparing 18th Century North African and Western European Institutions. *Comparative Studies in Society and History* 59 (1): 5–33.
Chambers D and Pullan B (1992) *Venice: A Documentary History 1450–1630*. Oxford: Blackwell.
Chojnacka M (2001) *Working Women in Early Modern Venice*. Baltimore: Johns Hopkins University Press.
Clancy-Smith J (2005) Women, Gender and Migration along a Mediterranean Frontier: Pre-Colonial Tunisia, c. 1815–1870. *Gender & History* 17 (1): 62–92.
Clarsen G (2014) Feminism and Gender. In: Adey P et al. *The Routledge Handbook of Mobilities*. London: Routledge, 94–102.
Colley L (2007) *The Ordeal of Elizabeth Marsh: A Woman in World History*. New York: Pantheon.
Concina E (1997) *Fondaci. Architettura, arte e mercatura tra Levante, Venezia e Alemagna*. Venice: Marsilio.
Costa P (1999) *Storia della cittadinanza in Europa*. Vol. 1. Rome–Bari: Laterza.
Craig LA (2009) *Wandering Women and Holy Matrons: Women as Pilgrims in the Later Middle Ages*. Vol. 138. Leiden: Brill.
Cresswell T and Uteng TP (2008) *Gendered Mobilities*. Aldershot: Ashgate.
De Beauvoir S (1973) *The Second Sex*. New York: Vintage Books.
De Munck B and Winter A (2012) *Gated Communities? Regulating Migration in Early Modern Cities*. Aldershot: Ashgate.

Di Pasquale F (2014) Civilizzare le civilizzatrici. Insegnanti italiane nello spazio mediterraneo fra Ottocento e Novecento. In: Deplano V. and Pes A. (eds) *Quel che resta dell'impero: la cultura coloniale degli italiani*. Milan–Udine, Mimesis, 169–89.

Dialeti A and Plakotos G (2015) Gender, Space and the Production of Difference in Early Modern Venice. *Genesis* 14 (2): 33–58.

Dieste M and Muriel García N (2020) A mi querido Abdelaziz…, de tu Conchita. Cartas entre españolas y marroquíes durante el Marruecos colonial. Madrid: Icaría.

Donati S (2013) *A Political History of National Citizenship and Identity in Italy, 1861–1950*. Stanford: Stanford University Press.

Donato KM (1992) Understanding U.S. Immigration: Why Some Countries Send Women and Others Send Men. In: Gabaccia D. (ed) *Seeking Common Ground: Multidisciplinary Studies of Immigrant Women in the United* States. Westport CT: Greenwood Press, 159–184.

Donato KM, Gabaccia DR, Holdaway J, Manalansan M and Pessar P (2006) A Glass Half Full? Gender in Migration Studies. *International Migration Review* 40 (1): 3–26.

Dursteler E (2011) *Renegade Women: Gender, Identity, and Boundaries in the Early Modern Mediterranean*. Baltimore: Johns Hopkins University Press.

Ferraro JM (2001) *Marriage Wars in Late Renaissance Venice*. Oxford–NewYork: Oxford University Press.

Ferraro JM (2018) Making a Living. The Sex Trade in Early Modern Venice. *The American Historical Review* 123 (1): 30–59.

Gabaccia D (1996) Women of the Mass Migrations: From Minority to Majority, 1820–1930. In Hoerder D. and Moch L. (eds) *European Migrants: Global and Local Perspectives*. Boston: Northeastern University, 90–111.

Gabaccia D and Iacovetta F (2002) *Women, Gender, and Transnational Life*. Toronto: University of Toronto Press.

Ginzburg C (2012) Our Words, and Theirs: A Reflection on the Historian's Craft, Today. In: Fellman S. and Rahikainen M. (eds) *Historical Knowledge: In Quest of Theory, Method and Evidence*. Newcastle upon Tyne: Cambridge Scholars Publishing, 97–119.

Greefs H and Winter A (2019) *Migration Policies and Materialities of Identification in European Cities: Papers and Gates, 1500–1930s*. London–New York: Routledge.

Green NL (2012) Changing Paradigms in Migration Studies: From Men to Women to Gender. *Gender & History* 24 (3): 782–98.

Guerry L and Thébaud F (2020) Éditorial. *Clio. Femmes, Genre, Histoire* 1 (51): 19–32. Available at: https://doi.org/10.4000/clio.17791 (accessed on 20 January 2022).

Hacke D (2004) *Women, Sex and Marriage in Early Modern Venice*. Aldershot: Ashgate.

Hancock AM (2016) *Intersectionality: An Intellectual History*. New York: Oxford University Press.

Hanley W (2017) *Identifying with Nationality: Europeans, Ottomans, and Egyptians in Alexandria*. New York: Columbia University Press.

Hannam K, Sheller M and Urry J (2006) Mobilities, Immobilities and Moorings. *Mobilities* (1): 1–22.

Hannerz U (1980) *Exploring the City: Inquiries Toward an Urban Anthropology*. New York: Columbia University Press.

Harzig C (2001) Women Migrants as Global and Local Agents: New Research Strategies on Gender and Migration. In: Sharpe P. (ed) *Women, Gender and Labour Migration: Historical and Global Perspectives*. London–New York: Routledge, 15–28.

Harzig C (2003) Immigration Policies: A Gendered Historical Comparison. In: Morokvasic M., Erel U. and Shinozaki K. (eds) *Crossing Borders and Shifting Boundaries*. Wiesbaden: VS Verlag für Sozialwissenschaften, 35−58.

Harzig C and Hoerder D (2009) *What Is Migration History?* Cambridge: Polity Press.

Herzfeld M (2005) Practical Mediterraneanism: Excuses for Everything, from Epistemology to Eating. In: Harris W. V. (ed) *Rethinking the Mediterranean*. Oxford: Oxford University Press, 45−63.

Herzog T (2003) *Defining Nations: Immigrants and Citizens in Early Modem Spain and Spanish America*. New Haven–London: Yale University Press.

Herzog T (2004) *Upholding Justice: Society, State, and the Penal System in Quito (1650-1750)*. Ann Arbor: University of Michigan Press.

Larsen J (2014) Distance and Proximity. In: Adey P., Bissell D., Hannam K., Merriman P. and Sheller M. (eds) *The Routledge Handbook of Mobilities*. London–New York: Routledge, 125-33.

Luibhéid E (2002) *Entry Denied: Controlling Sexuality at the Border*. Minneapolis: University of Minnesota Press.

Martini M and Mukherjee S (2019) Special Issue: *Migration, Institutions and Intimate Lives*. *Gender & History* 31 (3).

Morokvasic M (1984) Birds of Passage Are Also Women. *International Migration Review* 18 (4): 886−907.

Nirenberg D (2002) Conversion, Sex, and Segregation: Jews and Christians in Medieval Spain. *American Historical Review* 107 (4): 1065-93.

Phizacklea A (1983) *One Way Ticket: Migration and Female Labor*. London−New York: Routledge.

Piore MJ (1979) *Birds of Passage: Migrant Labor in Industrial Societies*. Cambridge: Cambridge University Press.

Pomata G (1998) Close-ups and Long Shots: Combining Particular and General in Writing the Histories of Women and Men. In: Medick H. and Trepp A. C. (eds) *Geschlechtergeschichte und Allgemeine Geschichte: Harausforderungen und Perspektiven*. Göttingen: Wallstein Verlag, 99−124.

Rappaport J (2014) *The Disappearing Mestizo: Configuring Difference in the Colonial Kingdom of Granada*. Durham, NC: Duke University Press.

Ravenstein EG (1885) The Laws of Migration. *Journal of the Royal Statistical Society* 48: 167−235.

Ravenstein EG (1889) The Laws of Migration. *Journal of the Royal Statistical Society* 52: 241−305.

Romani C (2008) Il corpo dell'esotismo: Cartografia, fotografia, cinema. *Le Globe: Revue Genevoise de Géographie* 148 (1): 107-28.

Rowbotham S (2002) Forward. In: Sharpe P. (ed) *Women, Gender and Labour Migration: Historical and Cultural Perspectives*. Vol. 5. London–New York: Routledge, xvi–xvii.

Sahlins P (2004) *Unnaturally French: Foreign Citizens in the Old Regime and After*. Ithaca–London: Cornell University Press.

Salzberg R (2019) Mobility, Cohabitation and Cultural Exchange in the Lodging Houses of Early Modern Venice. *Urban History* 46 (3): 398−418.

Sarnelli T (1924) Il Buri dei Negri tripolini. *Bollettino della Società Africana d'Italia*: 204-24.

Scarabello G (2006) *Meretrices. Storia della prostituzione a Venezia tra il XIII e il XVIII secolo*. Venice: Supernova.

Scott JW (1986) Gender: A Useful Category of Historical Analysis. *American Historical Review* 91: 1053–75.
Schettini L (2019) *Turpi traffici. Prostituzione e migrazioni globali 1890–1940*. Rome: Biblink.
Sharpe P (2001) *Women, Gender and Labour Migration: Historical and Global Perspectives*. London–New York: Routledge.
Sheila R (2002) Forward. In: Sharpe P. (ed) *Women, Gender and Labour Migration: Historical and Cultural Perspectives*. Vol. 5. London–New York: Routledge, xvi–xvii.
Sheller M and Urry J (2006) The New Mobilities Paradigms. *Environment and Planning* 38 (2): 207–26.
Siebenhüner K (2008) Conversion, Mobility and the Roman Inquisition in Italy Around 1600. *Past & Present* 200 (1): 5–35.
Sinke SM (2006) Gender and Migration: Historical Perspectives. *International Migration Review* 40 (1): 82–103.
Sorbera L (2006) Viaggiare e svelarsi alle origini del femminismo egiziano. In: Scrittori A. R. (eds) *Margini e Confini. Studi sulla cultura delle donne nell'età contemporanea*. Venice: Cafoscarina, 265–94.
Spadaro B (2018) Remembering the "Italian" Jewish Homes of Libya: Gender and Transcultural Memory (1967–2013), *The Journal of North African Studies* 23 (5): 811–33.
Stabili MR and Tirabassi M (2014) Donne migranti tra passato e presente. *Genesis* 13 (1).
Taraud C (2003) *Mauresques: femmes orientales dans la photographie coloniale 1860–1910*. Paris: Albin Michel.
Timmerman C, Fonseca M, Van Praag L, and Pereira S (2018) *Gender and Migration: A Gender Sensitive Approach to Migration Dynamics*. Leuven: Leuven University Press.
Tomas N (2006) Did Women Have a Space? In: Crum R. J. and Paoletti J. T. (eds) *Renaissance Florence: A Social History*. Cambridge: Cambridge University Press, 311–28.
Tucker JE (1985) *Women in 19th Century Egypt*. Cambridge: Cambridge University Press.
Tucker JE (2020) Women's and Gender History in the Middle East and North Africa, 1750–World War I. In: Meade A. T. and Merry E. W. (eds) *A Companion to Global Gender History*. Hoboken: Wiley, 399–414.
Von Tippelskirch X and Villani S (2017) Tra confini religiosi. *Genesis* 16 (2).
Zemon Davis N (1987) *Fiction in the Archives: Pardon Tales and Their Tellers in 16th century France*. Stanford: Stanford University Press.
Zucca Micheletto B (2022) *Gender and Migration in Historical Perspective: Institutions, Labour and Social Networks, 16th to 20th Centuries*. London: Palgrave Macmillan.

5 Handling distances as a key factor in social power dynamics

Marina Bertoncin and Andrea Pase

5.1 Introduction

In the Introduction to Section Two entitled "Qualities" of *The Routledge Handbook of Mobilities*, Adey et al. (2014) propose the concept of "understanding distance as a relation of mobility", an alternative to the conventional approach of analysing mobility as "an activity to overcome, annihilate or foreshorten distance". In this perspective, distance and closeness are analysed by investigating the social-spatial relations that are produced through mobilities (Adey et al., 2014: 104). Terms such as friction of distance, proximity and temporality frequently occur in that section (Cresswell, 2014; Larsen, 2014; Lyons, 2014). This inverted approach to mobility and its use of terminology is intriguing: the initial concept of mobility is viewed from the angle of space (and time). From this point of view, mobility is one of the ways of experiencing distance. Distance can also be acted upon by intervening on the territory (construction of barriers, communication, and circulation networks), on space-time, on the various forms of control, or by creating obstacles/facilitating relationships.[1] Lussault, the French geographer, identifies the constitutive element of the social construction of space in the double concept of separation/distance (2007: 45–69). There is a "separative principle" which constitutes the very essence of human space, making it possible to distinguish, name and act on different social realities. The materialisation of the separative principle is precisely the distance. Places, people and things are separate because they are mutually distant. If there is no distance, there is no space. As Elden (2013) notes, the Latin term *spatium* indicates what lies between the architectural elements of a composition (the columns of a temple) or between the different units of a deployed army. More precisely, it is an interval, the distance, that allows us to separate. Brunet (2009: 14–15) underlines how the Latin term *intervallum* indicates the void that separates—*inter*—two palisades of the Roman *vallum*, a trench defending a bastion. The original sense of space is, therefore, neither a *surface*, nor an extension, nor an area in some way defined, nor a container that exists autonomously regardless of any content. In this sense, it would reflect an essentialist concept of

DOI: 10.4324/9781003278665-7

space intended as *a surface in itself*, independent and abstract from any concrete relational content and historical evolution. On the contrary, space is the space-in-between subjects, objects and places, which, on the one hand, separates them but, on the other hand, connects them, arranges them *on the surface*, determines their order and their very visibility. The intrinsic nature of space is, therefore, relational and non-essentialist: it is the distance—or, as will soon be observed, the plurality of distances, in their multiplicity and changeability over time—that allows for the unfolding of substantial differences and of the relationships between them that intertwine on the surface.

The separative principle is what produces order, because there is no order without distinction, without the definition of differences and, as a consequence, the creation of names and classification systems. Bateson (1972: xxiii–xxvi) highlights how, in the archetypal account of biblical creation, the reality of the world emerges from the progressive separation of day from night, of the waters above from those below, of the sea from the earth, and of the different natural species through which the human denomination appears. For Schmitt (2003) too, order arises from separation, from a distinction that separates the cosmos from the chaos: the political and legal order anchors itself to a primordial differentiation of spaces. Each separation is the identification of a distance, which can be minimal but still effective. When distances are correctly arranged and substantial differences are put in their *place*—in the right order—reality manifests itself as a harmonic dimension: a cosmos.

What some perceive to be a well-ordered reality may be interpreted by others as an imposed order, a cage or a tightening set of constraints. The issue of *who* carries out the separation—defines the distances, establishes the order and names the differences—remains up for grabs: here, power comes into play, in its subtlest form, which is that of making some things visible while obscuring others, marking certain separations while cancelling others. As Schmitt states, the sovereign power belongs to those who establish the order, the primary distinction between an internal and external jurisdiction. The same sovereign power thus has the faculty to suspend its effectiveness through the proclamation of the state of exception (Schmitt, 2003; Agamben, 1995, 1996 and 2003). Distance and politics are closely intertwined because distance is constructed, not a given/taken for granted: it is a tool for political power.

The social need to "regulate distance" translates into "distance technologies" (defined as "techniques, rules and ideologies"), which activate co-presence and mobility (Lussault, 2007: 45–66). Co-presence reduces distance to a minimum and brings multiplicity together: it generates density and leads to an increase in coexisting diversities, as in the case of urban agglomerations. In contrast, for Lussault, mobility—in its dual nature of displacement and telecommunication—is based on distance and manages it. Returning to the case of urban agglomeration, co-presence and mobility are actually mutually reinforcing: in co-presence we find one mobility that takes the various forms of urban mobility and, specularly, mobility makes the connection of co-presence nuclei possible, as seen in the reticular structures of urban agglomerations. Nonetheless, both give rise to specific but interconnected territorial changes: urban expansions, concentrations of industries and shopping centres, circulation nodes and networks. Alongside the technologies of distance, Lussault contextualises the strategies of spatial separation, which consist of two complementary tools: denomination and delimitation. Denomination is the attribution of quality, i.e. the identification of differences in space and their cognitive stabilisation, while delimitation has various forms: material and immaterial limits, closed and open, clear and blurred (Lussault, 2007: 66–69). What makes Lussault's argument particularly persuasive is the close correlation he draws between separation and distance, viewing them as a single primordial problem that generates different technologies and spatial strategies. To elucidate this insight, this chapter will first examine the difference between suffered and desired distances, that is, by identifying a first power differential that distinguishes who can act on distances and who is compelled to endure them. Therefore, attention is focused on who is able to act on the distances and on the movements that this agency can generate. The next section addresses how it is possible to identify different dynamics of power, drawing on Harvey's (2006) discussion on the different distances that descend from the tripartition of space: absolute, relative and relational. In the conclusion, it will be demonstrated how distance has not only been central to the current pandemic crisis with its multiple transformations of mobility, but it is also linked to the next issue on the horizon: decarbonisation to combat climate change. The issue of distance is returning to the forefront and will continue to be of critical importance in the present and near future.

5.2 Distances on the move

Distances can be uneven: they can arise within highly dissymmetrical relational fields (Raffestin, 1980). Modelling (or shaping) of distance can be reduced, aimed at facilitating connections, or increased, oriented towards closure and separation. Furthermore, distance can be acted upon, desired or planned, or it can be suffered, forced or imposed. In one situation, social actors take an active role, while in the other, they are passive (albeit perhaps manifesting more or less hidden forms of resistance).

Two examples that could symbolise this ambivalence are gated communities, understood as a voluntary choice of isolation from the outside world, and refugee camps, where migrants are forced to live in isolation. In the first case, those who seek to distance themselves from the outside world establish the rules governing interactions with their surroundings. In the second case, a governmental authority imposes restrictions on migrants who are forced to stay in the refugee camps. Table 5.1 illustrates some situations that may occur: active versus those imposed are in the vertical columns, while the direction of the modelling—the reduction or increase of distance—is represented by the horizontal lines.

76 Bertoncin and Pase

Table 5.1 Distance: active/imposed, reduced/increased. Some examples

Distance	Desired/active	Feared/imposed
Reduced Opening / connection	Design, installation and management of connection infrastructures: circulation and communication networks Activation of commercial and cultural exchange flows Activation of resistance networks	Arrival areas of industrial or service relocation, land grabbing and raw material extraction (forced opening to the international market) Opening of access routes in equatorial forests (herringbone patterns) Areas affected by infrastructure projects (e.g. high-speed railways)
Increased Closing / interruption	Hermitages, gated communities, access controls on national borders, customs duties and protectionism, "Fortress Europe" Friction of terrain as "a weapon of the weak" (Scott, 2009 and Cresswell, 2014)	Ghettos, *lazzaretti*, refugee camps, urban suburbs and "red areas" during a pandemic Disconnections and slowdowns in exit, visa restrictions

Table 5.2 Actions on distance

	Creating proximity	Creating remoteness
Moving others (things and/or people)	Bringing something/someone closer to themselves (attracting)	Distancing something/someone from themselves (repelling)
Moving themselves	Bringing themselves closer to something/someone (approaching)	Moving themselves away from something/someone (leaving, escaping)

This chapter focuses on the active modifications of distance:[2] How can actors alter distance? Moreover, what are their intentions for fostering this alteration?

Actors could choose to move things or people or, alternatively, they could decide to move themselves in space. As for their intentions, it is possible to identify two objectives that actors may have in modifying distance: those who may wish to create proximity and those who may wish to create distancing. Table 5.2 presents four different movements that may occur with distance: the actors' intentions are in the vertical columns whereas the horizontal lines describe the preferred or compelled choice, that is, whether preferring or being compelled to move or, on the contrary, preferring or being compelled to remain still.

Handling distances as a key factor in social power dynamics 77

The four modifications of distance thus identified can be accomplished in very different spatial dimensions, which will be examined in the next section.

5.3. Handling distances

The world—in the sense of how actors experience it—can be handled, modified, adapted and shaped according to the needs of the different actors, bringing into play the possible modifications of distance. The very idea of handling implies manipulation: the hand, through the opposability of the thumb, enabled mankind's first active interaction with reality, beginning with chipping flint or holding a stick. It is the hand that initiates that first chain of measurement of space based on a bodily experience, the thumb and palm. Then, by extending an arm and taking a step, humans begin to measure and interact with distance. From this point forward, handling distance becomes an integral part of any project aimed at transforming reality. The Latin term *projectus* accurately describes the ability to throw forward, and then launch: the hand grasps, the arm extends and the *projectile* reaches the target. To further grasp this concept of how handling space is possible, it is necessary to return to the geographical concept of space. In Harvey's proposal (1973, 2006), space has three dimensions: absolute space, understood as a surface that can be measured using Euclidean geometry; relative space (time), defined as a space subject to different conditions one must face; and relational space (time), which is related to the relationship that social, economic and political actors establish with one another.[3]

In Table 5.3 we suggest how these three different dimensions of space generate different types of distance. First of all, we consider absolute distance, easily measurable with the Euclidean metric. Then we consider relative distance, which is dependent on different variables: the geomorphological and climatic situations (contextual); the infrastructural density of the territory (territorial: e.g. circulation and communication networks, urban agglomerations); the organisation of transport (technical means and management effectiveness); and, finally, the individual conditions at stake, the ability to deal with distance (hodological, which derives from the Greek term for journey (Janni,

Table 5.3 Types of space and distance (Bertoncin and Pase, 2022)

Type of space		Declination of distance	
Absolute space		Absolute distance	
TimeSpace	Relative	Relative distance	Contextual
			Territorial
			Organisational
			Hodological
	Relational	Relational distance	Psychological
			Positional

1984), meaning the objective conditions of individuals such as age, health, wealth and "value" of the passport). Finally, we consider relational distance, defined as the distance determined by the subjects within the social relationship. Two dimensions exist within relational distance: psychological distance and positional distance. The first is related to individual perceptions of distance (between oneself and another) or by collective subjects (between us and others), drawing on the construal-level theory: "... psychological distance is egocentric. Its reference point is the self in the here and now, and the different ways in which an object might be removed from this point—in time, in space, in social distance, and in hypotheticality" (Trope and Liberman, 2010: 440; Simandan, 2016). The second one deals with the "relational field" proposed by Raffestin (1980), where it is possible to identify the reciprocal distance assumed by individuals and collective subjects.

All these distances, including the absolute ones, can be manipulated, as we will see later. The interest of the actors is to modify the playing field to suit their own interests, to ensure that others play "with the slope against", to use a metaphor. As the following section demonstrates, distances are subject to the dynamics of power.

5.4 Distances at stake (or up for grabs)

Distances are not neutral, and their management translates as "a difference of power" (Lagendijk and Lorentzen, 2007: 462): in fact, one cannot ignore "the crucial role [that] power plays in the dynamic developments of spatial configurations". In other words, distances are created and modified as a way of expanding the power of some actors towards other actors and on space (Raffestin, 1980). Those with greater means and skills change distances more effectively; those who best modify distances gain information and energy and, in so doing, strengthen their position with respect to other actors. Table 5.4 identifies some dynamics of power tied to the management of distance.

While absolute distance cannot be modified, there are ways to exert control over it, particularly cognitively. Having a representation of absolute space and being able to determine the geographical coordinates of every possible location enables intervention, such as planning explorations or military campaigns. The dream of power is to be able to "see" everywhere and, to the extent possible, to instantaneously strike at a distance, as if distance did not exist and everything was perfectly legible. The powerful have always been girded by geographical representations: maps of the reign adorn the walls of the great palaces of power (for example, the *Palazzo Ducale* in Venice or the Vatican's Gallery of Maps). In reality, the great empires—particularly the global ones of the Modern Age, and primarily the Spanish and Portuguese Empires before them—had to grapple with the hard problem of governing from a distance. Confronted with journeys that lasted many months and fraught with great uncertainties, a "politics of knowledge" was developed over

Table 5.4 Types of distance and dynamics of power

Type of distance	Dynamics of power
Absolute distance	Overviewing
	Seeing from above (from satellites, drones and through video surveillance) and acting at a distance (remote control of civil and military technological georeferenced devices)
	Planning through representations of space: joining/separating on the map
	Establishing order (linking someone-something to a position on the maps)/defining order (projecting a legal and political order onto absolute space)
Relative distance	Changing the geomorphological condition (e.g. drilling a mountain, diverting a river)
	Opening/closing territories through the construction of infrastructural networks, the concentration of residences and activities in the centres, the erection of boundaries and checkpoints
	Organising and engineering the circulation of goods, passengers, information (technological evolutions, e.g. information and communication technologies or high-speed trains, and organisational innovations, e.g. online sales or standardisation of transport, see containerisation: Levinson, 2006)
	Facilitating or hindering the movement of individuals or social groups through the provision or non-provision of economic subsidies, network access points and visas
Relational distance	Withdrawing/opening up (of the subject, in a psychological dimension)
	Perceiving near/distant (what you want/what you fear)
	Including-excluding in social processes
	Moving up-moving down in the social hierarchy

time through maps, letters, books, itineraries and lists as a means of ensuring the effectiveness of the imperial *vision* (Castelnau-L'Estoile and Regourd, 2005; Gaudin, 2013; Gaudin and Valenzuela Márquez, 2015; Brendecke, 2016). Today's satellite systems for remote sensing and positioning, as well as the various forms of remote control and intervention, such as guided missiles and drones, all give concreteness to ancient aspirations. For bombardment operations, distance is now reduced to a screen that strikes "intelligently", which frames the space to be hit, with the decisive moment then occurring at the touch of a button, triggering an explosion thousands of kilometres away. Certainly, there will be "collateral damage" because reality can never be reduced to mere calculation. Due to devices that can be tracked and operated remotely, acting on a representation has today become acting on reality, which was until now the prerogative of the divine or magical thought. Furthermore, georeferenced representations can today stratify numerous layers of information, both current and historical, with continuous updating, and thus give rise to an "augmented reality" where interpretations and readings of the world can be amplified in ways previously unimaginable.

On the other hand, intervening with different conditionality can modify relative distance, starting with the contextual ones, that is, by trying to diminish the geomorphological and climatic constraints: mountains can be perforated; rivers and even maritime straits can be crossed by bridges or cut through with tunnels; and underground systems ensure free movement in hostile climates, even in the coldest winters. The most important modifications of relative distance have to do with territorial conditions and the organisation of movement. By intervening in a space, distance can be modified by bringing a location closer or by distancing it. There is an explicit link between the management of distance and a planning project (Brunet, 2009: 15): it is the effort of an actor that connects or separates two points in space, in this way bringing geographical areas closer or moving them farther apart. The management of distance can make a difference as a project develops within a territory. The intentionality of an actor determines whether distance is considered as an obstacle to be overcome or as a protective barrier against something potentially hostile or dangerous. According to Raffestin (1980), territorial strategies are to a great extent tied to the management of distance. For example, communication and movement networks construct space in response to the needs of the actors to come closer to determined nodes; on the other hand, a system of boundaries sets up a distance between areas, establishing thresholds that alter spatial continuity in order to separate the territories, thus creating discontinuity (Soja, 1971: 27–28).

Two actions are possible in terms of relative distance: the act of approaching and the "castling". Construction of communication and movement networks, and their technological modernisation, can compress relative distance: consider the advent of railways and then of today's high-speed trains. Other actions concern organisational arrangements for freight transport, such as the emergence of businesses specialising in the transport of goods in the Modern Age (Braudel, 1982) and the modern development of the logistics industry (Grappi, 2016). As a result of technical and organisational interventions in a territory, space is crumpled and the relative distances are compressed. Consequently, the centres of political and economic power tighten their relationship. The opposite action is the castling. The centres lock themselves in defensive barriers. The hostile or less important places remain at the peripheries of circulation networks; physical, administrative and political boundaries separate the territories, thus creating a breakdown in relative distance; and, consequently, impediments lengthen time and operating costs. Drawing on Elias Canetti (1960) who states: "All the distances that man has gathered around himself are driven by the fear of being touched", Brighenti further notes how distance is a crucial aspect for social life (2010: 223). For the sociologist, "Distance management entails finding out and defining critical distances, thresholds, points, lines and degree beneath and beyond which a given relationship is substantially transformed". In this way, "each territory is a zone of convergence of actors (and their forces) who attempt to manage their reciprocal visibilities and invisibilities—i.e. their reciprocal affections—*managing reciprocal distances*" (italics of Brighenti), so it is precisely through the management of openings and closings and the predisposition of networks and barriers that movement is facilitated or obstructed. From this point of view, openings or closings, approaching or castling are all aspects of the same process: the management of distance. Borders are the critical thresholds that interact with the flow. As a result, inequality exists between centres and peripheral spaces. As Lagendijk and Lorentzen (2007: 462) note, "[The] key mechanism of power and control, i.e. of granting access to places and resources, remain heavily founded upon territory-based practices". Relative distance is uneven:

> Especially for those living in less privileged areas, it is clear that access to good education, jobs, social security, healthcare service, decent housing, competitively priced products, or even the possibility to travel abroad, very much depends on places of birth and residence.
> (Lagendijk and Lorentzen, 2007: 462)

However, Raffestin (1980) reminds us that the game is not over and that, as history attests, the centres of power are always relocating in space: in our Modern Age, economic power passes from the Mediterranean to the Atlantic and, possibly, now to the Pacific. The path dependence resulting from territorial arrangements is not easy to modify because it originates from "the historically accumulated construction of transport infrastructures and of meeting places, both in a more material and virtual sense" and from "the shaping of territorially bounded spaces, along social, institutional, political and economic dimensions" (Lagendijk and Lorentzen, 2007: 460). An underestimation of these spatial inequalities can lead to the "revenge of places that don't matter" (Rodríguez-Pose, 2018), resulting in turbulence in electoral behaviour or in street protests that erode Western democracies, and not exclusively. Consider the French "yellow vest" (*gilets jaunes*) movement, or the urban riots in Santiago de Chile in 2019, or the populist vote expressed by the territorial peripheries in the Brexit referendum, or the recent political elections in Italy. Finally, again with regard to relative space, it is also possible to modify hodological conditions, for example by reducing public transport fares for certain social classes (workers, students and seniors), the preparation of itineraries for the blind or wheelchair users, and the setting up of humanitarian corridors for asylum seekers from war zones. Or, conversely, it is possible to further hinder those who are prevented from moving, by increasing transport prices or complicating the procedures for obtaining entry visas.

As far as relational distance is concerned, by examining the motivations that could explain social behaviour, the manipulation of distance responds to that fundamental ambivalence of human need discussed by Eibl-Eibesfeldt (1984): on the one hand, there is a need for a delimitation of closure, such as in the identification of a space for defence or for intimacy, which then enables self-recognition and the creation of privileged social relationships; on the other hand, there is the need for relationships, movement, opening up to the outside world and change.

Here, the psychological colouring of distance, in the perception of what is near and what is far, assumes a clear ambivalence: distance can arouse more fear because it is less known, yet distance can simultaneously stimulate interest in what is different—the dimension of otherness—which can enrich one's experience and relational life. The drive to shorten or increase the spatial, temporal, social or hypothetical psychological distance will depend on the direction chosen by the subject, individual or collective. In other words, it is contingent upon prevailing perceptions at any given moment, dependent on whether one's privacy or security is being protected, or upon the desire for contact with otherness. The collective dimension of psychological proximity or distance between us and others can be modified through narratives and policies that focus on the fear of difference (emphasising or inventing the dangers associated with contact with otherness), thus increasing psychological distance. Or, in contrast, it can be modified with narratives and policies that foster inclusion and enhancement of differences, thus decreasing the psychological distance between us and the others.

In relational distance, we argue that two dynamics of power are correlated. The first pertains to the sense of inclusion or exclusion in a specific relational field. The second deals with the position that an actor assumes while interacting in that same relational field. Taking these two dynamics into consideration, two perceptions can be identified: one of superiority and one of inferiority.

In order to proceed with the analyses of power dynamics in relational distance, we propose the following diagram that intersects these two oppositions (Figure 5.1).

The diagram identifies four different positions: in the first, the most favourable position, an actor perceives a sense of superiority in that s/he is part of or fully participatory in the relational field; in the second, an actor feels that s/he is part of it, yet in an inferior position (for example, s/he has less influence over others); in the third, the actor does not feel that s/he is part of a specific relational field but, at the same time, s/he is not interested, yet nevertheless s/he still retains a position of influence; in the fourth, the actor feels excluded from the relational field and perceives it as a position of inferiority in relation to others (the worst position). Inevitably, the actors' objective would be to move to a "more" favourable position (up, inclusion). In a given context, social mobility can be active, meaning it would be possible to move from one position to another through education and work commitment; in this way, at least the most gifted and capable individuals would be able to shorten the distances. If, on the other hand, the social context is rigid and impenetrable, thereby preventing social mobility between classes, the hierarchy would be

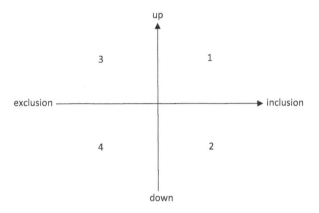

Figure 5.1 Relational distance and power dynamics.

predetermined: the weakest subjects, even if capable, would inevitably feel excluded, and discontent and tensions would grow over time.

5.5 Conclusion

Technical revolutions in the transport of goods and people and in the transmission of communication (especially with the development of ICTs: Information and Communications Technologies)—in constant acceleration during the 20th century—have certainly determined a "space-time compression" (Harvey, 1973), which has caused more than a few scholars to declare "the death of the distance", as the title of a well-known text by Cairncross (1997) states. In reality, "proximity studies" have demonstrated the role that proximity, or rather proximities, continues to play in the context of globalisation, both positively as a facilitator of innovation processes, and negatively as a result of the risks of lock-in associated with an "excess" of proximity (Boschma, 2004, 2005; Boschma and Frenken, 2003; Rallet, 1993; Torre, 2009; Torre and Wallet, 2014; Torre and Gallaud, 2022). In a similar vein, Morgan firmly objects to the "exaggerated death of geography" wrought by the ability of ICTs to transcend any distance. Indeed, the dissemination of information is one thing, its understanding is quite another (Morgan, 2004).

Unlike what has been hypothesised by those who, like Bauman (2000), support the advent of "smooth de-territorialised spaces" where power is "becoming 'extraterritorial', no longer bound by the resistance of space" (Urry, 2002: 267), according to Scott (2009) and Cresswell (2014), the "friction of distance" has shifted but is far from disappearing. It cannot, therefore, be said that "power is liquefied and separated from territory" (Urry, 2002: 268); rather, power continues to play with distances on multiple levels and in ever-changing ways. The "celebration of a borderless world, facilitated by new communications technologies and an integrated global economy" was perhaps declared prematurely, and "the neoliberal mythology of a frictionless world" conceals the proliferation of "holes and excesses" in "the dirty underside of the gl*O*bal" (Kapoor, 2018: xxii). Neoliberal globalisation maintains an *O* at its centre, a void, a darkness, from which destabilising unconscious materials emerge, creating psychological distances and hostility towards diversity (Kapoor, 2018: xix–xxxiv).

On the other hand, the abrupt shift in context and narratives associated with the spread of the pandemic, with the drastic increase in impediments to movement, with the sudden cooling of hypermobility, and with the success of definitions such as "social distancing", confirms that distance, in all its materiality and—if you prefer—brutality, had perhaps vanished, but had not vanished completely, and is always ready to reappear (Grasland, 2018). Global crises such as pandemics or global warming, both of which are accelerated—albeit in a different way—precisely by the frenetic circulation of people and goods (and viruses), reconfirm and update distance strategies as a key factor in social power dynamics. Covid-19 has established the return of the political nature of space with respect to the domination of the financialised economy in the age of unfolding globalisation. Everything changes in the face of a catastrophe: States, which seemed to have lost their grip on the world, have regained their role and self-determination by closing borders, even within countries, as with the declaration of "red zones", imposing distancing rules and limiting movement: therefore, and precisely, *handling* distances. Projecting distance has quickly regained prominence. It will remain so even after the pandemic's hoped-for conclusion because another crisis is clearly on the horizon, this one determined by climate change, forcing us to rethink "high-carbon mobility". Many businesses and municipalities on the cutting edge of innovation are already moving towards a new design of distances and proximity, as evidenced by "near working" experiences in the metropolis or the shortening of production and distribution chains, particularly for "strategic goods" such as masks or vaccines. The territorial implications will be far-reaching and profound: distance is back and is here to stay.

Notes

1 On distance, in relation to space, see: Brunet, 2009; Deza and Deza, 2009; Grasland, 2018; Gatrell, 1983, 2017; Pirie, 2009; Simandan, 2019; Bertoncin and Pase, 2022.
2 Distance suffered/imposed will not be discussed in this chapter, but will be the subject of further analysis.
3 On space and time see: May and Thrift, 2001; Bertoncin and Pase, 2022.

References

Adey P, Bissell D, Hannam K, Merriman P and Sheller M (eds) (2014) *The Routledge handbook of mobilities*. London, New York: Routledge.

Agamben G (1995) *Homo sacer. Il potere sovrano e la nuda vita*. Torino: Einaudi.
Agamben G (1996) *Mezzi senza fine. Note sulla politica*. Torino: Bollati Boringhieri.
Agamben G (2003) *Stato di eccezione*. Torino: Bollati Boringhieri.
Bateson G (1972) *Steps to an ecology of mind*. New York: Ballantine.
Bauman Z (2000) *Liquid modernity*. Cambridge: Olity.
Bertoncin M and Pase A (2022) Geographical proximity questioned. In: Torre A and Gallaud D (eds) *Handbook of proximity relations*. Cheltenham, UK, Northampton, MA, USA: Elgar, pp. 204–219.
Boschma RA (2004) Competitiveness of regions from an evolutionary perspective. *Regional Studies* 38(9): 1001–1014.
Boschma RA (2005) Proximity and innovation: a critical assessment. *Regional Studies* 39(1): 61–74.
Boschma RA and Frenken K (2003) Evolutionary economics and industry location. *International Review for Regional Research* 23: 183–200.
Braudel F (1982) *La Méditerranée et le monde méditerranéen à l'époque de Philippe II*. Paris: Colin.
Brendecke A (2016) *The Empirical empire. Spanish colonial rule and the politics of knowledge*. Berlin/Boston: De Gruyter.
Brighenti AM (2010) Lines, barred lines. Movement, territory and the law. *International Journal of Law in Context* 6(3): 217–227.
Brunet R (2009) Les sens de la distance. *Atala* 12: 13–32.
Cairncross F (1997) *The death of distance*. Cambridge, MA: Harvard Business School Press.
Canetti E (1984) *Crowds and power*. New York: Farrar, Straus and Giroux (*Masse und Macht*. Hamburg: Claassen, 1960).
Cresswell T and Merriman P (2008) *Geographies of mobility: practices, spaces, subjects*. London: Ashgate.
Cresswell T (2014) Friction. In: Adey P et al. (eds) *The Routledge handbook of mobilities*. London, New York: Routledge, pp.107–115.
De Castelnau-L'Estoile C and Regourd F (eds) (2005) *Connaissances et pouvoirs: les espaces impeériaux, XVIe–XVIIIe siècles, France, Espagne, Portugal*. Pessac: Presses Universitaires de Bordeaux.
Deza MM and Deza E (2009) *Encyclopedia of distances*. Berlin, Heidelberg: Springer.
Eibl-Eibesfeldt I (1984) *Etologia umana. Le basi biologiche e culturali del comportamento*. Torino: Bollati Boringhieri (*Die Biologie des menschlichen Verhaltens. Grundriss der Humanethologie*. München: Piper, 1984).
Elden S (2013) *The birth of territory*. Chicago: University of Chicago Press.
Gaudin G (2013) *Penser et gouverner le Nouveau Monde, au XVIIe siècle. L'empire de papier de Juan Diez de la Calle, commis du Conseil des Indes*. Paris: l'Harmattan.
Gaudin G and Valenzuela Márquez J (2015) Empires ibériques: de la péninsule au global. *Diasporas. Circulations, migrations, histoire* 25: 13–24.
Grappi G (2016) *Logistica*. Roma: Ediesse.
Grasland C (2018) Distance/proximité: la fin de la mort de la géographie? In: Mareï N and Richard Y (eds) *Dictionnaire de la régionalisation du monde*. Neuilly: Atlande, pp.132–136.
Gatrell AC (1983) *Distance and space. A geographical perspective*. Oxford: Clarendon.
Gatrell AC (2017) Distance. In: Richardson D, Castree N, Goodchild MF, Kobayashi A, Liu W and Marston RA (eds) *International encyclopaedia of geography: people,*

the earth, environment and technology. New York: John Wiley & Sons. https://doi.org/10.1002/9781118786352.wbieg0391

Harvey D (1973) *Social justice and the city*. London: Edward Arnold.

Harvey D (1990) *The condition of postmodernity*. Malden, Oxford: Blackwell.

Harvey D (2006) Space as a key word. In: Harvey D (ed) *Spaces of global capitalism: towards a theory of uneven geographical development*. London, New York: Verso, pp.119–148.

Janni P (1984) *La mappa e il periplo. Cartografia antica e spazio odologico*. Roma: Bretschneider.

Kapoor I (2018) *Psychoanalysis and the glObal*. Lincoln, NE, USA, London: University of Nebraska Press.

Lagendijk A and Lorentzen A (2007) Proximity, knowledge and innovation in peripheral regions. On the intersection between geographical and organizational proximity. *European Planning Studies* 15(4): 457–466.

Larsen J (2014) Distance and proximity. In: Adey P et al. *The Routledge handbook of mobilities*. London, New York: Routledge, pp.125–133.

Levinson M (2006) *The box: how the shipping container made the world smaller and the world economy bigger*. Princeton: Princeton University Press.

Lyons G (2014) Times. In: Adey P et al. *The Routledge handbook of mobilities*. London, New York: Routledge, pp.154–162.

Lussault M (2007) *L'homme spatial. La construction sociale de l'espace humain*. Paris: Seuil.

May J and Thrift N (2001) Introduction. In: May J and Thrift N (eds) *Timespace: geographies of temporality*. London: Routledge, pp.1–37.

Morgan K (2004) The exaggerated death of geography: learning, proximity and territorial innovation systems. *Journal of Economic Geography* 4(1): 3–21.

Olsson G (1965) *Distance and human interaction: a review and bibliography*. Philadelphia, PA: Regional Science Research Institute.

Pirie GH (2009) Distance. In: Kitchin R and Thrift N (eds) *International encyclopaedia of human geography*. Oxford: Elsevier, pp.242–251.

Raffestin C (1980) *Pour une géographie du pouvoir*. Paris: Libraires Techniques.

Rallet A (1993) Choix de proximité et processus d'innovation technologique. *Revue d'Economie Régional et Urbaine* 3: 365–386.

Rodríguez-Pose A (2018) The revenge of the places that don't matter (and what to do about it). *Cambridge Journal of Regions, Economy and Society* 11(1): 189–209.

Schmitt C (2003) *The Nomos of the earth in the international law of the Jus Publicum Europaeum*. New York: Telos (*Der Nomos der Erde im Völkerrecht des Jus Publicum Europaeum*. Berlin: Duncker & Humblot, 1974).

Scott JC (2009) *The art of not being governed. An anarchist history of upland southeast Asia*. Yale: Yale University Press.

Simandan D (2016) Proximity, subjectivity, and space: rethinking distance in human geography. *Geoforum* 75: 249–252.

Simandan D (2019) Distance. In: Kobayashi A (ed) *International encyclopaedia of human geography*. Oxford: Elsevier, pp.393–397.

Söderström O and Crot L (2010) *The mobile constitution of society: rethinking the mobility-society nexus*. MAPS, Working Paper 7. Neuchâtel: Université de Neuchâtel.

Soja EW (1971) *The political organization of space*. Resources Paper No. 8. Washington, D.C: Association of American Geographers.

Torre A (2009) Retour sur la notion de proximité géographique. *Géographie, Économie, Société* 11: 63–75.

Torre A and Wallet F (eds) (2014) *Regional development and proximity relations*. Cheltenham, UK, Northampton, MA, USA: Elgar.

Torre A and Gallaud D (eds) (2022) *Handbook of proximity relations*. Cheltenham, UK, Northampton, MA, USA: Elgar.

Trope Y and Liberman N (2010) Construal-level theory of psychological distance. *Psychological Review* 117(2): 440–463.

Urry J (2002) Mobility and proximity. *Sociology* 36(2): 255–274.

6 Map-mobilities
Expanding the field

Laura Lo Presti and Tania Rossetto

6.1 Introduction

From an experiential perspective, maps have always been involved in movement in a variety of ways. In their most general aspects, we encounter them as mediating objects that help humans to navigate and orient in space. By mainly treating them as tools of travel, we forget, however, that maps are also powerful images that attempt to simulate movement over their symbolic surfaces for several different purposes; and, precisely because of the value of what they represent and how they convey it, maps, in various forms, have circulated and continue to spread as travelling images. Let's think about the inscription of imaginary paths on the prehistoric rocky map of Bedolina, in Val Camonica (Italy) or the many portable road maps used to navigate the land since the antiquity and the wide spectrum of sizes, lines and colours of the sea-charts used by maritime explorers during the Middle Ages and the Age of Discovery. Let's think also about the flow maps that have appeared in atlases or newspapers over the last few centuries to illustrate migration, currents, trade goods and traffic, or the digital, interactive and immersive ego-centred mobile mapping practices that we are experiencing today through smartphones and sat-nav apps. Those taxonomies, flexibilities and inscriptions of movement infer that the map, either as a device or an image, cannot be easily dissociated from the mobile condition. Nevertheless, critical and humanist readings have often complained of the ontological fixity expressed by maps, mostly considered the quintessence of immobility, or, more extremely, referring to cartographic visuals as 'lifeless media' (Dodge, 2014: 519).

In a recent work built around the critique of a set of enduring preconceptions and common-sense hypotheses about cartography, map historian Matthew Edney (2019: 234) fairly affirmed that 'nothing about mapping is fixed and stable'. By contesting the ideal of cartography, that is a web of basic convictions about cartography as a universal and individual mode of spatial knowledge developed since the late 18th century with the adoption, by European states, of systematic territorial surveys, Edney endorses a history of maps that is instead capable of grasping the multifaceted,

DOI: 10.4324/9781003278665-8

diverse and dynamic existence of disparate mapping practices. Through a processual approach, he places particular emphasis on the dynamic ways in which maps are produced, circulated and used, and the multiple forms, including non-image ones, in which these practices emerge in varied contexts. Remembering that Western maps are 'semantically flexible as non-Western maps', he re-interrogates their histories, making a plea for considering 'not cartography, but mapping' (Edney, 2019: 235, 229). Methodologically, this rethinking of the history of maps goes beyond not only the normative vision of a continual technical progress of cartography, but also beyond the overly restrictive socio-cultural and political approaches that have enlivened map critique since the 1980s (Harley, 1989). The kind of processual and dynamic approach endorsed by Edney asks for less politically deconstructive and more empirically descriptive modes of inquiry. Indeed, Edney's call within the history of maps echoes the move already experienced in the mid-2000s by map theory, when a new wave of post-representational, emergent, processual cartographic thinking focusing on the continuous unfolding of mapping practices was established (Dodge, Kitchin and Perkins, 2009). Map scholars researching both contemporary and historical mapping acts are increasingly prompted to follow the fleeting existence of such mappings.

The advent of digital cartography has had a significant impact on the above-mentioned theoretical reorientations, given that the static image of the paper map, making a portion of territory immutable and freezing a moment in time, has been challenged by electronic navigation, transforming the logic of mapping from representations to coordinates (Rankin, 2017). In the digital mapping era, because of the changes in navigation techniques, maps went 'beyond cartography' and became subject to a more dynamic consideration. Yet we should appreciate how much the digital shift stimulated a re-evaluation of the navigational nature of cartography as a whole. Indeed, while proposing a navigational rather than a mimetic interpretation of maps in the digital age, November, Camacho-Hübner and Latour (2010) suggested that the crucial dimension of cartography as navigational applies also to pre-computer cartography. In this chapter, in the wake of the re-mobilisation of cartographic thinking and methodologies, and through a humanistic lens, we will consider three conceptual frameworks, namely cartographic navigations, circulations and animations, to provide a tentative overview of the ways in which the mobility, mobilisation and dynamism of maps may be articulated with reference to both past and present cartographic phenomena and cultures.

6.2 Navigations

Maps are often appreciated for their ability to let people navigate the space around them. As more appropriately argued by literary scholar Robert Tally Jr. (2011), constant navigation equates to the experience of *being in the world*. In this sense, the long history of the concept of 'the voyage of life' as a kind of imagined mapping of time-in-space is revealing, as Della Dora (forthcoming) shows, while viewing the ancient *navigatio vitae* metaphor 'as an evocative map of human existence'. Famously, literary theorist Fredric Jameson (1991) claimed a new aesthetic of *cognitive mapping* as part of a political project aimed at providing the postmodern subject with a heightened sense of its place in the global late capitalist economic and social system, merging the geographic totality evoked by modern mapmaking with the more mobile and situational experience evoked by pre-cartographic forms of mappings such as itineraries. Overall, we navigate when we try to find our place in society in relation to others, in orienting in space and time, in tracing a course, in daily travel, on the internet. All these experiences require different forms of mapping: mental, aural, emotional, embodied, inscriptive.

In narrowing the scope of navigation to the physical movement of the body, many maps of the past and the present would only be omitted from the horizon of mobility studies, because they have not been explicitly conceived for travel. Especially during the early Middle Ages, immediate location and the existential discovery of 'one's own space' (Classen, 2018) prevailed over long-distance journeys. Curiously, even many cartographic accounts and travel guides produced for pilgrimages to holy cities were destined to immobile people. In this respect, an element of medieval chronicle writing was specifically addressed to those who could not make a pilgrimage because of the expense of travel and the cloistered monastic life. The itinerary maps of Matthew Paris, presented in the famous *Chronica majora*, filled such physical stillness with an imaginative one, by inviting armchair travellers to travel virtually from London to Jerusalem, moving with their fingers along folded road maps and illustrated pages (Connolly, 1999). Mobilising an optic and tactile interaction, map-reading was itself a dynamic tool (Della Dora, 2009) and a form of mobility (Van Netten, 2020). As additionally outlined by Jacob (1996: 195), '[m]aps imply intellectual and visual motions' at different scales, since '[t]he map user is travelling not only through the areas and the places depicted but also through related levels of signs, reality and abstraction, through logical steps, through cultural fields'.

While much attention has been devoted to maps in the history of movement, travel and transportation (Akerman, 2006), theories of spatial navigation have been proposed through a different historical lens within visual and media studies' broader focus on images and representations. Verhoeff (2012), for instance, carried out a historical-comparative investigation of the nexus between movement in space and visual culture, delineating the 'visual regime of navigation' as 'a specific mode of interaction at the intersection of visuality and mobility' (Verhoeff, 2012: 133). Contemporary digital mobile mapping, the interaction it entails between screens and moving subjects, and the consequent redefinition of the representational map in terms of mobile experience, constitute a further variation and dramatisation of this historical visual regime of navigation. However, as Hind (2020: 133) suggests, in the last ten years we have been witnessing unprecedented 'developments in the form, scope, spread, cost, and integration of mobile maps, mappings, and navigation into, and across, contemporary society'. This has led to a consolidation of online mobile mapping within everyday life. The specific mobile-map experience that derives from functionalities which place the user at the centre of the map provided by GNSS (Global Navigation Satellite System) capabilities has been put forward as an accentuated form of ego-centric mapping. In fact, by enhancing the embodied nature of mapping, navigational mobile devices used on the move increase an ego-centric feeling and a form of digital narcissism (Reddleman, 2020) involving the 'spatial self' (Schwartz and Halegoua, 2015). If the embodiment of maps can be observed also with reference to paper ones (Rossetto, 2012), the possibility of switching rapidly from zenith to street views offered by digital devices enhances our sense of moving simultaneously across the map and the streets. The 'hodological space', a term used by Janni (1984) with reference to Antiquity to indicate the traversed, internally experienced space of the path, thus overlaps with the 'cartographic space', which is the space vertically viewed from the outside.

In the last few years, digital spatial navigation through smartphones or sat-navs has been researched extensively through an array of approaches and methodologies that encompass, not only a technical or cognitive point of view (see Liao et al., 2019 on eye-movement tracking of navigators), but also more-than-cognitive and practice-based perspectives, ethnomethodological and ethnographic investigations, field studies, and cultural and social understandings (see Speake, 2015; Laurier et al., 2016; Dalton and Thatcher, 2019; Duggan, 2020). There is a clear connection between these qualitative ways of researching cartographic practices on the move and the mobile methodologies endorsed by the New mobilities paradigm. Moreover, we should also note that many of these recent readings are inflected through a humanistic perspective. In fact, some readings of cartographic or geotagging practices have focused on the *experiential* dimension of navigation by adopting phenomenological approaches and ethnographic techniques, thus clearly contributing to a humanistic approach to the personal lifeworld of digital navigating *subjects* (see Hjorth, 2012; Duggan, 2017; Pink and Wilmott, 2020).

According to Duggan (2018: 33–34), 'maps have a common association with the practices of navigation yet this association is all too often thought about in simplistic terms as a straightforward mimetic process of finding one's way based on guidance of map'. He further proposed a denser and more complex way of conceptualising and conducting research, in which navigation is considered informed by 'process' thinking. A navigational take on maps, in fact, helps in considering them as entities that emerge and come into being through processes and events. This processual mode of thinking about maps, which transforms them from representations to performances (Gerlach, 2018), clearly establishes an important link to the mobility and humanities theory, which is deeply affected by process philosophy (Merriman and Pearce, 2017). Thinking about the *becoming* rather than the *being* of maps, then, entails considering and valuing also their lives, movements and circulations.

6.3 Circulations

The mobility of maps cannot be conceived exclusively in terms of a navigational performance, where people materially and imaginatively move from one place to another. Drawing on new concepts and ideas directly from the fields of visual anthropology and media studies, we consider additional perspectives that may expand the understanding of what constitutes map-mobilities: the circulation, migration and remediation of maps.

From a circulation perspective, meanings are produced, not only by the content that maps represent, but also by the place maps come to occupy to express their message, as well as their movements through different networks, which may involve intense acceleration in case of the virality of the maps' content but also limited diffusion that may decrease maps' value. This change of perspective in the study of maps does not devalue cultural theory but rather affirms that the generative work of representation could also shift from an attachment to the internal symbolism of the image to an analysis of the mobile, destabilising, dispersive and pervasive existence of cartographic images. In this respect, the term 'visual economy', coined two decades ago by anthropologist Deborah Poole, introduced a new sensitiveness over the movement of images, claiming an interest in 'not what specific images mean but, rather, how images accumulate value in a network system through the social processes of accumulation, possession, circulation and exchange' (1997: 9).

Such social processes, including an increasing interest in the 'life-cycles' of maps (Prior, 2012), have been central in historical analyses of cartography, especially conducted from the perspectives of material culture and history of science. As is well known, Latour (1987: 223) referred to cartography as a 'dramatic example' of the *immutable mobiles* invented during the modern age to ensure that Western domination was feasible at a distance. While the status of immutability was conferred by the ways in which, during the modern age, cartographic information gradually became standardised, universalised and fixed in the form of cartographic material objects, the status of mobility was conferred by the portability and transferability of the cartographic artefact, which became a vehicle used to transport Western spatial knowledge into different contexts with the aim of exploring, trading and colonising. The notions of centres of calculations and immutable mobiles derived from Latour (1987) have had a significant impact on studies on cartography of the modern age and imperial grounds (e.g., Brückner, 2017; Lobo-Guerrero et al., 2021).

Yet, if the notion of immutable mobiles highlights the relative stability of maps as objects that maintain the same shape while circulating across different locations and, in turn, stabilise the same networks and imaginaries of space they create, to speak of *mutable* mobiles, as recently argued by Perkins (2014), Lammes (2017) and Edney (2019), emphasises the instability of maps, the idea that they are constantly reinscribed and translated, and thus able to transform spatial imaginaries. This aspect emerged opportunely in *The Social Life of Maps in America, 1750–1860*, where Brückner attributes the increased circulation of cartographic objects to their new affordability in the market through which maps become objects of everyday life, produced for a much more heterogeneous audience. As newly consumer goods, maps appeared on newspapers, posters, specialised magazines, travel guides, pocket atlases, streets and daily gadgets. Recognising the changing and *ambulatory* nature of popular maps in America, Brückner suggests approaching them as 'things in motion' (2017: 244) that could prompt other questions 'about the relationship of maps and their materials, the production and consumption of cartographic knowledge, and – above all – the map's seemingly uncartographic uses' (2017: 47). Like commodities, maps become objects that people want to possess for their aesthetic value or for sentimental attachment, and their life and success depend upon where, when and how they circulate and how they are consumed. This means that, in the past as in the present, maps experience various circuits of mobility, and they are often supposed to travel to then become stationary and familiar objects to keep at home, in public squares, offices and cafes.

The mobile and unstable condition of images, including maps, suggests also retracing or following their possible journey and metamorphoses across several spatial-temporal contexts. In this respect, Latour considered maps as non-human actors to be followed according to the methodology of the actor-network theory. As applications of this method underline, 'it is in following maps through society and through history, as Latour might, that we can reveal the strength, fragility or indeed ambiguity of cartographic knowledge' (Oliver, 2011: 68). Engaging with postcolonial debates about the cartography of European expansion and its implications for constructing North American landscapes, Oliver (2011: 68) researched the social lives and afterlives of maps, paying attention to 'the way maps are actually engaged with by those using them', how 'they are employed and appropriated in different historical contexts', how they are 'made for specific purposes but then dispersed', thus showing how the power of maps often produces contradictions. According to Lee and LiPuma (2002: 192), circulation is usually conceived as a series of 'processes that convey meaning, rather than constitutive acts in themselves'. In fact, circulation does not designate only a space in motion but also a cultural phenomenon with its interpretative communities and dominant codes.

Drawing insights from previous seminal contributions, including the famous 1986 collection *The Social Lives of Things* edited by Arjun Appadurai, the thing-following method has been recently discussed (Hulme, 2017) with reference to the high-globalisation era in terms of 'unfollowability', fragmentation, gaps and ruptures. Indeed, following the movement of maps in the *cartosphere* today seems highly problematic, but we could think of exercises of map-following through the suggestions emerging from the field of visual studies, which is increasingly impacting the field of maps studies in terms of theories and methodologies. Zarzycka (2020: 177), from the field of photography studies, for instance, has recently proposed studying the *migration* (which is an alternative to the more common concepts of circulation or dissemination) of images across sites, media, bodies and screens in a contemporary visual economy. By tracing map-mobilities, the study of map migrations would highlight how travelling cartographic visuals are shared to involve diverse audiences, post-processed, variously appropriated, re-edited to express feelings, used to form affective communities and moved from digital to analogue formats to create tangible, visceral aesthetics. The Covid-19 pandemic, for instance, has been recently studied through a humanistic lens in an attempt to grasp the proliferation and rapid movement of maps, mapping practices, map-like objects and creative cartographies online as well as in tangible worlds (Pase et al., 2021). The pandemic offers a particularly relevant case study for understanding how maps are mobile in many different ways: as navigational devices through which people navigate turbulent terrains (Brice, 2020); as images that often move in viral ways; as tools that visualise, in (near) real time, huge amounts of data.

6.4 Animations

In traditional cartography, the relationship between image and movement has been a central point of discussion for geographers due to the limits that a non-interactive two-dimensional map faces to represent events as they unfold. For critical and humanistic geographers, a map, as the output of a geometric construction, cannot reproduce nuanced and fleeting expressions of movement over its surface. The representation of human and non-human dynamic processes on maps is in fact challenging, and map-makers and GIS (Geographic Information System) scientists have often envisaged different design strategies to optimally reproduce the flow and distribution of spatial phenomena. That of the geo-visualisation of movement has become a language with its conventional grammar and morphology, where choropleths, vectors, flow maps, cartograms, animated maps and the space-time cube have been generated over time to shape various dynamic spatial phenomena involving human and non-human actors, also following different social and political meanings of mobility (Dodge, 2014; Segal and Vannieuwenhuyze, 2020). The digital sphere has certainly provided cartographers, but also designers and artists, with new heuristic possibilities to experience motion through animation and inter-medial approaches, with the perception that 'mapping technology is outpacing cartographic theory' (Harrower and Fabrikant, 2008: 49).

Yet, as Caquard (2009) demonstrated, when professional cartographers produced their early animated maps in the 1960s, most of the features of modern digital cartography had been implemented through moving cinemaps, with the first examples of animated maps emerging in docudramas of the 1910s. Not by chance, the intertwining of map theories and film studies, as well as that of cartography and filmic experiments, constitutes a particularly vital field for valuing the multiple ways in which moving maps work. Let's think of the famous map in the headlines of the television series *Game of Thrones*, in which a cartographic artefact is endowed with mechanised movement – a kind of cartographic automaton. As Fidotta (2014: 263) stated, 'animated techniques do not just provide the map with motion, but also undermine most of its meanings by adding an element – movement – which integrates the world's static order into a flow of processes and changes'.

The progress in the animation of digital mapping has further driven the re-evaluation of cartographic representations as interfaces that 'move and refresh with the user' (Wilmott, 2017: 323). These digital mapping practices lived through mobile devices enhance our perception of the temporal mobilities of cartography (Lammes et al., 2018). Yet the various temporalities inherent to maps have also been recently researched with reference to pre-digital cartography and the ways in which a sense of time has been inserted into the spatial medium of maps across past centuries (Wigen and Winterer, 2020). If an essential role of maps in history has been to slow the speed of time by cementing movement in static images, contemporary data vividly sets to work to speed up time through geovisualisations. Indeed, today, we experience a generalised 'speeding up' of cartography connected to vast and growing streams of real-time data. So-called crisis-mapping, involving humanitarian assistance, disaster response, street crime, protests or infectious diseases, is particularly sensitive to the notions of velocity, rapidity and real-time reactions to the extent that, today, we could think of maps as artificially intelligent sensing cartographic machines (Mattern, 2018). As Hind (2020: 135) further suggests, the live-ness of mobile maps that are responsive to changing conditions 'is open to interpretation, however, with most offering only "near-real-time" as opposed to actual or "real-time" mapping'. For instance, the delayed temporalities of supposed near real-time cartographies that monitor migrants' sea crossing are particularly revealing of enduring cartographic frictions (see Lo Presti, 2019), while current real-time responsive forms of mapping have been critically interrogated by Chandler (2018) as forms of political governance that are focused on sensing fleeting appearances on the surface rather than analysing deep causes to adopt problem-solving structural actions. As Wilson (2017) noted, while the rise of GIScience can be seen as an elaboration on centuries of practice to capture time, the rapidity of the contemporary data set and the proliferation of crises call for animated mobile maps on the one hand, and continue to question the role of capture in the representational system of GIS on the other hand. For Wilson (2017: 74), in fact, animated maps reveal both the potentialities and the 'epistemological irreducibilities' in cartography. The pandemic has revealed, for instance, the frustrations deriving from the will to capture the spread of the virus across local, national and global spaces as well the problems emerging from the use of mapping technologies to monitor or limit the mobility of individuals and collectives through digital fences and tracings (Kitchin, 2020).

Technologically enhanced animated maps have been developed and cognitively analysed and, more recently, historicised, criticised and also theoretically endorsed as 'interventions for liveliness' (Wilson, 2017 and 2019). For Wilson, the figure of the 'map that moves' becomes a theoretical device for endorsing a non-representational view of cartographic liveliness beyond effectiveness. Drawing from the idea of the 'liveness' of maps as a kind of movement in/of cartography, we should also pay attention to how maps are growingly felt while coming to existence, and therefore theorised as entities with affective lives (Craine and Aitken, 2009; Rossetto, 2019). As fittingly reminded by Harrower and Fabrikant (2008: 50), 'animation has its roots in the Latin word *animare,* in English, "bring to life"'. In fact, an alternative way to consider the animation of maps is that of thinking about them as living entities. Although this kind of animation intersects with the more recent performative understanding of mapping practices and also with recent theories of visual agency, we should remember that the map has been traditionally fetishised as an agential actor. Emphasising the prosopopoeial nature of maps, many critics of cartographic discourse have highlighted how maps assert their powers, command and enforce actions, do something and get things done by speaking to their viewers/readers. Indeed, a speaking map introduces one of the most known and celebrated pieces of cartographic theory, namely Harley's (1989) seminal article 'Deconstructing the Map'. This article in fact opens with a literary quotation from *West with the Night*, a 1942 memoir by Beryl Markham, later praised as a classic of adventure writing, in which the author lets a map speak for itself: 'A map says to you, "Read me carefully, follow me closely, doubt me not". It says, "I am the earth in the palm of your hand. Without me, you are alone and lost"' (Markham, 1988: 215, cited in Harley, 1989).

Yet we could appreciate the liveness and agency of maps beyond these critical readings by intertwining this traditional reflection on the agency of maps with more recent visual theories that are studying the capacity of images to move, the vibrancy of material visual entities, the alien force of visual artifacts, the role of images as counterparts of humans, the empathy towards and human conversations with visuals (see Van Eck, 2015; Bredekamp, 2018). Following image theorist Hans Belting (2014), animating images means attributing to them a sort of corporeality as well as considering our own bodies as living organs for images. How do map users infuse a life force into maps? How do we experiment 'the force of [cartographic] representations' as entities that take part in the 'movement of life' (Anderson, 2019: 1128)? This could be an additional and less experimented angle to appreciate the movement of maps from a humanistic perspective.

6.5 Conclusion

Over recent years, huge theoretical, empirical and creative efforts have been made by cultural geographers and humanist thinkers to unsettle the allegedly static nature of maps and unravel the many faces of mobility expressed through them, often acknowledging those manifold forms of movement beyond the technicalities of professional cartography and – philosophically speaking – beyond issues of representation and representability. Contemporary map studies, which are driven by a (post)humanist afflatus rather than a technical concern, are in fact aimed at understanding the methods, subjects, networks, materialities and spatialities through which the cartographic imaginary is shaped and endowed with meaning in contemporary society. As we attempted to show in the course of the chapter, this stance requires giving more attention to the diverse roles that maps play in everyday mobile life, both in the past and the present. When adopting a cultural and humanistic lens, map-mobility appears an elastic concept (Rossetto, 2021) that embraces a much wider horizon of research possibilities. By grasping flows, movements, circulations, stories, feelings that involve mapping within the dense network of experience, map-mobilities open to a more widespread and boundless realm than that of cartography or mobile mapping. All the previously mentioned forms of map-mobilities involve, in fact, heterogeneous fields, knowledge and practices. The 'extroversion of cartography' (Lo Presti, 2018) – the sensitiveness toward mapping matured in artistic and humanistic fields – is just a hint of the longstanding seduction of the map as a navigational, travelling and communicational device. Contemporary artists, more recently collaborating with geographers and social scientists, are manifesting a certain propensity to discuss mobile phenomena, like globalisation, migration and diaspora, through a cartographic lens, including reflections on travel, networks, belonging, borders and immobility (Kelly, 2019; Lo Presti, 2020). Overlapping a plurality of mobile registers, artist Janetka Platun recently created a one-metre-diameter globe illustrating the route taken by her parents who arrived in London as post-war migrants from Poland (Sheringham et al., 2020). The globe was also *put in motion* by the artist who rolled the copper sphere all around the streets of London, Shrewsbury and Delhi, marking its surface with new lines and trajectories, but also with lively and fleeting encounters with strangers. Integrating the sculpture with four cameras, the globe was also endowed with the ability to see its own trajectories, reorienting the perception of movement from a human-centred to an object-centred position.

While critical readings have often dwelt on the many discrepancies and limits of cartographic representations, on what remains outside a map, in this chapter we have adopted a different sensitiveness, preferring to wonder where and how the map as a navigational, mobile and living image is leading and moving us, trawling through the past and present for an expansion of the map-mobilities field.

References

Akerman JR (ed) (2006) *Cartographies of travel and navigation*. Chicago: University of Chicago Press.
Anderson B (2019) Cultural geography II: The force of representations. *Progress in Human Geography* 43(6): 1120–1132.

Appadurai A (1986) *The social life of things: commodities in cultural perspective*. Cambridge: Cambridge University Press.
Belting H (2014) *An anthropology of images: picture, medium, body*. Princeton, NJ: Princeton University Press.
Bredekamp H (2018) *Image acts: a systematic approach to visual agency*. Berlin and Boston: Walter de Gruyter.
Brice J (2020) Charting COVID-19 futures: mapping, anticipation, and navigation. *Dialogues in Human Geography* 10(2): 271–275.
Brückner M (2017) *The social life of maps in America, 1750–1860*. Chapel Hill: University of North Carolina Press.
Caquard S (2009) Foreshadowing contemporary digital cartography: a historical review of cinematic maps in films. *The Cartographic Journal* 46(1): 46–55.
Chandler D (2018) *Ontopolitics in the Anthropocene: an introduction to mapping, sensing and hacking*. London: Routledge.
Classen A (ed.) (2018) *Travel, time, and space in the Middle Ages and Early Modern Time*. Berlin, Boston: De Gruyter.
Connolly DK (1999) Imagined pilgrimage in the itinerary maps of Matthew Paris. *The Art Bulletin* 81(4): 598–622.
Craine J and Aitken S (2009) The emotional life of maps and other visual geographies. In: Dodge M, Kitchin R and Perkins C (eds) *Rethinking maps: new frontiers in cartographic theory*. London and New York: Routledge, pp.167–184.
Dalton C and Thatcher J (2019) Seeing by the Starbucks: the social context of mobile maps and users' geographic knowledge. *Cartographic Perspectives* 92: 24–42.
Della Dora V (2009) Performative atlases: memory, materiality, and (co-)authorship. *Cartographica* 44(4): 240–255.
Della Dora V (forthcoming) 'Most grievously tossed in the stormy sea of life': mapping spiritual voyages in Byzantium. In: Mihail Mitrea (ed) *Mapping the sacred in Byzantium: construction, experience and representation*. Edinburgh: University of Edinburgh Press.
Dodge M (2014) Mappings. In: Adey P, Bissell D, Hannam K et al. (eds) *The Routledge handbook of mobilities*. New York: Routledge, pp.517–533.
Dodge M, Kitchin R and Perkins C (eds) (2009) *Rethinking maps: new frontiers in cartographic theory*. London and New York: Routledge.
Duggan M (2017) The cultural life of maps: everyday place-making mapping practices. *Livingmaps Review* 3: 1–17.
Duggan M (2018) Navigational mapping practices: contexts, politics, data. *Westminster Papers in Communication and Culture* 13(2): 31–45.
Duggan M (2020) Spatial media and cycling spaces: a theory of coded attractors. *Area* 52(2): 322–328.
Edney M (2019) *Cartography: the ideal and its history*. Chicago: University of Chicago Press.
Fidotta G (2014) Animated maps. *NECSUS: European Journal of Media Studies* 3(1): 263–294.
Gerlach J (2018) Mapping as performance. In: Kent AJ and Vujakovic P (eds) *The Routledge handbook of mapping and cartography*. London; New York: Routledge, pp.90–100.
Harley JB (1989) Deconstructing the map. *Cartographica* 26(2): 1–20.
Harrower M and Fabrikant S (2008) The role of map animation in geographic visualization. In: Dodge M (ed) *Geographic visualization: concepts, tools and applications*. Chichester, UK: Wiley, pp.49–65.

Hind S (2020) Mobile mapping. In: Kobayashi A (ed) *International encyclopaedia of human geography (2nd Edition)*. Amsterdam: Elsevier, pp.133–140.
Hulme A (2017) Following the (unfollowable) thing: methodological considerations in the era of high globalisation. *Cultural Geographies* 24(1): 157–160.
Jacob C (1996) Toward a cultural history of cartography. *Imago Mundi* 48: 191–198.
Jameson F (1991) *Postmodernism, or, the cultural logic of late capitalism*. London: Verso.
Janni P (1984) *La mappa e il periplo: cartografia antica e spazio odologico*. Rome: G. Bretschneider.
Kelly M (2019) Mapping Syrian refugee border crossings: a feminist approach. *Cartographic Perspectives* 93: 34–64.
Kitchin R (2020) Using digital technologies to tackle the spread of the coronavirus: panacea or folly? *The Programmable City Working Paper* 44. https://progcity.maynoothuniversity.ie/wp-content/uploads/2020/04/Digital-tech-spread-of-coronavirus-Rob-Kitchin-PC-WP44.pdf
Lammes S (2017) Digital mapping interfaces: from immutable mobiles to mutable images. *New Media & Society* 19(7): 1019–1033.
Lammes S, Perkins C, Gekker A et al. (2018) *Time for mapping: cartographic temporalities*. Manchester: Manchester University Press.
Latour B (1987) *Science in action*. Cambridge, MA: Harvard University Press.
Laurier E, Brown B and McGregor M (2016) Mediated pedestrian mobility: walking and the map app. *Mobilities* 11(1): 117–134.
Lee B and LiPuma E (2002) Cultures of circulation: the imaginations of modernity. *Public Culture* 14(1): 191–213.
Liao H, Dong W, Huang H et al. (2019) Inferring user tasks in pedestrian navigation from eye movement data in real-world environments. *International Journal of Geographical Information Science* 33(4): 739–776.
Lobo-Guerrero L, Lo Presti L and dos Reis F (2021) *Mapping, connectivity and the making of European empires*. Latham: Rowman and Littlefield.
Lo Presti L (2018) Extroverting cartography: 'seensing' maps and data through art. *Journal of Research and Didactics in Geography* (J-READING) 7(2): 119–134.
Lo Presti L (2019) Terraqueous necropolitics: unfolding the low-operational, forensic, and evocative mapping of Mediterranean sea crossings in the age of lethal borders. *ACME: An International Journal for Critical Geographies* 18(6): 1347–1367.
Lo Presti L (2020) The migrancies of maps: complicating the critical cartography and migration nexus in 'migro-mobility' thinking. *Mobilities* 15(6): 911–929.
Mattern S (2018) Mapping's intelligent agents. In: Bargués-Pedreny P, Chandler D and Simon E (eds) *Mapping and politics in the digital age*. London and New York: Routledge, pp.208–224.
Merriman P and Pearce L (2017) Mobility and the humanities. *Mobilities* 12(4): 493–508.
November V, Camacho-Hübner E and Latour B (2010) Entering a risky territory: space in the age of digital navigation. *Environment and Planning D: Society and Space* 28(4): 581–599.
Oliver J (2011) On mapping and its afterlife: unfolding landscapes in northwestern North America. *World Archaeology* 43(1): 66–85.
Pase A, Lo Presti L, Rossetto T et al. (2021) Pandemic cartographies: a conversation on mappings, imaginings and emotions. *Mobilities*, Epub ahead of print 11 January 2021. DOI: 10.1080/17450101.2020.1866319
Perkins C (2014) Plotting practices and politics: (im)mutable narratives in OpenStreetMap. *Transactions of the Institute of British Geographers* 39(2): 304–317.

Pink S and Hjorth L (2012) Emplaced cartographies: reconceptualising camera phone practices in an age of locative media. *Media International Australia* 145(1): 145–155.

Poole D (1997) *Vision, race, and modernity: a visual economy of the Andean image world.* Princeton, NJ: Princeton University Press.

Prior A (2012) British cartographic representations of Africa c.1880–c.1915. *Imago Mundi* 64(2): 242–243.

Rankin W (2017) *After the map: cartography, navigation, and the transformation of territory in the 20th century.* Chicago: The University of Chicago Press.

Reddleman C (2020) *I am here: cartographic abstraction and digital narcissism in GPS selfies.* In: *20 years of seeing with GPS: Perspectives and Future Directions*, London, King's College, 12 June.

Rossetto T (2012) Embodying the map: tourism practices in Berlin. *Tourist Studies* 12(1): 28–51.

Rossetto T (2019) *Object-oriented cartography: maps as things.* London and New York: Routledge.

Rossetto T (2021) Not just navigation: thinking about the movements of maps in the mobility and humanities field. *The Cartographic Journal.* Epub ahead of print 8 January 2021. DOI: 10.1080/00087041.2020.1842144

Schwartz R and Halegoua GR (2015) The spatial self: location-based identity performance on social media. *New Media and Society* 17(10): 1643–1660.

Segal Z and Vannieuwenhuyze B (eds) (2020) *Motion in maps, maps in motion: mapping stories and movement through time.* Amsterdam: Amsterdam University Press.

Sheringham O, Platun J, McAvinchey C et al. (2020) Globe's encounters and the art of rolling: home, migration and belonging. *Cultural Geographies* 27(2):177–199.

Smith TA, Laurier E, Reeves S, et al. (2019) 'Off the beaten map': navigating with digital maps on moorland. *Transactions of the Institute of British Geographers* 45(1): 223–240.

Speake J (2015) 'I've got my sat nav, it's alright': user's attitudes towards, and engagements with, technologies of navigation. *The Cartographic Journal* 52(4): 345–355.

Tally RT (2011) On literary cartography: narrative as a spatially symbolic act. *Nano: New American Notes Online*, 1. Available at: https://nanocrit.com/issues/issue1/literary-cartography-narrative-spatially-symbolic-act (accessed 5 February 2021)

Van Eck C (2015) *Agency and living presence: from the animated image to the excessive object.* Berlin: De Gruyter.

Van Netten D (2020) The new world map and the old: the moving narrative of Joan Blaeu's *Nova Totius Terrarum Orbis Tabula* (1648). In: Segal Z and Vannieuwenhuyze B (eds) *Motion in maps, maps in motion: mapping stories and movement through time.* Amsterdam: Amsterdam University Press, pp.33–55.

Verhoeff N (2012) *Mobile screens: the visual regime of navigation.* Amsterdam: Amsterdam University Press.

Wigen K and Winterer C (2020) *Time in maps: from the age of discovery to our digital era.* Chicago: University of Chicago Press.

Wilmott C (2017) In-between mobile maps and media: movement. *Television & New Media* 18(4): 320–335.

Wilmott C (2020) *Mobile mapping: space, cartography, and the digital.* Amsterdam: Amsterdam University Press.

Wilson MW (2017) *New lines: critical GIS and the trouble of the map*. Minneapolis and London: University of Minnesota Press.
Wilson MW (2019) Maps that move. In: Kurgan L and Brawley D (eds) *Ways of knowing cities*. New York: Columbia University Press, pp.237–249.
Zarzycka M (2020) Still images on the move: theoretical challenges and future possibilities. In: Durde M and Tormey J (eds) *The Routledge companion to photography theory*. London and New York: Routledge, pp.176–187.

7 Narrative mobilities
Moving texts from representation to practice

Giada Peterle

7.1 Introduction: setting narrative geographies in motion

This chapter enters the interdisciplinary debate on mobility and the humanities from a specific narrative geographical perspective. In the following paragraphs, I interpret texts as opportunities to represent and enact mobile practices, looking at narrative representations of mobility from a relational, more-than-representational and geocritical perspective. The chapter proposes a mobile geocritical approach for *moving narrative geographies* from representation to practice by bringing into dialogue recent debates in literary geography, spatial literary studies, literary urban studies and literary mobilities (Ameel et al., 2015; Finch et al., 2017; Gurr, 2021; Pearce, 2016, 2017, 2018; Saunders, 2010; Tally, 2011, 2021).

As I have discussed more thoroughly elsewhere (Peterle, 2021: 9), a *narrative geographical approach* analyses the entanglements between real and fictional, textual, and material spaces, exploring the prolific exchange between the narrative representations of space, place, maps and mobilities, and the spatial practices that are activated by them. Inspired by creative and art-based approaches in the geohumanities, I see *narrative geographies* as an opportunity to engage with narratives as research practices, rather than mere objects of analysis. Thus, a narrative geographical approach experiments with narrative forms as storytelling practices: narratives represent creative means for activating plurivocal stories, producing uncharted spatial meanings and deconstructing dominant spatial discourses about cities, places, spatial identities and mobilities. This approach rejects an instrumental and purely representational use of literature, texts and narrative or artistic representations; instead, it considers the contents and peculiar forms of different languages, types and genres of narration to discover how they shape unpredicted spatial visions.

In this chapter, I propose a focus on mobilities from a narrative geographical perspective, focusing on a mobile-centred approach to what we may call *narrative mobilities*. Here, narrative mobilities will be explored through a processual and relational approach inspired by literary geographies (Anderson, 2014; Saunders and Anderson, 2016), which reads narrative representations as emergent practices that are situated in space and time and performed in different contexts. In this view, the roles of texts, authors, and readers are equally important, as are their different engagements and positionalities. Thus, if narrative geographies examine narrative representations as processes, from conception to composition and circulation (Hones, 2014), the same applies to narrative mobilities. Likewise, if a narrative geographical approach is a critical interdisciplinary perspective for analysing narratives from a space-centred point of view, then narrative mobilities embrace a mobile-centred perspective for analysing texts. Both are creative modes of thinking and practising cross-disciplinary research, interpreting spaces as archives of stories and using stories as tools to actualise different spatial meanings and activate new trajectories for spatial action.

The first section explores the relationship between the new mobilities paradigm and literary studies through the so-called field of literary mobilities. The next section proceeds by interpreting texts as "mobile events", through rethinking Sheila Hones' idea of texts as "spatial events" (Hones, 2008) from a mobile point of view. The final section, which aims to set narrative geographies in motion, sketches the further opportunity of moving from the analysis of narrative representations of mobilities to the engagement with narrative methods to conduct mobility research. Following Marco Caracciolo's "enactivist approach" to texts (2012, 2014), I propose *enacting narrative mobilities* to interpret storyworlds as meaningful constellations of mobilities that are not limited to the space of the page but are able to influence our mobile practices in the material world. Caracciolo's view of texts as triggers for spatial action and cognitive orientation in real life helps in the blurring of the boundaries between the narration of mobile practices and the enactment of those same practices in real space. This could represent a further opportunity for mobility scholars, art-practitioners, literary geographers and researchers working in the humanities to explore creative and narrative-based methods from a specific mobile angle. Thus, narrative mobilities are an opportunity to find new and "vital methodologies" (Sheller, 2015) that place narrative representations and practices at the centre of research-creation endeavours in mobility studies.

7.2 Reading literary mobilities: texts as dynamic provocations in mobility studies

Literary texts can play a significant role in the interdisciplinary debate that involves scholars in cultural geography, the social sciences and the humanities around the forms, practices, structures and meanings of cultural mobilities. While many social scientists are still debating the extent to which textual representations of mobilities "constitute 'data' of the kind that can substitute, or be used alongside, that garnered from living subjects or other forms of empirical evidence" (Merriman and Pearce, 2017: 502), recent works on literary mobilities have attempted to trace the long-lasting contribution of literature and the "role of literary studies in the pre-history of the 'mobilities turn'" (Aguiar et al., 2019: 5). By exploring the relationship between texts and mobilities from an interdisciplinary angle, these works demonstrate the extent to which the "new mobilities paradigm" has been influenced, since the very beginning, by scholars working outside the social sciences' disciplinary boundaries, using texts as their primary sources. Some scholars have even moved a step further, not just tracing the past history of this interdisciplinary collaboration, but also demonstrating the role that texts may play in the future in revitalising the theoretical and methodological debate around mobilities (Sheller and Urry, 2006, 2016). Even though there "remains a reluctance to regard the textual realm as intrinsic to our lived experience rather than merely a representation of it" (Merriman and Pearce, 2017: 503) and, in some disciplinary contexts, their "subjective" and "fictional"' dimensions still represent a limitation in the reliability of narrative sources, it is precisely these unique features of narratives that are increasingly seen as an opportunity for productive contamination among disciplines.

Scholars in mobility studies

> are using what they find in texts not as evidence of how people perceive, think or feel in the material world but rather as prompts to model theoretical possibilities which may, in turn, be put to work alongside more empirical data.
>
> (Merriman and Pearce, 2017: 502)

As Peter Merriman and Lynne Pearce suggest,

> when we allow for the fact that experiences of mobility are not confined to the "now"—but have been central to past practices as well as current memories—there is a strong counter-argument that retrospective representations of movement through literary and other texts are no less evocative, important, lively, and dynamic than ethnographic "data" captured "on the move".
>
> (2017: 498)

According to this perspective, literary texts should neither substitute more traditional data sources in the social sciences nor be considered less reliable references simply because of their fictional, rather than mimetic, dimension: "it is not the subjective and/or fictional status of the text that is the obstacle here"—Merriman and Pearce affirm—"but rather the 'old-fashioned' realism that clings to the way we think about the world and how we 'know' it" (2017: 503). Moving beyond a mere representational function, texts project our future imaginations, rather than simply registering our past and present experiences of movement. They present potential areas of spatial intervention rather than static recordings of movements happening outside the space of the page.

In their volume *Mobilities, Literature, Culture*, Aguiar et al. present "not only the interdisciplinary origins, but also the multi-disciplinary applications, of the mobilities paradigm" (2019: 5–6), showing how textual sources are able to chart the entanglements of mobilities at different scales and capture different forms of movement over time. To a certain extent, cultural and literary studies have always worked on representations of mobilities, even if movement was not at the centre of the analysis: reflections on the disparate forms, genres and subjects of mobilities' representations have been part of studies connected to travel writing, urban modernity and migration, to mention but a few. Moreover, scholars in post-colonial, diaspora and cultural studies have discussed cultural representations of mobilities through the connection between mobility, identity and power, giving a significant contribution to the debate on mobilities, also in the social sciences. Moving from the works by Edward Said (1993), Paul Gilroy (1995) and James Clifford (1997) to more recent contributions (Aguiar, 2011; Green-Simms, 2017), post-colonial studies have focused on the relationship between mobility and power in disparate geographical and historical contexts. For many thinkers, mobility is the subject/object of cultural representations but, more importantly, the "basic conceptual 'building-block' of thought as well as of the life-world in general" (Merriman and Pearce, 2017: 502). The mobile geocritical approach presented in the following paragraphs stems from a processual theoretical understanding of texts. It considers mobilities as objects/subjects of narrative representations, understands the semantic sphere connected to mobilities as a source for theoretical contaminations and conceptual explorations, and interprets movement as an intrinsic part of the cognitive experience of writing/reading a text. Narratives could also become practices for carrying out mobility research, thus contributing to methodological innovation.

Beyond providing a potential field for methodological experimentation, narrative mobilities also represent an opportunity for drawing an interdisciplinary mobilities agenda that places the imaginary and metaphoric power of narrative forms at the centre of its theoretical thinking. Indeed, narrative representations do not merely register our memories of past mobilities; rather, they inform our "fantasies of the future" mobilities (Aguiar et al., 2019: 26). Through their unique language and metaphorical reasoning, texts shape our mobile thinking. The humanities' contribution to mobility studies helps to reframe urgent contemporary issues, such as "migration and displacement, travel and tourism, sustainable transport and care for the environment (including its heritage), to mention but a few" (Aguiar et al., 2019: 26) from a metaphoric, imaginative, subjective, descriptive, but also embodied, more-than-human, geopolitical, cultural and critical interdisciplinary perspective. Cultural representations are still often analysed from a merely representational perspective. A mobile geocritical approach aims to show how critical approaches in literary geography and spatial literary studies could contribute to the ongoing debate around cross-disciplinary mobility research through a processual understanding of texts.

7.3 Towards a mobile "geocritical" approach: narrative movement and texts that move

According to Mimi Sheller and John Urry, "accounting for mobilities in the fullest sense challenges social science to change both the objects of its inquiries and methods of its research" (Sheller and Urry, 2016: 208): this claim, if seen from a narrative geographical perspective, becomes a challenge that could also apply to geoliterary approaches and "geocritical explorations" of literary mobilities (Tally, 2011). The mobility paradigm requires us to "open up all sites, and places, and materialities to the mobilities that are already always coursing through them" (Sheller and Urry, 2006: 209), which includes types of spaces, subjects, and practices whose connection to mobility is less automatic, or explicit, but still relevant. Although mobile approaches to texts have already considered these kinds of mobile objects of study, recent works suggest reading texts through a dynamic lens that interprets the practices of writing and reading texts as intrinsically mobile. My proposal is to integrate literary approaches to geography and geocritical perspectives in literary studies with literary mobilities (i.e. examination of texts from within mobility studies) in order to investigate how these interdisciplinary fields might enrich each other. This critical encounter could lead not just to a plurivocal interpretation of narrative representations of mobilities, but especially to a mobile-centred perspective that could inform the conceptual tools of textual analysis beyond the boundaries of mobility studies.

In his geocritical reasoning, Eric Prieto interprets literature as a powerful source for deconstructing obsolete explanatory models and providing laboratories for unexplored representational practices and objects of study in geographical research, urban planning, architecture, and environmental studies (2012: 9): as discussed above, narratives represent valuable references, including for exploring new directions in mobility studies. In his seminal volume *Geocriticism: Real and Fictional Spaces* (2007), Bertrand Westphal, who is considered to be the father of *geocriticism*, proposes starting from a single real place. In Westphal's approach, the author and the single literary work are pushed to the background in order to put the narrative stratifications of single places at the centre of the comparative geo-centred analysis. Starting from here, Prieto moves his gaze towards a broader field of research involving not just single, mappable places with specific geographical coordinates, but also "types of places" that are associated with one another through shared features, traits, and properties. Attempting to question "the limits of geocriticism", Prieto (2011: 22–3) considers sites that may be spread around the globe, comparable because of the shared traits that make it possible to conceive of them as part of the same category. Prieto's comparative approach is based on the identification of common traits in different spatial and textual contexts, rather than on the presence of different narratives that co-exist in the same place. He even takes his geocritical "explorations" one step further when he leaves the reliability of geographical coordinates behind, thinking of "modes of spatial practice" as a potential area of interest:

> Another, more abstract but also more far-reaching extension to Westphal's approach would be to focus not on places nor even kinds of places but on modes of spatial practice. After all, some branches of geography are less interested in mapping out the physical distribution of spatial entities than in the study of the various modes of spatial awareness and activity. [...] This kind of approach suggests a mode of literary analysis that would organize the study of literary texts in a way that converges neither on singular places nor on categories of place but on behavioural aptitudes and strategies.

This suggestion by Prieto moves towards a dynamic rather than static perspective on literary representations: "new perspectives in literary geography" (Brosseau, 2017) could be centred on the behavioural aptitudes, spatial practices, and mobile strategies we use to navigate both real and textual spaces. Mobile practices such as walking and driving, mapping, losing, and finding ourselves again in the city are experiences that characterise our daily rhythms and lives, perceptions and emotions. Our movements and the spatialities that emerge from those mobile experiences not only influence the material space in which we move but also inform our experience of narrative mobilities, triggering an endless co-constitutive process between material spaces, practices, subjects and their narrative representations. According to Marco Caracciolo (2011), the reader's virtual body is constantly informed by real-life experiences when it attempts to reconstruct the narrative space. Indeed, "moving *is* knowing" (Ingold, 2010: 134), and spatial knowledge is an open-ended process composed of an alternation of conditions of traversing and resting both within and outside the space of the page. For this reason, a mobile geocritical gaze moves along the literary routes traced by both authors and readers of narrative texts, and understands the practices of writing/reading as a mobile process of spatial knowing.

A mobile geocritical perspective is not limited to the representation of mobilities within narratives; rather, it also influences methodological and theoretical reasoning concerning texts and their intrinsic mobile and dynamic essence. Alan Latham et al. (2009: 34) argue that the metaphors we employ to describe reality are more than simple imaginative suggestions, as they often "come, in all sorts of ways, to define this reality", influencing the way in which we interpret and, therefore, live in it. Thus, the leading metaphors of an explorative geocritical approach "on the move" (Cresswell, 2006) all belong to the semantic field of movement, motion, transition, transit, translation, processuality, and enactment. Looking closer, a mobile essence seems to be part of the geocritical approach since its first theorisation by Westphal, as he affirms: "Geocriticism will work to map possible worlds, to create plural and paradoxical maps, because it embraces space in its *mobile* heterogeneity" (Westphal, 2011: 73).

7.3.1 Narrative constellations of mobile chronotopes

A mobile geocritical approach investigates the expected objects of a mobility perspective on literature: these would comprise, for example, literary representations of means of transport, "landscapes of movement" (Cosgrove, 2006; Peterle, 2017), and mobile infrastructures, but also mobile bodies, subjects, practices, and emotions. Cars, trains, undergrounds, and trams are often connected to specific literary figures whose practices define not simply their modes of movement but also their character and socio-spatial relationships. These literary "on the move" types include, for example, the traditional figure of the flâneur/flâneuse, the double perspective of the car driver and passenger, and the commuter and the migrant; thus, the practices of walking, commuting, driving, cruising, and cycling define their characterisation as literary figures as much as their trajectories across (literary) space (Pearce, 2019, 2018, 2017, 2016; Peterle, 2016). At the same time, a mobile geocritical approach should be capable of rethinking traditional concepts and tools used for the analysis of literary texts from a mobile angle; one of these concepts is the chronotope. The chronotope has been employed as a useful conceptual tool in various fields, such as narratology, reception theory, and cognitive approaches to literary theory and gender studies (Bemong et al., 2010). The concept of chronotope is particularly intriguing because of its ability to connect not only time and space, but also the material world and fictional spaces within narratives. Interestingly, chronotopical analyses have crossed the boundaries of literary studies, garnering the attention of geographers as a result of the concept's intrinsic spatial nature. As suggested by James Lawson (2011: 389):

> The chronotope of a given novelistic genre corresponds closely to a real-world chronotope that prevailed when the genre first emerged [...]. This establishes a connection or "bridge" between narrative and real-world chronotopes that is crucial to using narrative form as a method of knowledge.

The chronotope, which serves as a "bridge" between the real and fictional worlds, does not only operate one way, with real chronotopes influencing narrative ones in a mere mimetic relationship between literature and reality. On the contrary, literary chronotopes have the capacity to configure the real world (Howell and Beckingham, 2015: 935) through a mutual exchange between pages and places. Chronotopical reading can be embraced, according to what Julian Holloway and James Kneale suggest, "to reveal the social, cultural, and political context of the time (and place) in which they were written" (2009: 147). Furthermore, chronotopical representations appear to be significant in both narrative organisation and the expression of a unique, spatio-temporal world view (Bemong et al., 2010: 8). On the one hand, the "wheres" and "whens" in which texts have appeared influence their chronotopical form, style, and spatio-temporal organisation; on the other, the forms themselves reveal crucial understandings of the spatio-temporal contexts in which texts have emerged, making them readable and cognitively accessible. As a result of its dynamic openness, the chronotope appears as a plastic concept to be adapted to a geocritical perspective "on the move". Exploring specific mobile chronotopes (emerging from practices, subjects and types of spaces connected to mobilities) or, in general, reading chronotopes from a mobile angle could open up mobility research to useful contaminations with literary critical analysis. Thus, a mobile geocritical perspective explores the possibility of not only considering static places—for example, the city, the crossing or the road, as suggested by more traditional geocritical approaches—but also, the moving elements and practices as possible narrative chronotopes. Moving elements, such as the car, the underground, trains and trams, to mention but a few, can be interpreted as mobile chronotopes bridging the narration and experience of movement.

The analysis of mobile chronotopes makes the co-constitution of real and textual spatial experiences visible. For example, where driving "has become in a quite concrete sense a whole way of life" (Latham et al., 2009: 31), the study of the way in which literary narratives have been modified according to the automobile perspective becomes a significant means of reading urban "car-only environments" (Urry, 2004: 30). Similarly, the attention paid by social scientists and geographers to the phenomenologies of car use, for example from "automotive emotions" and "embodied sensibilities" to the emergence of "car cultures" (Sheller, 2004: 221–2), adds further critical tools to interpret texts through different critical lenses, as the many works by Pearce on automobilities show. Given the importance accorded to automobilities as a set of spatial practices, embodied experiences, and affective emotions, the car itself could be interpreted as a mobile chronotope through which temporally located world views can be read. The analysis of the car as a mobile chronotope helps to link the different impacts of automobilities at the different spatial, geographical, architectural, and narratological levels. Through its central narrative role and the way in which it determines space-time representation, the figure of the protagonist, and the development of the plot, the car provides a narrative mobile space in which the present age of mobility finds its chronotopical expression.

Following this mobile-centred approach to narrative representations, the road's traditional chronotope can also be reinterpreted from a mobilised perspective. Roads have always been fundamental lines connecting pages and places. They represent cognitive arteries pulsating through concrete and textual spatialities, guiding readers' and authors' routes through texts and beyond. A mobile geocritical reading of the road's traditional chronotope, therefore, requires a deep engagement with those embodied receptions,

110 *Peterle*

spatial perceptions, and performative experiences that occur along these narrative threads suspended between pages and places. The individuation of chronotopical lines connecting narrative and material landscapes of movement can be interpreted as a mobilising research practice aimed at transforming narrative representations of mobilities into performative practices. Thus, mobile chronotopes act as a stimulus to move from page to action, from text to landscape, and to bodily perform the implicit mobile routes that emerge from narrative representations.

7.3.2 Moving with(in) narratives: enacting the "mobile event" of the text

In this section, I would like to move on by thinking about narrative mobilities from an enactivist and relational perspective. Inspired by contemporary works in literary geography and spatial literary studies, I interpret texts as writing and reading experiences as well as mobile events that contribute to the co-production of pages and places (Saunders and Anderson, 2016). According to relational literary geographies, the text "is a site of ongoing composition" (Anderson, 2014; Saunders and Anderson, 2016: 116) that does not create a realm "outside the time and space of the world" (McLaughlin, 2016: 124). According to David McLaughlin, the text, the author, and the reader are not separated but entangled, and the literary work and the world are immersed within each other. This analysis stems from a critical mindset that is processual and, I would argue, mobile in its own right. Angahard Saunders and Jon Anderson define their relational approach to literary geographies as a journey, namely a mobile experience that "is less concerned with cartographically rendering the fictional world and more interested in examining how the real and imagined come together and move apart" (2016: 115–6). Moving backwards, this kind of mobile critical attitude is also present in Marc Brosseau's literary geography (1995), especially when he compares the reading practice to that of walking on the sidewalk. Brosseau's seminal work seems to anticipate the need to connect the kinetic experience of movement in the material world with that of the reader, whose cognitive involvement is stimulated by the author's stylistic choices:

> [These kinetic descriptions] somehow reproduce, by simple juxtaposition, the spatial and temporal succession of the elements of the urban landscape: reading the text is like walking on the sidewalk. Eyes walk along the lines, like fingers following the beads of a rosary. Words and styles, tempo and pace, syntax and stride, become tangible, almost concrete.
>
> (1995: 100)

According to the geoliterary approach proposed by Brosseau, the reader and the urban walker are two figures whose movements appear to be very similar. This comparison took another step forward when relational literary geographies recently suggested interpreting texts as spatial events (Hones, 2008,

2014) and the practices of writing/reading as emerging, contextual, and relational spatial experiences. As we have seen, Ingold connects movement, and especially walking, to the practice of knowledge-making: "the wayfarer knows as he goes along", he affirms (2010: 134). Interestingly, when he describes the figure of the wayfarer, Ingold further affirms that "someone who knows well is able to tell, in the sense not only of being able to recount stories of the world, but also of having a finely tempered perceptual awareness of his surroundings" (134). This way, he connects the practices of walking and knowing to that of telling stories and, implicitly, to that of the three figures of the wayfarer, the reader and the narrator:

> In short, whereas the Kantian traveller reasons over a map in his mind, the wayfarer draws a tale from impressions in the ground. Less a surveyor than a narrator, his aim is not to "classify and arrange", or "to place every experience in its class", but rather to situate each impression in relation to the occurrences that paved the way for it, presently concur with it, and follow along after. In this sense his knowledge is not classificatory but storied, not totalizing and synoptic but open-ended and exploratory.
> (Ingold, 2010: 135)

Like Brosseau's urban walker, Ingold's wayfarer brings stories (narratives) and worlds closer through movement (mobile practices). In his enactivist approach, Caracciolo relates readers' perception of fictive spaces with their own intimate, emotional, and qualitative experiences of lived places: narrative texts ask readers to enter fictional worlds and call upon their preceding spatial experiences to re-construct those fictional projections; in the same way, however, the spatial skills and abilities acquired through this "readers' virtual body tour" (2011: 131–2) reflect themselves from fictional into real experiences. The reading practice can be interpreted as an active exploration of the environment, a lived, albeit virtual, spatial experience that readers use as a cognitive tool to orient themselves in the real world as well. As a result, narrative mobilities have an actual influence on our cognitive abilities to move across material spaces and vice versa. According to Caracciolo, storyworlds should be interpreted as meaningful collections of places which authors, while writing, and readers, while reading, can experience through embodied, intimate and emotional reactions (2013: 430), having an intrinsically mobile, and not simply spatial, essence. Whereas Caracciolo maintains that narrative *spatio-centred* passages trigger in authors' and readers' minds the same cognitive strategies they use for perceiving and comprehending reality (2011: 119–20), I contend that narrative *mobile-centred* passages can trigger in authors' and readers' minds the cognitive strategies they use for moving across and orienting themselves in the material world. Understanding texts as triggers for spatial action and cognitive orientation in real life allows us to move narrative mobilities from space representation to practice, from the representation of mobile practices, chronotopes, and subjects in narrative space to the understanding of those same representations as enactments, spatial events and cognitive explorations of mobilities that impact on material worlds, experiences, and emotions. Thus, texts are no longer single products whose reception is predetermined by their static ontic security. Instead, texts are actions that unfold through the embodied spatial practices of writing/reading and producing/acquiring knowledge through narrative movement.

7.4 Mobility and the geohumanities: enacting narrative mobilities as research practices

In their seminal introduction to the special issue of *Geoforum* (2002) entitled *Enacting Geographies*, Dewsbury et al. propose a serial logic of the unfinished that would be able to recognise, undergo, and embrace, rather than define and explain, the ongoing exceeding essence of the world and, therefore, the unfolding essence of research itself. They invite us to embrace a kind of spatial thinking that is focused on processually registering experience and *presenting* research, rather than on steadily representing fixed thoughts: "We want to work on *presenting* the world, not on representing it, or explaining it", they affirm, interpreting "representation not as a code to be broken or as an illusion to be dispelled, but rather representations are apprehended as *performative* in themselves; as *doings*" (2002: 438). If theory is always practical, the borders between spatial representations and (research) practices have definitely fallen in favour of a pluralistic, open-ended process of experiencing/knowing space. These suggestions seem to be able to cross geography's disciplinary boundaries, involving all those scholars in the humanities who might be interested in thinking of both texts as mobile and spatial events and representations as practices. Starting from these "tactical suggestions" (2002: 439), the mobile geocritical approach I tried to present in the previous sections proposes a shift from the simple, mostly static analysis of narratives towards the actual production of narrative mobilities by mobility scholars; enacting narrative mobilities, thus, means embracing mobile-centred narratives as practices that orient ourselves in the world, rather than as mere objects of research.

This proposal is inspired by the constant attempt to experiment with new methodologies within mobility studies, as well as the invitation to embrace creativity "as a mode of critical exploration" (Hawkins, 2013: 53), within creative geography. Recent years have witnessed a kind of explosion of mobile methods aimed at moving with objects of research. As Merriman observes, "these methodological experimentations in mobility studies are partially inspired by the arts and the humanities" (2014: 171–2). Following Merriman, these experimentations do not necessarily provide us with a deeper understanding of mobilities because of their creative and innovative character; rather, a constant dialogue between more traditional and innovative methods would provide mobility scholars with a wider range of possibilities to conduct mobility research. As he further observes, "critical, creative, practical and academic interventions can occur in all manner of ways, and the work of arts and humanities scholars and practitioners provides excellent examples of critical mobilities research practice" (2014: 173). This interest within mobility research in creative methods, inspired by the arts and the humanities, seems to trace a further connection between mobility and the emerging field of the geohumanities. Indeed, the recent (re)appearance of a so-called "creative turn" in geography and the declared "urgency" to experiment with creative approaches and methodologies seems to draw a potential area of intersection that moves a step forward in the ongoing dialogue between "mobility and the humanities" (Pearce and Merriman, 2018), through the mediation of creative, interdisciplinary, and mobile research in the geohumanities. As Harriet Hawkins affirms, creative geographies have become increasingly vibrant in the last decade, proposing research strategies that "re-cast geography's interdisciplinary relationship with arts and humanities scholarship and practices" by bringing geographers to work "as and in collaboration with artists, creative writers and a range of other arts practitioners" (2015: 262–3).

My proposal is to think of narrative mobilities as an opportunity to bring *mobility studies and the geohumanities* together and contribute to this ongoing interdisciplinary debate through an approach that begins with a close dialogue between literary geography, spatial literary studies, and the geohumanities: as I postulated in this chapter's opening paragraphs, I see narrative mobilities as an opportunity to engage with narratives as research practices in mobility research, with cultural representations of mobilities becoming dynamic research routes to follow, rather than being mere objects of analysis. Thus, a mobile geocritical approach experiments with narratives as mobilising storytelling practices and creative means that activate plurivocal discourses about mobile spaces, landscapes, bodies, subjects, identities, and practices involving audiences beyond academic boundaries. The renewed exchange between geography, the arts, and the humanities, in the field of the geohumanities, has endorsed the exchange between geographical and literary modes of approaching texts: this could be a starting point for experimenting with creative, mobile-centred narratives in mobility research. Whereas geographers' creative writings have embraced literary modes of storytelling to gain a more subjective, embodied and intimate narration of geographical research, likewise, mobility scholars could experiment with narrative methods and the composition of stories as a prolific tool to explore the potentialities of representations as practices of research. Significantly, this mutation would not simply affect the way in which mobility research can be told and re-told, but also how it influences the way in which mobile thinking is provoked and research is thought, conducted, and developed. If this "urgency" to embrace a more creative approach to spatial issues and to re-cast traditional methods of research has not yet reached the interdisciplinary field of literary geographies, resulting in an experimental and creative set of geocritical research products and doings, narrative mobilities could become a bridging interdisciplinary area to begin experimenting with a space-centred creative approach to texts through a mobile-centred perspective. Mobility and the (geo)humanities represent an expanding field of interdisciplinary exchange that poses methodological and critical challenges. The approach proposed in this chapter embraces creativity as a mode of critical thinking that opens new experimental ways to approach, read, and produce mobile narratives in the humanities.

References

Aguiar M (2011) *Tracking modernity: India's railway and the culture of mobility*. Minneapolis: University of Minnesota Press.

Aguiar M, Mathieson C and Pearce L (eds) (2019) *Mobilities, literature, culture*. London: Palgrave Macmillan.

Ameel L, Finch J and Salmela, M (eds) (2015) *Literature and the peripheral city*. London: Palgrave Macmillan.

Anderson J (2014) *Page and place: ongoing compositions of plot*. Amsterdam: Rodopi.

Bemong N, Borghart P, De Dobbeleer M, Demoen K, De Temmerman K and Keunen B (eds) (2010) *Bakhtin's theory of the literary chronotope: reflections, applications, perspectives*. Ghent: Academia Press.

Brosseau M (2017) In, of, out, with, and through: new perspectives in literary geography. In: Tally RT Jr (ed.) *The Routledge handbook of literature and space*. Abingdon: Routledge, pp. 9–27.

Brosseau M (1995) The city in textual form: Manhattan Transfer's New York. *Ecumene* 2(1): 89–114.

Caracciolo M (2014) *The experientiality of narrative: an enactivist approach*. Berlin: De Gruyter.

Caracciolo M (2013) Narrative space and readers' responses to stories: a phenomenological account. *Style* 47(4): 425–444.

Caracciolo M (2012) Narrative, meaning, interpretation: an enactivist approach. *Phenomenology and the Cognitive Sciences* 11(3): 367–384.

Caracciolo M (2011) The reader's virtual body: narrative space and its reconstruction. *Storyworlds: A Journal of Narrative Studies* 3: 117–138.

Clifford J (1997) *Routes: travel and translation in the late 20th century*. Cambridge: Harvard University Press.

Cosgrove D (2006) Carto-city. In: Abrams J and Hall P (eds) *Else/Where: mapping – new cartographies of networks and territories*. Minneapolis: University of Minnesota Design Institute, pp. 148–157.

Cresswell T (2006) *On the move: mobility in the modern western world*. Abingdon: Routledge.

Dewsbury JD, Harrison P, Rose M and Wylie J (2002) Enacting geographies. *Geoforum* 4(33): 437–440.

Finch J, Ameel L and Salmela M (eds) (2017) *Literary second cities*. London: Palgrave Macmillan.

Gilroy P (1995) *The Black Atlantic: modernity and double consciousness*. Cambridge: Harvard University Press.

Green-Simms LB (2017) *Postcolonial automobility: car culture in West Africa*. Minneapolis: University of Minnesota Press.

Gurr JM (ed.) (2021) *Charting literary urban studies: texts as models of and for the city*. Abingdon: Routledge.

Hawkins H (2015) Creative geographic methods: knowing, representing, intervening. On composing place and page. *Cultural Geographies* 22(2): 247–268.
Hawkins H (2013) Geography and art. An expanding field: site, the body and practice. *Progress in Human Geography* 37(1): 52–71.
Holloway J and Kneale J (2009) Dialogism (after Bakhtin). In: Kitchin R and Thrift N (eds) *International encyclopedia of human geography*. Amsterdam: Elsevier, pp. 143–149.
Hones S (2014) *Literary geographies: narrative space in "Let the Great World Spin"*. Berlin: Springer.
Hones S (2008) Text as it happens: literary geography. *Geography Compass* 2(5): 1301–1317.
Howell P and Beckingham D (2015) Time-geography, gentlemen, please: chronotopes of publand in Patrick Hamilton's London trilogy. *Social & Cultural Geography* 16(8): 931–949.
Ingold T (2010) Footprints through the weather-world: walking, breathing, knowing. *Journal of the Royal Anthropological Institute* 16: 121–139.
Latham A, McCormack D, McNamara K and McNeill D (2009), *Key concepts in urban geography*. London: Sage.
Lawson J (2011) Chronotope, story, and historical geography: Mikhail Bakhtin and the space-time of narratives. *Antipode* 43(2): 384–412.
McLaughlin D (2016) The work and the world: mobilities and literary space. *Literary Geographies* 2(2): 122–127.
Merriman P (2015) Mobilities I: departures. *Progress in Human Geography* 39(1): 87–95.
Merriman P (2014) Rethinking mobile methods. *Mobilities* 9(2): 167–187.
Merriman P and Pearce L (2017) Mobility and the humanities. *Mobilities* 12(4): 493–508.
Pearce L (2019) Trackless mourning: the mobilities of love and loss. *Cultural Geographies* 26(2): 163–176.
Pearce L (2018) "Walking out": the mobilities of love. *Mobilities* 13(6): 777–790.
Pearce L (2017) "Driving-as-event": re-thinking the car journey. *Mobilities* 12(4): 585–597.
Pearce L (2016) *Drivetime: literary excursions in automotive consciousness*. Edinburgh: Edinburgh University Press.
Pearce L and Merriman P (2018) *Mobility and the humanities*. Abingdon: Routledge.
Peterle G (2021) *Comics as a research practice: drawing narrative geographies beyond the frame*. Abingdon: Routledge.
Peterle G (2017) Moving beyond Venice: literary landscapes of movement in northern Italy's "diffused city". In: Ameel L, Finch J and Salmela M (eds) (a cura di) *Literary second cities*. Basingstoke: Palgrave Macmillan, pp. 217–240.
Peterle G (2016) Moving literature: the car as a mobile chronotope in Don DeLillo's *Cosmopolis*. *Rivista Geografica Italiana* 124: 281–300.
Prieto E (2012) *Literature, geography and the postmodern poetics of place*. New York: Palgrave Macmillan.
Prieto E (2011) Geocriticism, geopoetics, geophilosophy, and beyond. In: Tally RT Jr (ed.) *Geocritical explorations: space, place, and mapping in literary and cultural studies*. New York: Palgrave Macmillan, pp. 13–27.
Said E (1993) *Culture and imperialism*. New York: Vintage Press.
Saunders A (2013) The spatial event of writing: John Galsworthy and the creation of fraternity. *Cultural Geographies* 20(3): 285–298.

Saunders A (2010) Literary geography: reforging the connections. *Progress in Human Geography* 34(4): 436–452.

Saunders A and Anderson J (2016) Relational literary geographies: co-producing page and place. *Literary Geographies* 1(2): 115–119.

Sheller M (2015) Vital methodologies: live methods, mobile art, and research-creation. In: Vannini P (ed.) *Non-representational methodologies: re-envisioning research*. Abingdon: Routledge, pp. 130–145.

Sheller M (2004) Automotive emotions: feeling the car. *Theory, Culture & Society* 21(4–5): 221–242.

Sheller M and Urry J (2016) Mobilizing the new mobilities paradigm. *Applied Mobilities* 1: 10–25.

Sheller M and Urry J (2006) The new mobilities paradigm. *Environment & Planning A: Economy and Space* 38(2): 207–226.

Tally RT Jr (ed.) 2021 *Spatial literary studies: interdisciplinary approaches to space, geography, and the imagination*. Abingdon: Routledge.

Tally RT Jr (ed.) (2011) *Geocritical explorations: space, place, and mapping in literary and cultural studies*. New York: Palgrave Macmillan.

Urry J (2004) The "system" of automobility. *Theory, Culture & Society* 21(4–5): 25–39.

Westphal B (2011) *Le Monde plausible. Espace, lieu, carte*. Paris: Éditions de Minuit.

Westphal B (2007) *Geocriticism: real and fictional spaces*. New York: Palgrave Macmillan.

Afterword

Peter Merriman
ABERYSTWYTH UNIVERSITY

In our introductory article to the special issue of *Mobilities* on 'Mobility and the humanities', Lynne Pearce and I highlighted the long and rich tradition of scholarly thinking and creative practice which has focussed on movement, circulation, travel, transport, and mobility through the lens of the arts and humanities (Merriman and Pearce, 2017). We were quite clear. Mobilities research is not simply undertaken by social scientists. Concepts of movement and mobility reoccur throughout centuries of humanities scholarship, ranging from ancient philosophy and history, to recent scholarship in transport history, literary studies, and archaeology, and experimental creative approaches in art, design, and performance. The chapters in this section demonstrate the breadth of arts and humanities scholarship that has been and is being conducted on themes of mobility, movement, and circulation, covering movements of scientific knowledge, global commodities, and gendered bodies, and practice-attuned scholarship that focuses on maps and literary texts as dynamic mobile technologies which are in process and becoming.

A central theme of a number of chapters is the *materialities* of movement, considering what moves, why, and how. We are provided with an understanding of how movements are qualified and quantified, and how they are multiple rather than singular occurrences or events. These qualities are important, whether we are discussing the mobility of commodities such as silver and aluminium, or the experiences of mobile human bodies. In their chapters on the 'mobility of pictures' and 'map-mobilities', respectively, Elena Canadelli and Laura Lo Presti/Tania Rossetto draw upon Bruno Latour's famous typology of materiality and mobility in which he distinguishes between objects and technologies that are mutable mobiles, mutable immobiles, immutable mobiles, and immutable immobiles (see Latour, 1986, 1987; Law and Mol, 2001). This typology is useful for considering some of the changing qualities of the many 'things' which move or stay relatively still in social, economic, and political networks, but it is important not to forget that Latour also focuses upon other qualities, including the invention of objects that are 'presentable, readable, and combinable' (Latour, 1986: 7).

DOI: 10.4324/9781003278665-10

There are, of course, many different theoretical approaches to materiality that can attune us to the complexity of relations between material 'bodies' of different kinds, including approaches focussing on hybridity, cyborgs, existential 'withness', affect, processuality, vibrant materialism, and non-representational theories (see e.g. Heidegger, 1962 [1927]; Thrift, 2008; Bennett, 2010; Merriman, 2022). Putting aside the question of how we theorise materiality, and instead foregrounding the issue of *relations* and *ontology*, such alternative approaches can highlight how 'our' sense of *being, relating*, and *moving* as humans is affected or shaped by an innumerable number of relations with other 'bodies' and 'things' (cf. Rose, 1996) – with the caveat, of course, that there is no single uniform 'our', as our personal senses of self and being may be shaped by many factors, including our gender, sexuality, race/ ethnicity, physical ability, and cultural background. Our ontologies are continually reworked and performed as we *become* simultaneously individualised and collectivised map-readers, airline-passengers, manuscript-collectors, and book-readers. Perhaps the most famous examples of such relational 'couplets' in mobility studies are the 'hybrid' or 'cyborg' figures of the 'car-driver' (Lupton, 1999 and Sheller and Urry, 2000) or 'human-car co(a)gent' (Michael, 2000). In his discussion of 'the driver-car', sociologist Tim Dant prefers the term 'assemblage' to both 'cyborg' and 'hybrid', because he feels that the latter terms tend 'to fix and reify the assemblage' and imply a permanent combination of entities:

> While the car can be seen as a mobility aid for the able-bodied, human subjectivity is in no sense constituted by getting into a car; it is a temporary assemblage within which the human remains complete in his or her self.
>
> (Dant, 2004: 62)

While there are differences between the many uses of concepts like assemblage, cyborg, and hybrid, for me Dant (2004) misses the point, focussing upon the materialities of these configurations at the expense of the ontologies, sensations, and identities which emerge through and cut across the materialities of the 'car-driver'. As I stated in response in 2006:

> Dant appears to operate with a rather narrow conception of hybrids and cyborgs, and a somewhat essentialist construction of subjectivity that overlooks the multiple, partial and ongoing shaping of human subjectivity in relation to a variety of things in different spaces and times.
>
> (Merriman, 2006: 89)

These things may include transport vehicles, tools, digital interfaces, maps, weapons, food, and much more. As the chapters in this section reveal, people's engagements with things are not simply 'one-way' acts of 'consuming' commodities or of 'reading' texts. Indeed, arts and humanities scholars working across fields like history, literary studies, cultural studies, and cultural and historical geography have paid close attention to the many cultural, political, and economic processes and relations that have been involved in the production, circulation, consumption, and interpretation of mobile things, and in more recent times there has been a concerted effort by theorists – especially in traditions like phenomenology and post-structuralism – to highlight and apprehend the fleeting qualities of movements.

In my own discipline, the post-structuralist geographer Nigel Thrift famously coined the phrase 'non-representational theory' to refer to a broad range of traditions of thinking that have valued practices, process, and movement (Thrift, 1996), but the prefixing of this new theoretical brand with a negative – 'non' – has always been seen as problematic (see Lorimer, 2005, 2015). What could have been named 'mobile practice theory' or 'process theory' was instead given a name that is frequently taken to infer that researchers should not concern themselves with those things that are referred to as 'representations' (see Nash, 2000 and Lorimer, 2005). However, Thrift's key concern was to cast 'a critical light on theories that claim to re-present some naturally present reality', rejecting representational models of thought in favour of theories of 'thought-in-action' and 'presentation' (Thrift, 1996: 7). The things we commonly refer to as 'representations', then, must be approached differently, as dynamic 'presentations', and central to debates surrounding 'non-representational theory' was the question of how best to apprehend elusive and transient mobile practices, i.e. what methods and methodologies to adopt (Vannini, 2015).

In an early article, Thrift (1993: 98) positioned 'practical methodological problems' at the heart of any renewed focus on practices and movements, while in several later pieces he criticised geographers for focussing on a narrow range of textual methods and media in communicating their research (Thrift, 2000a):

> Current work in cultural studies and cultural geography still draws on a remarkably limited number of methodologies – ethnography, focus groups, and the like – which are nearly always cognitive in origin and effect. Non-representational work, in contrast, is concerned with multiplying performative methodologies which allow their participants equal rights to disclosure, through relation rather than representation.
>
> (Thrift, 2000a: 244)

To counteract this tendency, Thrift suggested that cultural geographers should adopt more open-ended, experimental approaches influenced by the performing arts (Thrift, 2000b). His arguments clearly resonated with scholars focussing on contemporary events, but many historically oriented scholars suggest that historical methods could also be used to understand past practices and performances, with fleeting practices, movements and atmospheres leaving traces in the historical record (see Merriman, 2005 and Griffin and Evans, 2008).

Thrift's writings on non-representational theory and mobile practices influenced many mobility theorists, ranging from an 'interested sceptic' like Tim Cresswell (see Lorimer, 2005: 85 and Cresswell, 2012: 98), to more sympathetic commentators such as Peter Adey, David Bissell and myself (see Adey, 2017; Bissell, 2010a, 2019 and Merriman, 2012). A number of social scientists focussed their attention on the implications of non-representational theories for mobilities methods, but these scholars were nearly always focussing on 'live' mobile practices in the present (Spinney, 2009, 2011 and Sheller, 2015), and many turned to technologically driven methods for tracking movement and recording moving images and sounds (see Fincham et al., 2010; Büscher et al., 2011 and Vergunst, 2011). As the geographer J.D. Dewsbury remarked more broadly of the kinds of methods being deployed to study non-representational practices and affects:

> Often when confronted with the desire to do performative research the knee-jerk reaction is to speed fast into devising a research project that involves animating knowledge by using video capture of one form or another: the 'only way' to get at practice and performance, and any other present-tense action.
>
> (Dewsbury, 2010: 325)

Video technologies were quickly embraced for their seeming ability to capture and record real-time/ live events, body movements, gestures and the visual layout of the environments in which acts take place. Due to the relatively confined or dynamic spaces and environments involved in mobile practices like cycling and car driving, as well as the interruptions caused by researchers travelling with participants, it is not surprising that some mobility scholars turned to digital cameras and GPS tracking technologies to try and capture the fleeting, dynamic and embodied qualities of moving bodies (see Laurier et al., 2008; Laurier, 2010; Spinney, 2006, 2011, et al.).[1] At times, these methods have formed part of a broader approach that includes more traditional social science methods such as interviews, and they have certainly added to the methodological repertoire and range of 'data' available for mobility scholars working in the social sciences. My concern is that a number of scholars seem to have positioned such 'live', participative, non-representational and mobile methods as being more effective or accurate at apprehending certain events and experiences than reflective methods like interviews and diaries, or more text-based methods (see Spinney, 2009, 2011 and Vergunst, 2011). Of course, this has never been an option for historically oriented scholars researching mobility practices, events and technologies in the past.

The chapters in this section demonstrate how a broad range of arts and humanities approaches and methods can be useful for understanding movement and mobility, from archival research to experimental geohumanities approaches to narratives and texts. Rather than speaking of 'mobile methods', it is perhaps more helpful to highlight the sheer range of methods and methodologies that can be useful when trying to trace, understand and apprehend movements and fixities of different kinds. There is a danger that a focus only on specialist 'mobile methods' or 'non-representational methods' leads scholars to generate what David Bissell (2010b: 56) has called an *overanimated* mobile subject', where the focus is on action, movement and change at the expense of 'other corporeal subjectivities', and distinctive experiences of stillness, slowness, waiting and boredom (see also Bissell, 2007, 2008 and Bissell and Fuller, 2011). These methods also miss a lot of the 'action', including the background actions which form the social, political, legal and cultural contexts in which movements are enabled, regulated and acquire meaning. These 'contexts' are rarely 'captured' in video recordings, but they do leave traces in the archival record which are examined by mobility historians.

The final point I want to make about this section, as well as the rich vein of scholarship that it represents, is that it covers a very broad time period (ranging from the 15th century to the present day), something that is often missing from research in transport and mobility history. Transport history scholars have largely focussed on 19th and 20th century transport modes – railways and canals, and later steam ships, motor vehicles, bicycles and air travel – with limited examination of earlier practices and transport modes (Divall, 2014). In the UK and USA, this temporal focus probably relates to the field's close affiliation with the fields of business history, the history of technology, and amateur enthusiast and preservation movements. Until recently, relatively little dialogue and debate seems to have occurred between the fields of transport history *and* related areas such as histories of exploration and empire, ancient history, global history, military history, literary studies and history of cartography, although some studies have started to explore these interfaces (see Spiers, 2017; Mathieson, 2015; Pearce; Merriman and Lambert, 2020).

Note

1 There is a distinct shift in Laurier's ethnographic research from his earlier ethnographic study of mobile company representatives in the late 1990s, where he sat in the passenger seat of the participants' vehicles (e.g. Laurier, 2004), to later video ethnographies of car travel where participants activated video cameras fixed to their dashboards (Laurier et al., 2008 and Laurier, 2010).

References

Adey P (2017) *Mobility* (Second Edition). London: Routledge.
Aguiar M (2011) *Tracking modernity: India's railway and the culture of mobility.* Minneapolis: University of Minnesota Press.

Bennett J (2010) *Vibrant matter: a political ecology of things*. London: Duke University Press.
Bissell D (2007) Animating suspension: waiting for mobilities. *Mobilities* 2(2): 277–298.
Bissell D (2008) Comfortable bodies: sedentary affects. *Environment and planning A* 40(7): 1697–1712.
Bissell D (2010a) Passenger mobilities: affective atmospheres and the sociality of public transport. *Environment and planning D: society and space* 28(2): 270–289.
Bissell D (2010b) Narrating mobile methodologies: active and passive empiricisms. In: B Fincham, M McGuinness & L Murray (eds) *Mobile methodologies*. Basingstoke: Palgrave Macmillan, pp.53–68.
Bissell D (2019) On edge: writing non-representational journeys. In: CP Boyd and C Edwardes (eds) *Non-representational theory and the creative arts*. London: Palgrave Macmillan, pp.351–358.
Bissell D and Fuller G (eds)(2011) *Stillness in a mobile world*. London: Routledge.
Brown K and Spinney J (2010) Catching a glimpse: the value of video in evoking, understanding and representing the practice of cycling. In: B Fincham, M McGuinness & L Murray (eds) *Mobile methodologies*. Basingstoke: Palgrave Macmillan, pp.130–151.
Büscher M, Urry J and Witchger K (2011) Introduction: Mobile methods. In: M Büscher, J Urry & K Witchger (eds) *Mobile methods*. London: Routledge, pp.1–19.
Cresswell T (2012) Nonrepresentational theory and me: notes of an interested sceptic. *Environment and planning D: society and space* 30(1): 96–105.
Dant T (2004) The driver-car. *Theory, culture, and society* 21(4–5): 61–79.
Divall C (2014) Mobilities and transport history. In: P Adey, D Bissell, K Hannam, P Merriman and M Sheller (eds) *The Routledge handbook of mobilities*. London: Routledge, pp.36–44.
Dewsbury JD (2010) Performative, non-representational and affect-based research. In: D DeLyser, S Aitken, M Crang, S Herbert and L McDowell (eds) *The SAGE handbook of qualitative research in human geography*. London: Sage, pp.321–334.
Fincham B, McGuinness M and Murray L (eds) (2010) *Mobile methodologies*. Basingstoke: Palgrave Macmillan.
Griffin C and Evans A (2008) On historical geographies of embodied practice and performance. *Historical geography* 36(1): 5–16.
Heidegger M (1962 [1927]) *Being and time*. Oxford: Blackwell Publishing.
Lambert D and Merriman P (eds)(2020) *Empire and mobility in the long 19th century*. Manchester: Manchester University Press.
Latour B (1986) Visualization and cognition. *Knowledge and society* 6(6): 1–40.
Latour B (1987) *Science in action: how to follow scientists and engineers through society*. London: Harvard University Press.
Laurier E (2004) Doing office work on the motorway. *Theory, culture & society* 21(4–5): 261–277.
Laurier E (2010) Being there/seeing there: recording and analysing life in the car. In: B Fincham, M McGuinness and L Murray (eds) *Mobile methodologies*. London: Palgrave Macmillan, pp.103–117.
Laurier E, Lorimer H, Brown B, Jones O, Juhlin O, Noble A, Perry M, Pica D, Sormani P, Strebel I, Swan L, Taylor AS, Watts L and Weilenmann A (2008) Driving and passengering: notes on the ordinary organisation of car travel. *Mobilities* 3(1): 1–23.
Law J and Mol A (2001) Situating technoscience: an inquiry into spatialities. *Environment and planning D: society and space* 19(5): 609–621.

Lorimer H (2005) Cultural geography: the busyness of being more-than-representational. *Progress in human geography* 29(1): 83–94.
Lorimer H (2015) Non-representational theory and me too. In: P Vannini (ed.) *Non-representational methodologies: re-envisioning research.* London: Routledge, pp.177–187.
Lupton D (1999) Monsters in metal cocoons: 'road rage' and cyborg bodies. *Body and society* 5: 57–72.
Mathieson C (2015) *Mobility in the Victorian novel: placing the nation.* London: Palgrave Macmillan.
Merriman P (2005) 'Operation motorway': landscapes of construction on England's M1 motorway. *Journal of historical geography* 31(1): 113–133.
Merriman P (2006) 'Mirror, signal, manoeuvre': assembling and governing the motorway driver in late fifties Britain. *The sociological review* 54 (s.1): 75–92.
Merriman P (2012) *Mobility, space and culture.* London: Routledge.
Merriman P (2014) Rethinking mobile methods. *Mobilities* 9(2): 167–187.
Merriman P (2022) *Space.* London: Routledge.
Merriman P and Pearce L (2017) Mobility and the humanities. *Mobilities* 12(4): 493–508.
Michael M (2000) *Reconnecting culture, technology and nature.* London: Routledge.
Nash C (2000) Performativity in practice: some recent work in cultural geography. *Progress in human geography* 24(4): 653–664.
Pearce L (2016) *Drivetime: literary excursions in automotive consciousness.* Edinburgh: Edinburgh University Press.
Rose N (1996) *Inventing our selves: psychology, power, and personhood.* Cambridge: Cambridge University Press.
Sheller M (2015) Vital methodologies: Live methods, mobile art, and research-creation. In: P Vannini (ed.) *Non-representational methodologies.* London: Routledge, pp.140–155.
Sheller M and Urry J (2000) The city and the car. *International journal of urban and regional research* 24(4): 727–757.
Spiers EM (2017) *Engines for empire: The Victorian Army and its use of railways.* Manchester: Manchester University Press.
Spinney J (2006) A place of sense: a kinaesthetic ethnography of cyclists on Mont Ventoux. *Environment & planning D: society & space* 24(5): 709–732.
Spinney J (2009) Cycling the city: movement, meaning and method. *Geography compass* 3(2): 817–835.
Spinney J (2011) A chance to catch a breath: using mobile video methodology in cycling research. *Mobilities* 6(2): 161–182.
Thrift N (1993) For a new regional geography 3. *Progress in human geography* 17(1): 92–100.
Thrift N (1996) *Spatial formations.* London: Sage.
Thrift N (2000a) Afterwords. *Environment & planning D: society & space* 18(2): 213–255.
Thrift N (2000b) Introduction: Dead or alive? In: I Cook, D Crouch, S Naylor and JR Ryan (eds) *Cultural turns/geographical turns.* Harlow: Prentice Hall, pp.1-6.
Thrift N (2008) *Non-representational theory.* London: Routledge.
Vannini P (ed.) (2015) *Non-representational methodologies: re-envisioning research.* London: Routledge.
Vergunst J (2011) Technology and technique in a useful ethnography of movement. *Mobilities* 6(2): 203–219.

Section 2
Ideas

8 Mobility
The word and the thing

Lucio Biasiori

> It is never a waste of time to study the history of a word. Such journeys, whether short or long, monotonous or varied, are always instructive. But in every major language, there are a dozen or so terms, never more, often less, whose past is no food for the scholar. But it is for the historian, if we give the word historian all its due force [...]. They alone can enable us to follow and measure, perhaps rather slowly but very precisely (language is not a very rapid recording instrument), the transformations which took place in a group of those governing ideas which man is pleased to think of as being immobile because their immobility seems to be a guarantee of his security.
>
> (Febvre, 1929: 219)

It is difficult to say whether Lucien Febvre would have placed the history of the word "mobility" among the competences of the simple scholar or historian. If this distinction still makes sense today, there would be no harm in also having carried out a work of pure scholarship, given that there is a dearth of studies devoted to the formation of the analytical category of mobility in European languages. However, this chapter wagers that a history of the word mobility is the work of a historian and that it may also help other experts in the human and social sciences to reflect on a term that has had such increasing success in recent decades to the point of creating its own disciplinary field—*mobility studies*. The fact that Febvre concluded his sentence by alluding to the false sense of security that gives human beings confidence in the immobility of the words they use argues in favour of this wager.

The purpose of this essay is to trace the historical (rather than the archaeological) semantics of the word "mobility".[1] I will concentrate mainly on the early modern period because that is when the category originated and gained popularity.

From the classical world through the Renaissance, the early modern age inherited a very negative meaning for the Latin term *mobilitas* and its derivatives in the Romance languages. For the Romans, *mobilitas* principally had a psychological meaning: it was mainly thoughts that were mobile.

DOI: 10.4324/9781003278665-12

"What is more shameful than inconstancy, levity, mobility?" Cicero asks himself in his *Philippicae* (7, 9).² But whose thoughts are they? Of women, mainly—we still have a hint of this in the famous aria of Giuseppe Verdi's Rigoletto "La donna è mobile" ("The woman is mobile"). Yet they are also the thoughts of non-Romans, such as the Numidians described by Sallust in the *Bellum Iugurtinum* 56, 5: "The Numidians behave with such mobility".³ And, finally, of those who belonged to the lower strata of the population, such as slaves, whose mobility was also physical, given that they always had to obey the demands of their masters. Latin comedy featured the figure of the *servus currens* (running servant) and, for centuries to come, mobility, both physically and psychologically, would be a natural attribute of slaves, as the Jesuit Alfonso Salmerón (1604: 280) writes in the second half of the 16th century: "as prudence or cunning is attributed to the serpent, simplicity to the dove and rapacity to the wolf, thus is mobility to the slave".⁴

However, common people in general were also considered to be especially subject to *mobilitas* and, therefore, volatile and unreliable: for example, the historian Tacitus (*Histories*, 5, 8, 3) spoke of kings "driven out by the mobility of the common people",⁵ whilst Livy (24, 31, 14) and Seneca (*Hercules furens* 170) compared the "*mobile vulgus*"—an expression destined for greatness, as we shall see—to a breeze that continually changes direction, or to a wave whose movement overwhelms all.⁶

To show the elasticity of this prejudice of race, gender and class against the physical and psychological mobility of the subalterns, there is nothing more effective than to observe this image.

Figure 8.1 F. Del Cossa, Palio di San Giorgio, fresco, Ferrara, Palazzo Schifanoia.

It is the fresco of the month of April, which Francesco del Cossa painted for the Duke of Ferrara, Borso d'Este. The subject is the Palio di San Giorgio, a race not only for horses but also for Jews (the errant people *par excellence*) and prostitutes—the *mulieres vagae* as they were dubbed, a term that alludes to both the volatility of their lustful nature (*vaghezza*) and their quintessentially vagrant trade. Despite its poor state of conservation, we can detect a powerful contrast between the frenetic mobility of the individuals running in the lower register and the distant, almost indifferent immobility of the nobles observing the scene from the upper one.

This concept was set into motion, if not into debate, at the beginning of the early modern era.

In his *Discourses on Livy* (I, 58), Machiavelli takes issue with the very definition of *mobile vulgus* given by Livy himself: "without trying to use either authority or force", Machiavelli asserts that inconstancy "of which writers accuse the multitude, all men individually can be accused of it, and chiefly princes, for he who is not regulated by the laws will commit the same errors as the ungoverned multitude" (Machiavelli, 1989: I, 313).[7]

The same attitude of rejection of the principle of authority leads to the resemantisation of the old, negative concept of mobility in two additional fields of cultural production. The first is that of printing, where—in the words taken from the *Encyclopédie*—"the mobility of characters is the foundation of the printing industry".[8] The second is that of cosmology. From the early modern age onwards, the term mobility assumes an increasingly dual nature: on the one hand, as we shall see, it does not lose that earthly connotation, aimed at defining the physical and psychological movements of social actors. On the other, however, mobility begins to increasingly refer to the property inherent in celestial bodies—the Earth, in particular—that enables them to move. The most succinct on this point was the abbot Jean-Antoine Nollet, a physicist, in his *Leçons de physique expérimentale* (Nollet, 1745: 177, my translation): "We must not confuse Mobility with Motion; these are two entirely different Things. The first is a Property common to all Bodies; the other is a State outside of which they are often considered but is not essential to them".

This impalpable quality of mobility—the cause, rather than the effect, of movement—was at the heart of the concept's criticisms. One of these came from the physician and poet Richard Blackmore (1712: vv. 321–28) in his philosophical poem *Creation*, an early modern version of Lucretius' *On the Nature of Things*, intended to serve as an expression of a cosmological point of view similar to that of John Locke, who was somewhat sceptical when it came to theories of movement.[9]

> This problem, as philosophers, resolve:
> What makes the globe from West to East revolve?
> What is the strong impulsive cause, declare
> Which rolls the pond'rous orb so swift in air?
> To your vain answer will you have recourse,
> and tell us 'tis ingenite, active force,
> Mobility, or native pow'r to move,
> words which mean nothing, and can nothing prove.

"Mobility" is, therefore, something that causes the "revolution" of celestial bodies. In other words, what happens to "mobility" is the same as what happens to another controversial term of the soft and hard sciences: revolution. The term revolution also passes continuously between sky and earth to indicate the movements of the planets around the sun (as in the *De revolutionibus orbium coelestium* of Copernicus) and the internal upheavals of states (Rey, 1989; Benigno, 2017: ch. 4).

In a pre-Copernican and qualitative vision of the cosmos, this continuous passage of terms such as *mobilitas* or *revolutio*, from physical bodies to political bodies, is based on a material affinity between the biological foundations of the microcosm (man) and the macrocosm (the universe). With the new, quantitative vision of the cosmos the analogy shifts at the level of method and language, so that the laws of nature serve as a model for the laws of society, and the vocabulary of post-Galilean mechanics is applied to political bodies.[10] 17th century political theories adopted the natural sciences as a model, thus replacing the organological or corporational metaphors describing society as a body with mechanical ones. The latter were in no way better grounded than the biological terms they replaced, but they expressed a new conviction: society ceased to be an immediate product or reflection of nature and became an artificial body, a product of man's choice and work, and not of his alleged "social instincts" (Funkenstein, 1986: 342).

A clue to this more general trend is contained in the term "mobility" when referring to people. This is an evolution of the Latin phrase with which, as we have seen, the principal Latin historians called the people: "*mobile vulgus*". In early modern English society especially, the formula spread so widely that the adjective "mobile" became a noun. Between the 1600s and 1650s in England, the simple use of the term "mobile" was often a derogatory reference to the people. Beginning in the second half of the 17th century and continuing for at least another two centuries, the adjective "mobile" was increasingly replaced by the abstract "mobility", which became a term used to refer to everything that was not "nobility". The *New General English Dictionary* (1740) contains coexisting definitions of the two meanings discussed thus far:

> Mobility is sometimes applied to the meaner or lower rank of vulgar people, or to an assembly that commits riots and disorders; and sometimes to the aptitude or facility of any body or thing to move; and in this sense it is applied to the earth by the modern astronomers.
> (Dyche, 1740, s.v.)

We do not have much data to tell us what happened to the word *mobility* during the English Civil War (1642–51), even if one cannot help but notice that, in the second half of the 17th century, the term had already appeared in such a profoundly negative context that it was even used to describe the somatic features of those who were the bearers of that characteristic: "The head rounde signifieth, mobilitie, vnstablenes, forgetfulnesse, smale discretion and lytle wysedome in the man" (Warde, 1562). Certainly, when the royalists called the Puritan members of the New Model Army *roundheads*, they were referring to their haircuts. Perhaps, however, their attention would not have been drawn to the shape of their heads had their view not already been shaped by a negative prejudice against the popular classes, whose psychological mobility was strong enough to even alter the shape of their skull.

For Hobbes (1650, F3v), instead, it was the environmental conditions that mattered, and it was the "mobilitie, blustering, and impuritie of the Air" that was breathed in urban districts that caused the "insincereness, inconstancie, and troublesom humour of those that dwell in populous Cities".[11]

From the 1690s onwards, the contracted form of "mobility" was preferred, a word that we still use today in some ways identical—although not entirely—to that of the late 1700s: "mob".

In the same year in which Dyche's vocabulary registered the use of "mobility" as an amphibious term between the sky and the slums of London and also indicated its use as a synonym for "riot", the Jacobite lawyer Roger North pinpointed the precise space-time coordinates for its contraction into "mob". This took place in 1670 at the meetings of the Green Ribbon Club, the headquarters of the Whig opposition to the restoration of the Stuart Monarchy after the death of Cromwell in 1658:

> I may note that the Rabble first changed their Title, and were called the Mob in the Assemblies of this Club. It was their Beast of Burden, and called first, *mobile vulgus*, but fell naturally into the Contraction of one Syllable, and ever since is become proper English.
> (North, 1740: 574)

From the point of view of a filo-absolutist political man such as North, the *mob* as a political subject would thus have emerged for the first time, not autonomously, but as a result of an elite's desire to establish its own "beast of burden", a pack mule capable of carrying all the weights that the Whigs were unwilling to carry themselves.

The great realist novelist Henry Fielding, another observer of the situation in England in the mid-1700s, confirms this impression:

> It may seem strange that none of our political Writers, in their learned Treatises on the English Constitution, should take Notice of any more than three Estates, namely, King, Lords, and Commons, all entirely passing by in Silence that very large and powerful Body which forms the fourth Estate in this Community, and have long been dignified and distinguished by the name of THE MOB.[12]

The fact that the "mob" was referred to as the "fourth estate" is fairly significant: first of all, because it is one of the first instances that an idea, destined for a bright future, appears in history; and second, and above all, because the concept of a "fourth estate" refers—exactly like that of "Third estate" during the French Revolution—to something indistinct, where the only point in common between those who are a part of it is that they do not belong to the other two, or three, estates.

Fielding's equivalence of "fourth estate" and "mob" enables us to understand how that large swathe of the population was perceived by the ruling classes: as something undifferentiated and thus ready to be used for their own ends. To be *mobilised* for their own ends, in fact. It is during this period that the word "mob" increasingly assumes a nuance that is no longer associated with movement in a psychological sense, but with movement in a political sense. Since the late 17th century, "mobility", "mobile" and their abbreviation "mob" have been used less and less to define people in their psychological inconstancy and increasingly to define the moment in which this inconstancy takes the form of direct political action in a revolt or a riot. Suffice it to say that Edward Chamberlayne's book on the state of England, which has about twenty editions starting from 1669, only records the effects of the "popular tumults (which are called the mobile)" from 1694 (Shoemaker, 2004: 111–12).

The Whig and Tory desire to take over the "mobile" and to channel it for their own ends is visible in a memorable way in a broadside ballad of 1682: *An Excellent New Hymne to the Mobile, exhorting them to Loyalty* (Figure 8.2).

The ballad finds its *raison d'être* in the Exclusion Bill, with which Parliament forbade the younger brother of Charles II—the Catholic James—from succeeding to the throne in favour of the eldest of his illegitimate sons, the Protestant Duke of Monmouth. It was precisely around the issue of whether or not to accept the Exclusion Bill that the schism developed between the Whigs and the Tories. The King's opposition to the provision led to the Rye House Plot (1683), in which some Whig Parliamentarians attempted to assassinate Charles II and his brother, James.

The ballad itself was presented as Whig propaganda text ("it's for liberty we plot / and for the publick good / by making bishops go to pot"), but the last line of every verse, which also gave the song its title, clarified that what had been written had to be interpreted "the clean contrary way". This competition of opposing political messages to guide "the mobile" would not have been clear to everyone if the true nature of the song—"a popish Libell"—had not been written immediately below the title.

Paradoxically, despite all attempts to transform it into a depersonalised force capable of being used to foment political unrest, the "mob" retained its own characteristics.

E.P. Thompson's essay on the moral economy of the English popular classes began precisely from the debate "against the loose employment of the term 'mob'" and the desire to restore its agency (Thompson, 1971: 76). Unlike earlier historiography, which had interpreted the 18th century food riots simply as "rebellions of the belly" unleashed by crowds without political agendas, Thompson demonstrated "the notion of legitimation" behind their behaviour. In his view, men and women in the crowd were informed by the belief of defending traditional customs and a coherent traditional view

Mobility: The word and the thing 133

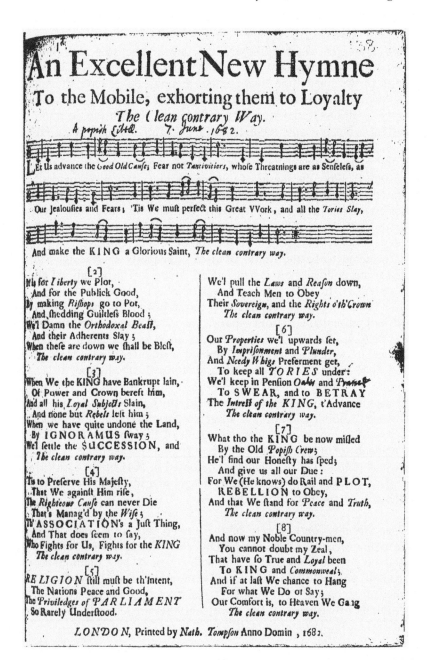

Figure 8.2 *An Excellent New Hymne to the Mobile, exhorting them to Loyalty*. Cover page. Courtesy of Huntington Library.

of social obligations and economic functions, which he called "the moral economy" (Thompson, 1971: 79).

As with all other classics, *The Moral Economy* can also be examined with new questions that may help address the issues raised here. Indeed, there is a wealth of documentation surrounding the point that I have attempted to make thus far, namely the growing ambiguity of the term "mob", which is no longer used just to describe the people responsible for the riots and their inconstancy, but the riots themselves. In 1757, for example, when Hannah Pain of Kettering complained to the judges that the baker was profiting from the price of bread, the baker "raised a mob upon her" (Thompson, 1971: 106). In 1766, the sheriff of Gloucestershire announced that "a Mobb was rais'd in these parts by the blowing of Horns & consisting entirely of the lowest of the people such as weavers, mecanicks, labourers, prentices" (Thompson, 1971: 110). The sheriff's respect for the rioters who behaved "civilly" demonstrates that, despite all the attempts to depoliticise it, the "mob" was considered to be the bearer of its own requests, increasingly difficult to control by political power and, indeed, holders of a potentially alternative sovereignty. In 1758, a pamphleteer from Bristol controversially called it "your law-giving mob", complaining to the justices of the peace that the people had prevented him from exporting his grain from the Severn and Wye valleys (Thompson, 1971: 95). Eight years later, the noblemen of Fareham in Hampshire were even warned to prepare themselves "for a Mob or Sivel war", which would "pull George from his throne" (Thompson, 1971: 127). The more the ruling classes tried to depersonalise the "mob", the more it recognised itself as an independent political entity.

The term "mobility", simply as a reference to the people, was not entirely abandoned in support of the concrete result of this popular fretfulness. We have evidence of it, particularly interesting given its late date, in the work *Portraits of Children of the Mobility,* composed in 1841 by the satirical journalist Percival Leigh, with drawings by the popular illustrator John Leech.

Who was the mobility for Leigh?

> The Mobility are a variety of the human race, otherwise designated, in polite society, as "The Lower Orders", "The Inferior Classes", "The Rabble", "The Populace", "The Vulgar" or "The Common People". Among political philosophers, and promulgators of Useful Knowledge, they are known as "The People", "The Many", "The Masses" and "The Millions". By persons of less refinement, they are termed "The Riff-raff" and "The Tag-rag-and-bobtail".
>
> (Leigh, 1841: 1)

Leech succeeded in satirising the nobility through the irony elicited in the reader by the narrator's excessively snobbish approach.

> The word Mobility is said to be derived from the Latin term Mobilis, fickle, or moveable; as Nobility is from Nobilis, noble. But what can be

more fickle than fashion, what more vulgar than constancy? The heads of society, too, are quite as moveable as its tails. The Nobility are continually in motion; moving in good company, moving in Parliament, moving about the world. If we are to take up the Mobility as vagrants, we must set down the Nobility as tourists; there are some real travellers among the Mobility, though most of their journeymen lead a sedentary life. If the former are moved by Punch and Shakespeare, the latter are equally so by Rubini and Bellini.

(Leigh, 1841: 2)

Here again we find, repeated in the mid-19th century, that link between mobility of bodies, thoughts and emotions that we have attempted to untangle for the early modern centuries. With great accuracy, the author even made reference to an earlier three-and-a-half-century-old obsession of Europe's ruling classes, that of the existence of a counter-society of vagabonds with their own rules, institutions and language, perpetually plotting to overthrow the established order: "we might describe its followers as probationers belonging to the Society of Mendicants; an order, it would seem, which Henry VIII could not entirely suppress" (Leigh, 1841: 14). The persistence of the belief in a counter-society of vagrants in the much later words of Leigh leads us to believe that it was not only the instability and psychological inconstancy, but also the physical mobility of the strata of the population that did not own property that could foment the class vision that lies behind the characterisation of the people as "mobility". As the most original scholar of this myth of anti-society villains has observed, "there is evidently a relationship between what Le Goff has defined '*mobilité des hommes du Moyen Age* [...] *extreme, deconcertant*' and the recurrent sense of general insecurity that gnaws at the medieval soul" (Camporesi, 1973: xxx).

However, there was another spectre haunting Europe in the 1840s, and this had nothing to do with the bands of vagabonds that troubled Henry VIII and Luther's dreams. Leigh informed his readers about this:

Our readers may, perhaps, have read of a set of people called Socialists, whose chief characteristic is a community of property and of almost everything else; and who, besides, live huddled together in colonies, and are not very scrupulous in their behaviour.

(Leigh, 1841: 12)

Four years later, Friedrich Engels' *The Condition of the Working Class in England* (1845) painted a picture of children of the mobility that contrasted with Leigh's amusing, but ultimately nauseating outlook. It was, in fact, immediately after the publication of *Portraits* that the term mobility, which had by now been definitively replaced by derivatives of the German *Proletariat*, shed its references to the lower social classes and assumed the meaning that we still attribute to it today.

At this same juncture, however, it also assumed a certain fluidity of its own. Perhaps inherited also from its use as a term for the energy that propels celestial bodies, the term's fluidity has certainly become the central aspect of its success.

In their *plaidoyer* for the application of the category of mobility in the human sciences, Merriman and Pearce (2017) trace an intellectual genealogy of its use by scholars in these fields. At the same time, this is also a somewhat impressionistic trajectory—little more than name-dropping from Lucretius to Julia Kristeva. Perhaps we should concentrate our focus on the first of the modern authors which Merriman and Pearce perceptively place at the origin of the union between mobility and humanities: Henri Bergson.

Winner of the Nobel prize for literature in 1928, and the first example of a "jet professor", Bergson was not only a pioneer of academic mobilities (Dervin, 2010), but he also played a significant role in the development of the concept of mobility in the academic sphere.

Above all, in his last book, La pensée et le mouvant, Bergson placed the reflection on mobility at the origin of his entire philosophical system:

> Ever since my university days, I had been aware that duration is measured by the trajectory of a body in motion and that mathematical time is a line; but, I had not yet observed that this operation contrasts radically with all other processes of measurement, for it is not carried out on an aspect or an effect representative of what one wishes to measure, but on something which excludes it. The line one measures is immobile, time is mobility. The line is made, it is complete; time is what is happening, and more than that, it is what causes everything to happen.
>
> (Bergson, 1934: 10)

Therefore,

> to pass from intellection to vision, from the relative to the absolute, is not a question of getting outside of time (we are already there); on the contrary, one must get back into duration and recapture reality in the very mobility which is its essence.
>
> (Bergson, 1934: 33)

There could easily be many more quotes, but the point underlined by Bergson is just one: "The essential object of society is to insert a certain fixity into universal mobility" (Bergson, 1934: 95).

If my reconstruction is correct, the concept of mobility as a fluid that permeates all of society, which is now endorsed by most exponents of mobility studies in the humanities, should be traced back to the equivalence between reality and mobility established by Bergson, at the level of both the natural and human sciences.[13]

The Anglophone reception of Bergson's collection of writings *La pensée et le mouvant* was particularly influential. Not only was this his last book, subsequently charged with the importance of a spiritual testament (Gontarski, 2011: 66), it was also translated into English as *The Creative Mind: An Introduction to Metaphysics*, in this way facilitating the equalisation of the themes it covers with the basic theme of Bergson's philosophy—*l'évolution créatrice*—while also giving them the form of an introduction to metaphysics, as reflected in the subtitle.

The Creative Mind or *La pensée et le mouvant*, however we wish to call it, was originally published in 1934 and translated into English in 1946, but contained lectures and conferences held between 1903 and 1923. Precisely because of its strangely delayed fortune, Bergson's work had the effect of reintroducing into the post-World War II years a point of view that dated back to a very different historical period, such as that immediately following the First World War. In France, his "philosophie de la mobilité" had already been sharply criticised, for instance by the philosopher Julien Benda who, in two books—(a) *Bergson et la philosophie de la mobilité* and (b) *Sur le succès du bergsonisme* (Benda, 1912 and 1914)—had highlighted the potentially irrational position of Bergson and the other *mobilistes*. According to them, thought no longer proceeded from a fixed stage A to a fixed stage B, but abandoned all fixity to instead embrace an "incessante mobilité" (Benda, 1912 and Grogin, 1978). In Benda's view, this was an incorrect way of dragging the results of the natural sciences, such as Einstein's special theory of relativity or Heisenberg's uncertainty principle, into the field of the social and human sciences.

Benda provided the same diagnosis in his most famous work, *La Trahison des Clercs* (1927), translated into English the following year as *The Betrayal of the Intellectuals*. As was observed at the time, Benda's condemnation of the intellectuals who were indeed betraying the eternal values of humanity and universal brotherhood in the name of contemporary political values (race, nation and class), was nothing more than a development of his positions on Bergson and Bergsonism.[14] This interpretation is certainly unilateral. However, it picks up an important point, that is, the tendency by Benda to see the Bergsonian "philosophie de la mobilité" invading, as a fluid, theories which were also politically and philosophically opposed to it, such as the dialectic materialism of Marx:

> Dialectical materialism also repudiates reason by the fact that it intends to conceive of change not as a succession of fixed, as well as infinitely close, positions, but as an "incessant mobility" that ignores all fixity; or even, to use its labels, as a pure "dynamism," unharmed by any "staticism." In this, too, although many deny it, it is a reprise of the Bergsonian thesis, which exalts the embrace of movement in itself, as opposed to a succession of fixed points, however close, which is in fact quite different. Now, such an attitude decrees the formal abjuration of reason, since it is proper of reason to immobilise the things it deals with, at least as long as it deals with them, while a pure becoming, which by its essence excludes

any identity with itself, can be the object of a mystical adhesion, but not of a rational activity.[15]

Emphasising whether Benda was right or wrong does not matter here—the links between Marxism and Bergsonism certainly cannot be reduced, if only for chronological reasons, to a simple filiation of the former to the latter. Benda's warning against applying the label of "mobility" to any phenomenon found in the natural sciences, however, can also apply to the human sciences. Today, we are not confronted with the scientific revolution of Heisenberg and Einstein, but the economic, social and cultural revolution brought about by globalisation and the processes of the more or less forced mobility of men, goods and ideas it has triggered. In order to understand these mobility-related phenomena, the researcher cannot depend on an immediate reflection between reality and his or her analysis, inserting every object of study both past and present into the field of the *mobility turn*. "The true image of the past flits by. The past can only be captured as an image that flashes up at the instant of its recognition, never to be seen again" (Benjamin, 1940: 390, slightly revised).

From this point of view, perhaps, what has been accomplished here—which is not a deconstruction, but a reconstruction of the category of mobility and of the social actors who have embodied it from time to time—may have value.

Notes

1. My thanks go to Tullio Viola and Rosa Salzberg for their criticisms, as well as to all the participants in the "Mobility and Humanities" project.
   Contrary to what the title implies, this study owes little to Foucault (1966) and much to Benveniste (1966: 249): "the 'meaning' of a linguistic form is defined by the totality of its uses, their distribution, and the types of associations therefrom. In the presence of identical morphemes with different meanings, one must ask oneself whether there is some use in which the two meanings converge. The answer is never given in advance. It can only be found after a careful study of all the contexts in which the form may appear".
2. "*Quid est inconstantia, levitate, mobilitate turpius*"?
3. "*Tanta mobilitate sese Numidae gerunt*".
4. "*Ut enim prudentia, sive astutia serpenti tribuitur, columbae simplicitas, lupo rapacitas, ita servo mobilitas*".
5. "*Mobilitate volgi expulsi*".
6. "*Quam vana aut levi aura mobile vulgus esset*"; "*Fluctu ... magis mobile vulgus*".
7. This defence of *mobilitas*—even if Machiavelli never used this term—had its origins in his vision of the relationship between man and nature. As he wrote to his friend Francesco Vettori on 31 January 1515, "Anybody who saw our letters, honoured friend, and saw their diversity, would wonder greatly, because he would suppose now that we were grave men, wholly concerned with important matters, and that into our breasts no thought could fall that did not have in itself honour and greatness. But then, turning the page, he would judge that we, the very same persons, were light-minded, inconstant, lascivious, concerned with empty things.

And this way of proceeding, if to some it may appear censurable, to me seems praiseworthy, because we are imitating Nature, who is variable; and he who imitates her cannot be rebuked" (Machiavelli, 1989: II, 961). As we shall see, this comparison between the sciences of what Machiavelli also calls "nature" and the human sciences in the name of the common mobility of their objects of study, will be a constant that would extend, through Goethe, as far as Bergson.

8 "*La mobilité des caracteres fait le fondement de l'Imprimerie*" (Diderot, D'Alembert, 1751).
9 "Locke's attitude towards mechanical philosophy can reasonably be described as positive, but it was significantly more cautious than those of his most eminent philosophical contemporaries in continental Europe" (Milton, 2001: 221). On this issue, see also Anstey (2011).
10 Hirschman (1991, 8) observed the same phenomenon for the opposite of revolution: "The couple 'action' and 'reaction' came into current usage as a result of Newton's third law of motion, which stated that 'to every Action there is always opposed an equal Reaction'. Having thus been singled out for distinction in the then outstandingly prestigious science of mechanics, the two concepts spread to other realms and were widely used in the analysis of society and history in the 18th century".
11 I concur with what Aradau wrote (2016) with regard to Cresswell's (2006) application of the category of mobility to the political philosophy of Hobbes: "The centrality of mobility for Hobbes (and Harvey), morphing into the centrality of mobility for modern citizens, risks diluting the constitutive role that Hobbes's absolutism played in his political theory". As can be seen from the above passage, Hobbes used the term within environmental determinism. From a semantic point of view, Cresswell's analysis (2006: 20) is very astute, albeit limited to dictionaries and to the English language.
12 Henry Fielding, *The Covent-Garden Journal*, 47, Sat., June 13 1752, quoted by Shoemaker, 2004: 12.
13 As is nearly always the case, Bergson was by no means the first to get there: Machiavelli and, later, as has been said, Goethe had already insisted on the common mobility of human creations and natural creations: "What has a structure is immediately transformed, and if we wish to gain a living insight (*Anschaun*) into nature, we too must remain mobile and malleable (*beweglich und bildsam*), following the example set by nature" (Goethe's words are quoted by Ginzburg, 2017: 351, my translation).
14 "However, the next book, *Sur le succes du bergsonisme*, is all-important here, for it contains, at the very least, the whole theme of the *Trahison*" (Niess, 1947: 3, n. 5).
15 I have chosen to translate this personally because the last English translation, that of Roger Kimball (2006), ignores the reference to the debate on *mobilité* between Benda and Bergson.

References

Anstey PR (2011) *John Locke and natural philosophy*. Oxford: Oxford University Press.
Aradau C (2016) Political grammars of mobility, security and subjectivity. *Mobilities*, 11(4): 564–574.

Benda J (1912) *Le bergsonisme ou une philosophie de la mobilité*. Paris: Mercure de France.
Benda J (1914) *Sur le succès du bergsonisme*. Paris: Mercure de France.
Benda J (1927) *The betrayal of the intellectuals*. Boston: Beacon Press, 1928.
Benda J (1945) De la mobilité de la pensée selon une philosophie contemporaine. *Revue de Métaphysique et de Morale* 50(3): 161–202.
Benigno F (2017) *Words in time: a plea for historical re-thinking*. London: Routledge.
Benjamin W (1940) On the concept of history (transl. Jephcott E). In: Eiland H, Jennings M (eds) *Selected Writings*, 4. Cambridge Mass: Harvard University Press, 2006, pp. 389–411.
Benveniste E (1966) Semantic problems in reconstruction. In: *Problems in general linguistics*. Miami: University of Miami Press, pp. 249–265.
Bergson (1934) *The creative mind: an introduction to metaphysics*. New York: Citadel Press, 1946 (original title *La pensée et le mouvant*).
Blackmore R (1712) *Creation. A philosophical poem demonstrating the existence and providence of a God in seven books*. London: Buckley.
Camporesi P (1973) *Il libro dei vagabondi*. Turin: Einaudi.
Cresswell T (2006) *On the move: mobility in the modern Western world*. London: Routledge.
Dervin F (2010) Bergson, précurseur des mobilités académiques contemporaines? *Les Cahiers de Framespa* (online).
Diderot D and D'Alembert JB (1751–) *Encyclopédie, ou dictionnaire raisonné des sciences, des arts et des métiers*. Paris: Le Breton., s.v. *imprimerie*.
Dyche T (1740) *A new general English dictionary*. London: Ware, 1740.
Febvre L (1929) Civilisation: evolution of a word and a group of ideas. In: Burke P (ed) *A new kind of history: from the writings of Febvre*. New York: Harper & Row, 1973, pp. 219–257.
Foucault M (1966) *Les mots et les choses. Une archéologie des sciences humaines*. Paris: Gallimard (English translation: *The order of things: an archaeology of the human sciences*. New York: Pantheon, 1970).
Funkenstein A (1986) *Theology and the scientific imagination: from the Middle Ages to the seventeenth century*. Princeton: Princeton University Press.
Ginzburg C (2017) *Storia notturna. Una decifrazione del sabba*. Milan: Adelphi.
Gontarski SE (2011) "What it is to have been": Bergson and Beckett on movement, multiplicity and representation. *Journal of Modern Literature* 34(2): 65–75.
Grogin RC (1978) Rationalists and anti-rationalists in pre-World War I France: the Bergson–Benda affair. *Historical Reflections / Réflexions Historiques* 5(2): 223–231.
Hawke M (1655) *The right of dominion, and property of liberty, whether natural, civil, or religious*, London: T.C.
Hirschman AO (1991) *The rhetoric of reaction: perversity, futility, jeopardy*. Cambridge Mass: Harvard University Press.
Hobbes T (1650) *Discourse upon Gondibert, an heroick poem written by Sr. William D'Avenant with an Answer to it by Mr. Hobbs*. Paris: Guillemot.
Leigh P (1841) *Portraits of children of the mobility, drawn from nature by J. Leech with memoirs and characteristic sketches*. London: Bentley.
Machiavelli N (1989) *The chief works and others*, ed. and trans. by A. H. Gilbert, 3 vols. Durham and London: Duke University Press.
Merriman P and Pearce L (2017) Mobility and the humanities. *Mobilities* 12(4): 493–508.

Milton JR (2001) Locke, medicine and the mechanical philosophy. *British Journal for the History of Philosophy* 9(2): 221–243.
Niess RJ (1947) Evolution of an idea: Julien Benda's "La trahison des clercs". *The French Review* 20(5): 383–392.
Nollet JA (1745) *Leçons de physique expérimentale*. Paris: Guerin.
North R (1740) *Examen: Or, an enquiry into the credit and veracity of a pretended complete history, shewing the perverse and wicked design of it.* London: Gyles.
Rey A (1989) *Révolution: historie d'un mot*. Paris: Gallimard.
Salmerón A (1604) *Commentariorum in epistolas B. Pauli tomus secundus*. Cologne: Hierat.
Shoemaker R (2004) *The London mob: violence and disorder in 18th century England*. London: Bloomsbury.
Thompson EP (1971) The moral economy of the English crowd in the 18th century. *Past & Present* 50(1): 76–13.
Warde W (1562) *The most excellent, profitable, and pleasant booke of the famous doctour and expert astrologien Arcandain or Aleandrin [...] with an addition of phisiognomie very delectable to reade, now newly tourned out of French into our vulgar tonge by Williamd Warde*. London: Rowbothum.

9 Tyrannical mobility, dictatorial mobility

Francesca Cavaggioni, Luca Fezzi and Flavio Raviola[1]

Very recent studies have softened the originality of the historical significance of archaic Greek tyranny, interpreting it as a simple variant of the physiological and essentially constant presence of monarchical or apical figures of power who were at the helm of Hellenic cities since the 8th century BCE. Similarly, the 'classical' Roman dictatorship has recently been the object of a deep reassessment, tending to reduce it to a supplementary and/or additional instrument with respect to the ordinary magistracies, not conceived as an *extraordinarium auxilium* until its last applications at the time of the dramatic confrontation with Hannibal. However, if we read the ancient texts from a purely phenomenic point of view, in relation to tyranny, we always find the persistent underlining of the strong impact on the *poleis* from individuals who, whatever their name or the qualification they bear, exhibit a power felt to be excessive and undue by the rest of the community; in relation to dictatorship, we always find the capacity of an equally strong power, even if programmatically limited in time, to manage situations of serious crisis (or perceived or envisaged as such). In these cases, the words *tyrannos* and *dictator* or the 'de facto' tyrant and dictator continue to possess specific evidence and substantial disruptiveness and lend themselves to being studied as historical objects in various ways pertaining to the category of mobility. More specifically, the final history of the dictatorship in Rome with Sulla and Caesar constitutes a case of singularly creative renewal of this institution, and yet at the same time exhausts its possibilities of adapting or reconciling itself, in other words, of *moving* with its mutations within the republican rules of the Roman 'city-state'.

9.1 The case of archaic Greek tyranny

9.1.1 The mobility of tyranny as a historical phenomenon

The idea of tyranny moves and travels with the very name of *tyrannos*. The idea originated in a non-Greek environment and then *moved* to a Greek context. It is well known that the word is not Hellenic in origin, but derives from Asia Minor. The first Greek author to mention it, at least among the

DOI: 10.4324/9781003278665-13

remaining literary sources, is Archilochus (fr. 19 West; see also fr. 23 West), who implicitly attributes *tyrannis*, already using the abstract term, to Gyges, the great king of Lydia, who appears to represent a particularly concentrated paradigm of political, military and territorial authority. For the poet, the tyranny held by Gyges is to be considered a desirable condition of power within a Hellenic sphere, even if the poet does not seem to be wanting it for himself, nor does he envy it in those who might exercise it. Archilochus knows that other Greeks might aspire to obtain it and exercise it in their *poleis*. At the same time, the paradigm is still Oriental: the reference is to Gyges.

With Archilochus, the idea of tyranny, therefore, moves metaphorically from Asia to Greece. The foreign model of the Lydian tyrant is perceived as similar to that of some Greek *monarchoi*, who were dominating their *poleis*.

For the identification of a clear example of mobility of the idea of tyranny in the Greek world, the following considerations can be made. Ever since the Homeric tradition, the Greek language has had a customary and specific term to indicate rulership or, if one prefers, the role of community leader: *basileus*, in the singular, identifies with clarity and immediacy the figure of the 'leader', who is normally a role inherited from father to son. The fact that at a certain point (at the time of Archilochus, or shortly before, in any case, in the middle of the 7th century BCE) a new word was introduced to refer to the command or 'reign' of an individual over the *polis* means that while the word *basileus* continued to translate the notion of an essentially traditional and consensual hereditary monarchy, it might have failed to render other different connotations, which were now required either by new developments in the way of being and presentation of that same monarchy, or by the introduction of a drastically new type of leading figure or ruler. The latter undoubtedly arose for reasons and developments internal to city societies and the structures and dynamics concerning their nobility, but it was clearly inspired directly by the great micro-Asiatic dynasties.

The novelty in both cases could be objective, in fact, but also a product of a polemical perception on the part of political adversaries within a *polis*. For example, Alcaeus (fr. 348 Voigt) at around 600 BCE, in Mytilene, on the island of Lesbos, bitterly remarks that 'The Mytilenians have made Pittacus a tyrant!'. Actually, most ancient authors agree in presenting this new type of leading figure, the *tyrannos*, and its monarchical rule as a novelty. The exercise of power is now more violent and arbitrary than the community could traditionally accept. This is thus the result of a movement: whether the movement from East to West was merely that of a *word*, an analogical image, or whether it was in some way that of the *thing* itself, i.e. the transfer of the institutional model of tyranny, it developed in Greece by imitation of a role and a style of power firmly established and rooted in Asia Minor.

For the purpose of this paper, I will limit myself in analysing, in what follows, the movement of the idea of tyranny in space and time in continental Greece. A well-established tradition sees the tyranny of Corinth with the family of the Cypselids preceding (with a chronological range of 657–584

BCE) those of Sicyon with the Orthagorids (c. 640–540), and Megara with Theagenes (c. 630).

It is worth noting the spatial advance of the tyrannical regime on a regional scale, with the Isthmus of Corinth as its starting point, as well as its development in a matter of years. It is also worth noting that Sicyon and Megara border on Corinth, on opposite sides of the Isthmus. Theagenes is also the father-in-law of an unsuccessful Athenian tyrant, Cylon, who around 630, or immediately before, tried and failed to seize power because of the rapid reaction of the hoplitic community, the entire Athenian army, which blocked him and all his men on the Acropolis. Significantly, in Thucydides' account (1.126.2-11), there is explicit complicity in the coup on the part of his father-in-law, Theagenes, who supplies mercenaries to his son-in-law Cylon. We see here the attempted reproduction of a tyranny, almost by duplication or a form of gemmation.

These examples clearly show that along the Isthmus route and at the entrance to the Peloponnese, a number of great aristocratic families or individuals with a high aristocratic profile seem to have gradually implemented a shared plan to seize power at home. While in the case of Theagenes and Cylon a conscious and planned cooperation is evident, in the case of Sicyon and Megara one must at least admit a conscious imitation, induced by the close spatial proximity of the tyrannical initiative of Cypselus in Corinth. In any case, it is important to note here the transmission of a form of lordship via territorial propagation, with a rather obvious geographical coherence. This, I suggest, testifies to a capacity for mobility and diffusion that appears inherent to the tyrannical model and the styles of power that this model conveys.

In the decades after the events discussed, the tyranny was finally established in Athens with Pisistratus. It was imposed (perhaps in 546) with the help of many allies, including Lygdamis, a mercenary commander from the island of Naxos who supplied armed manpower to the Pisistratids. Once firmly established in power, Pisistratus, taking advantage of the naval force that Athens had at its disposal at the time, installed Lygdamis as tyrant in Naxos (Herodotus 1.61.4; 1.64.1-2): again, a form of gemmation, an almost genetic reproduction of a tyranny on the basis of geographical or at least strategic proximity (between Athens and Naxos, the sea is a fast and natural communication route).

9.1.2 *Tyranny as a mobility factor*

Up to this point, we have discussed tyranny as a model or practice of power that spreads through space as well as time. However, it is possible to consider tyranny also as something that moves, and sets in motion, either elements within the *polis* or the whole *polis* itself.

If one considers the home policy of the tyrannies and its effects, one gets the impression that these were a factor of social mobility within the cities they ruled. The tyrant seems to have been a catalyst or accelerator of certain phenomena of economic and, indeed, social ascent of large and different civic groups from both the city itself and the countryside. This seems directly proportional to the tyranny's impact within, and on, the community, and decisive for the present and future developments of the community itself.

Archaic tyrannies were established, persisted and returned to *poleis* in which land ownership and distribution were usually very unbalanced, in the sense that large sections of the population were substantially deprived of it. On the other hand, the literary tradition from the 5th century onwards (Herodotus *in primis*) attests to tyrants and tyrannies, precisely in the area of the Isthmus of Corinth, who, especially in the 7th century BCE, had been capable of causing the violent removal of agricultural property at the expense of the aristocracy: for example, Herodotus says of Cypselus that 'he exiled many of the Corinthians, deprived them of much of their wealth but, even more importantly, he deprived them of their lives' (5.92.ε2).

We never have any *explicit* mention, either in the very few contemporary texts or in later ones, of the possibility that the land had been redistributed by some tyrants to the *demos*, or at least to the poorer section of it. But Solon's words allow us to understand that such an action might have taken place sometimes and somewhere. I am referring in particular to a passage from the *Athenaion politeia* of the Aristotelian school (*Ath. pol.* 12.3): in justifying his actions (approximately between 600 and 590) as arbiter, legislator and rebalancer of a situation of very serious social and economic degradation in Athens at the end of the 7th century, he admits that his reforms displeased everyone, both the rich and the noble, and the people, *demos*, i.e. the poor or *kakoi*, and in particular he recalls that the *kakoi* came insistently to beg him to assume tyrannical power; but Solon had refused because, he said, 'I do not like to do something with the violence of tyranny (*biai tyrannidos*), nor give an equal share of the homeland's fat land to the bad and the good' (fr. 34 West, ll. 7-8; see also fr. 32 West), in other words to the *kakoi* and the *esthloi*, the poor and the nobles, respectively. This last point is significant: in Solon, the notion of tyrannical power is automatically connected to the idea of redistribution of land to the poor, achieved through *bia*, 'violence', that is 'inherent in', or 'typical of tyranny', as the Greek literally reads the abstract genitive *tyrannidos*. Interestingly, this time we do not depend on a classical or later source, but on an author who lived and worked at the turn of the 7th and 6th centuries, which is the period of the great tyrannies in Greece that developed not far from Athens, such as those of Periander in Corinth and Cleisthenes in Sicyon.

The Solonian text thus assumes considerable importance as it possibly informs us also on the historical authenticity of revolutionary practices implemented outside of Athens by certain tyrannies, at least the most dynamic ones, as early as the second half or the last decades of the 7th century. It allows us to reflect on the impact that tyrants' actions had on those who suffered and those who benefited from them; actions, it must be understood, centred on agrarian redistributions in favour of the *kakoi* and on their transformation into small landowners.

My following argument will be exclusively deductive. I will limit myself to reflect on the case of Athens because it is sufficiently paradigmatic.

Combined data from literary and epigraphic sources dated to the 5th and 4th centuries indicate that most members of the society of isonomic and democratic Athens (a period that covers nearly 190 years) were landowners. There was a considerable spread of medium-sized landed property and a widespread presence of small, particularly fragmented landed property.

And yet in the *Athenaion politeia* we are informed that Solon was asked to intervene by the *demos* because the vast majority of it did not possess land and was forced to go into debt and to work in the fields of the rich (*Ath. pol.* 2; 4.5-5.2), as well as was unable to pay the rent or usufruct agreed upon on the concessions of the landowners with the products of their own harvest. Solon himself confirms this, when he stresses, as we have seen in the passage above, that in the Athens of his time there was a hunger for land and the *kakoi* expected that his reforms would result in an agrarian distribution in their favour. Solon then clearly states that he had not touched the properties of the rich and that, indeed, this had not even crossed his mind (also fr. 34 West, ll. 7-8).

On the other hand, when Athens' very long democratic experience began in 510, it is certain that the isonomic reform of Cleisthenes did not deprive the aristocracy or the newly rich from the tyrannical period of their properties.

Yet, already at the outset of the Athenian democratic period, agrarian property was owned by many Athenians and was distributed even at the level of small allotments. So, who gave this land to so many Athenians? My impression is that the tyranny, that is, the 'reign' of Pisistratus and his son Hippias, a very strong and lasting monocratic experience (from 561, and permanently from 546 to 511), capable of deeply affecting the fabric of Athenian society, was decisive in rebalancing the land ownership situation in Athens. Although no ancient text tells us that Pisistratus and Hippias distributed land to the *kakoi*, this possibility can be at least postulated.

9.1.3 Conclusion

The Athenian case study is a fitting example of the ability of tyranny to produce social and economic ascendancy, to set the entire society of the *polis* in motion and make it more dynamic than it was before. We would come to similar conclusions if we considered other elements such as productive and mercantile activities, monumental and public buildings, and foreign policy, all areas in which tyrants, or some tyrants, seem to have played a truly propulsive and mobilising role.

Tyranny, therefore, certainly refers to a power that is violent, irregular, illegitimate and difficult to accept in the long term in the context of 'republican' community customs and traditions. The same power, however, as

I argued in this paper, is also capable of imprinting strong stimuli for changes on the entire *polis* system. It is precisely for these aspects that the figure of the *tyrannos* came to be perceived within the collective consciousness as a paradigm of effective and efficient civic government.

And it is precisely the distinguishing characteristics of mobility and dynamism of this phenomenon that may have favoured the consolidation of traditions concerning the most ancient Hellenic tyrannies, ensuring their survival in the great shipwreck of the memory of archaic Greece.

9.2 The case of early and mid-republican Rome

In ancient accounts, the emerging picture of the Roman dictatorship is of an 'immobilising' office, a magistracy that paralyses both fellow citizens and enemies with fear and blocks any unnecessary activity in the supreme effort to save the *res publica*. Even so, the institution can be analysed under the lens of mobility too. Unfortunately, it is impossible here to deal with the subject exhaustively: so we will limit ourselves to identifying some of its most representative aspects.

9.2.1 Onomastic mobility

Introduced in Rome in 501 or 498 BCE (Liv. 2.18; Dion. Hal. 5.73), the dictatorship shows signs of some mobility even from its earliest stages, marked by a change of title. According to scanty passages from Cicero, Varro, Longus and Festus, the original name of the dictator was *magister populi*, and he only later assumed the title of *dictator* (spec. Cic. *Rep.* 1.63; *Leg.* 3.3.9; Varr. *LL* 5.82; 6.61; Sen. *Ep.*108; Fest. p. 216 L.). It is a matter for discussion how, when and why this passage took place: the sources, in fact, allude cursorily to the two titles and offer different etymological explanations, one emphasizing the dictator's authority (being built on the comparative *magis*, 'more') and the other the procedure of appointment ('the one who is named', that is, appointed by a consul rather than elected). However that may be, there is an undeniable mobility of the word. And such a mobility can only imply a mobility in Roman perceptions of the office: whether a different emphasis of some specific feature (either of the authoritative dimension, or of the very method of appointment, as already observed), or rather, different institutions.

In fact, it is well known that these data prompted some scholars to ascribe to the dictatorship a special role in the passage from monarchy to republic. According to their view, the consulship—an annual collegiate magistracy of two equal members—cannot be advised all at once and out of nothing; there must have been an intermediate stage, in which the king was replaced by a single annual magistrate (perhaps together with a junior colleague or colleagues). The dictatorship, or some prototype of it, so it was held, originally represented this link; and only later, with the creation of the consulship, did it become extraordinary, retained only for use in emergencies.

9.2.2 Mobility of models, mobility of readings

Similar problems arise when investigating the possible antecedents of dictatorship. Within a tradition focused on Rome, only Dionysius (5.73-74) is concerned with the question, proposing two opposing hypotheses. For him, the Romans took the dictatorial power from the Greeks, and more precisely from the office of the *esimneti*, described by Theophrastus as 'elective tyrants': they were chosen by the *poleis*, not continuously, but when needed, as often and for as long a time as seemed convenient, especially in times of political unrest, just as in the case of the aforementioned Pittacus. In the same passage, however, Dionysius admits that Licinius Macer, a historian of the Sullan age, referred instead to Alba Longa, the metropolis of Rome; according to Licinius, the inspiration came from the Albans, because they firstly replaced their extinct royal line with annual magistrates, vested with the same powers of the kings, and called them dictators.

The dictatorship as a product (or name) in movement is thus flanked by the idea of a dictatorship as the product of a spatial and cultural movement: that is, at the roots of the office there is a shift—to Rome from outside—of a kind of power, which can evidently be transferred and reproduced elsewhere. The input, indeed, is variably identified, spatially (Greek world v. Latin world) and legally (extraordinary office, connected to the resolution of a conflict v. regular annual office); and it is variably understood and motivated. Rejecting the Licinian thesis by saying that he is not interested in 'where the Romans took the name from', the Halicarnassian seems, in fact, to circumscribe the weight of the Alban precedent to the onomastic level. As for the magistracy comprehended under that name, he seems instead to perceive it as an 'example of authority' that can be reproduced within *any* magisterial system: it responds, so Dionysius claims, to a physiological necessity of such form of government, inevitably subject to corruption and, therefore, sometimes induced to temporarily restore tyrannical powers in order to curb it (5.74.1-4).

A mobility of readings and interpretations, drawing different images of dictatorship, thus overlaps a mobility of names and models. On the other hand, the available sources are no older than the 2nd century BCE, and the bulk of it is at least a century later. The knowledge they had about the archaic dictatorship was for the most part inadequate and lacking. Besides the gaps of information, moreover, every author had his own agenda, and revisited the data for his personal goals. As regarding Dionysius, for example, it is clear that, referring to the *esimneti*, he wanted to claim a privileged relationship with the Greek world for Rome, a leitmotiv of his reconstruction of the archaic history of the *Urbs*, intended to counter the anti-Roman prejudices then circulating in the Greek and Greek-speaking world (1.4).

Besides the question of ancestry, when we consider how the ancient historians portray and explain the inception of the office, widely varying assessments emerge again. While all the sources are consistent in presenting the political innovation as a response to a crisis, the nature of the crisis, the real purpose, and the powers of the new magistrate are variably defined. Where Livy (2.18) and others (Cic. *Rep.* 1.63; Pomp. *Dig.* 1.2.2.18; Eutr. 1.12.1; Oros. 2.5.4; Ioann. Ant. *frg.* 80.1 R.; cfr. Plb. 3.87.7-9) refer to serious military threats, thus assigning primarily military character to the dictator, Dionysius emphasises the conflicts within the city, the need to impose obedience on the commons, excluded from power and wealth and reluctant to participate in military service. Thus, he describes the dictatorship as an elite's solution to circumvent the citizens' right of appeal and so crash popular agitation: namely, as a domestic repressive means (5.70; cfr. Cic. *Leg.* 3.3.9; Lyd. *Magg.* 1.36; Zon. 7.13).

Similarly, in an attempt to explain the unusual, not to say unique, power held by the dictator—a power 'greater' than that of regular magistrates—the ancient authors stress different features. They in turn emphasise his unaccountability, the absence of collegiality, the repressive power and the exemption from the constraints that normally delimit magisterial action. In this vein, the *novum genus imperii*, as Cicero defines it (*Rep.* 2.56), is ambiguously classified, and sometimes it is associated with royal power (Ioann. Ant. *frg.* 80.1 R.; Zon. 7.13-14), or with tyranny (Dion. Hal. 5.70.2 and *passim*; Ioann. Ant. *frg.* 80.1 R.), when not related to the affirmation of autocratic power by Caesar and later Augustus (Eutr. 1.12.1; Ioann. Ant. *frg.* 80.1 R.; Zon. 7.13-14), or even assimilated, in Eutropius (1.12.1), to the *imperii potestas* of the late 4th century CE.

9.2.3 Quantitative mobility

Beyond the beginning, signs of mobility also appear in the application of dictatorship over the centuries. In fact, despite being an integral component of the Republican system, frequently resorted to, the magistracy shows a desultory rhythm of employment, more irregular than the extraordinary character would imply. Regardless, periods of frequent recourse (as in the second half of the 4th century or at the time of the Second Punic War, 218–201) alternate with periods of rarefaction (as in the remaining 3rd century) or oblivion of the office (in the 120 years between the end of the Hannibalic war and Sulla's rise).

9.2.4 Mobility of functions and duties

The functions assigned to dictators are no less varied. In most cases the extraordinary magistrates were appointed to perform a military task and, to a lesser extent, to deal with domestic unrest. From 363 onwards, anyway, dictators are also entrusted with minor tasks of a different nature: such as holding elections or performing religious duties, not to say other tasks, attested only once in the sources.

The needs prompting the appointment of a dictator are also far from being uniform. In most cases, the dictatorships seem to be the natural response to a serious crisis, to a military, domestic or religious emergency, such as to jeopardise the very survival of the *civitas*. Nonetheless, in some instances—particularly highlighted by recent scholarship and concentrated above all in the second half of the 4th century, when dictatorships were most frequent—the appointment seems to have functioned as a supplementary or additional instrument, in order to carry out more or less routine tasks, when the regular magistrates were otherwise engaged.

9.2.5 Mobility in time and space

Investigating further developments, such as the evolution of dictatorial powers over time, would go beyond the limits conceded here. At any rate, the issue of spatial mobility deserves a mention at the very least. As with the *flamen Dialis*, the priest responsible for the cult of Jupiter, so too the dictator appears anchored to a space. He had to be appointed on Roman territory (or, at least, within a Roman camp); and for a long period he operated within a circumscribed perimeter, restricted to the bounds of Italy (Liv. 27.5.15). Admittedly, a change in the rule is recorded, though only at the middle of the 3rd century: in 249 BCE, A. Atilius Caiatinus, named dictator after a heavy defeat, first led an army outside of Italy (Liv. *Per.* 19.3). It is very difficult, however, to evaluate this turning point: following a military defeat, a leadership crisis (not without judicial consequences), a scandalous appointment of a former dictator, forced to resign, the innovation was, perhaps, of little moment and much debated (Liv. *Per.* 19.2; Suet. *Tib.* 2.2).

9.2.6 Mobility as a result of dictatorial action

As well as being a product of mobility, the dictator is also, like the tyrant, a factor of mobility. Compared to the Greek example, however, this dimension does not leap to the fore, nor does it take on the same disruptive features. At least in its canonical portrait, the Roman dictatorship is the magistracy of the *status quo*; it is not understood as a means of changing, but rather as a *remedium* to safeguard and/or re-establish the pre-existing structures.

Paradigmatic examples are the stories of Sp. Cassius, Sp. Maelius and Manlius Capitolinus. In the ancient accounts, they attempt to favour the underprivileged part of the population by agrarian and wheat distributions and the partial remission of debts—measures that heralded social and economic mobility (not without political repercussions) in a city burdened by great inequalities. In doing so, they are traditionally associated with the idea of personal power, not without tyrannical overtones: nonetheless, they are not dictators. Rather, at least according to the mainline tradition (not without variants), they are stopped by dictators, Maelius by Cincinnatus, at the hands of his all-too-zealous *magister equitum*, Capitolinus by Cornelius Cossus (Liv. 4.13-15; 6.11, 14-16).

That said, there is also the dictator Valerius, who, in 494, after a victorious military campaign, tried to solve the problem of indebted people, though unsuccessfully (Liv. 2.31.7-11).

Tyrannical mobility, dictatorial mobility 151

In the decades following the so-called Licinio-Sextian laws—which, in 367, gave plebeian access to consulship and marked a decisive turning point in the struggle of the orders—many dictators, in various ways, intervened in the political sphere. In the middle of the 4th century, for example, some dictators, vested with military or electoral functions, worked to bring the consulship back into the hands of the patricians, influencing in some way the course of the elections (Liv. 7.21.1-2; 22.1 and 10-11; 24.10-11). Some decades later, on the contrary, Publilius Philo, while dictator in 339, passed three laws most favourable to the plebs and disadvantageous to the nobility, that represented an important landmark in the long struggle for plebeian equality (Liv. 8.12.12-17). Again, in 314, another extraordinary magistrate, C. Maenius, was charged to investigate anti-Roman sentiment in Campania and then electoral conspiracies in Rome, but was in his turn accused of corruption by the conservative elite (Liv. 9.26.5-22).

These episodes are difficult to evaluate due to a revised and updated tradition. From these stories, however, emerges a dictatorship capable of 'setting in motion' the structures of the *res publica*, redesigning the geography of the group in power, amid a political society still in formation, in which a new *élite* based on census was being painstakingly constituted and defined. And, perhaps, this very possibility of having an impact, which the dictatorship sometimes lays claim to, is not the least of the many reasons that lead, shortly afterwards, to reducing its adoption, confining it to limited and, therefore, more controllable tasks, until the Hannibal catastrophe reopens the game.

9.2.7 Mobility as a connotative feature of dictatorship

From the foregoing discussion, we derive a multifarious picture. This picture already baffled the ancients, so much so as to lead Dionysius (5.77) to wonder why the Romans had long been ignorant of the tyrannical nature of dictatorship, revealed only by Sulla. And Dionysius' astonishment is echoed by modern historians, who often tend to treat the dictatorship as an unusual office, antithetical to the Roman values; or to isolate some of its components in search of its most authentic and original profile.

On the contrary, discrepancies apparently affecting the office are indeed an inherent part of the office itself. This is the best way to explain them, as the result of the institution's intrinsic dynamism.

Within a constantly evolving Republic (so much so as to be nowadays interpreted as a sequence of distinct *res publicae*), the dictatorship was not static and was responsive to changes in the political system. On the other hand, being extraordinary and linked to the performance of a particular task, beyond any other office it was marked by temporariness and contingency. Thus, it changed significantly over time, shifted in character, adapted to new needs, was implemented and vested with new meanings. We can therefore identify mobility as a connotative and distinctive feature of the dictatorship: only in this way is it possible to grasp the essence of an institution that, established a hundred times between the end of the 6th and the 3rd century BCE, represented for many men the highest *honos* of their career.

9.3 The case of the late republican dictatorship

A traditional anchor, the dictatorship was unable to save the *res publica* vessel from being sucked into the vortex of events. Indeed, closer examination reveals that its very weight, which had become ungovernable due to the acceleration, had contributed to drive the hull to the very place where it should not have gone.

How was this possible? Firstly, through a transformation, a 'distortion' of the institution, which in this period ended up taking on a disturbing negative aspect, an effect that Dionysius of Halicarnassus (5.77.4) attributes to the example of Lucius Cornelius Sulla, who, almost at the end of 82 BCE, revived the institution after 120 years. There had probably been a debate going back to 129 BCE, the object of which was, after the instability caused by the assassination of Tiberius Sempronius Gracchus, the conferring of a dictatorship on Publius Cornelius Scipio Aemilianus. In any case, Sulla's moment was a central one in the history of the dictatorship, and it played a decisive role in the development of its image. The figure of Sulla, as well as this pivotal moment in political history, has been the object of several interpretations, and a significant role was played by the subsequent propaganda.

Gaius Julius Caesar who, in December 49 BCE, was to take over the office again, thirty years after Sulla's death, did not understand the reasons for his 'predecessor's' abdication (Svet. *Iul.* 77.2). In the meantime, between 54 and 52 BCE, there had been a debate on whether to give the dictatorship to Gnaeus Pompeius Magnus, which ended in a deadlock due to too much fear of the institution. Nevertheless, Caesar managed to force the issue, making the dictatorship assume its broadest boundaries ever, both in time and space.

This was the final transformation of an already mobile institution which, under Sulla and Caesar, became even more mobile and, in turn, a disturbing vehicle of mobility, with ultimately lethal results.

9.3.1 Mobility in 'models'

When an institution is created to 'freeze' particularly mobile features, it must necessarily adapt to them; its various repropositions, even intuitively, must therefore differ from each other. In the case of Sulla, there were already great specificities: in the mode of appointment, which passed through a *lex publica* and an *interrex*, and, as we shall see more clearly later, in the duration and objectives of the dictatorship (both of which are the subject of debate but, in any case, exceeding previous practice). In this regard, it is sufficient to note the impression that Sulla's measures were conceived as those of a 'founder' (in accordance with illustrious 'models', such as Solon and Romulus). For Caesar, the 'model' was that of his ancient political rival, Sulla; even his first appointment did not conform to the practice because it took place in his absence via a *lex publica* and pronounced by a praetor (while the two 'legitimate' consuls had fled to Thessalonica); the outcome of this and many other manipulations, as we shall see, was that of a dictatorship by then devoid of all limits in space, time and objectives.

9.3.2 Mobility in judgments

Two such central, relatively close and necessarily connected events—also in ancient political theory and propaganda—constitute a single problematic nucleus (even if, due to the breadth of material, they are generally the subject of separate critical reflections in the modern age). However, the discussion could be taken back even further: both events also influenced the perception (and tradition) of previous dictatorships. As far as Sulla is concerned, tradition is hostile to him; modern criticism, generally maintaining a tyrannical view of his power, has split between a 'monarchical' view—already held by Appian (*BC* 1,463)—and an 'aristocratic' one, the latter compatible with the exhumation of ancient emergent dictatorships. For the *popularis* Caesar, on the other hand, more flattering judgments were not lacking, especially in modern criticism. If, of course, all this is linked with great problematicity to the concept of 'Caesarism', the attempts to revive—not only theoretically—the ancient dictatorial 'models' seem to have almost regularly favoured those of earlier eras.

9.3.3 Mobility in purpose

In both cases, the dictatorships had very broad objectives. In Sulla's, there were the missions of writing laws and of consolidating the *res publica*, never attested before (*legibus scribundis et rei publicae constituendae causa*, even if the latter could be an explanation of the more generic *rei gerundae causa*). The impression—obtainable from Appian (*BC* 1,465-470)—is that his measures are organised like those of a 'founder': choice of magistrates, legislation on the subject, appointment of the senate, reconstitution of the people, and colonisation of *terra Italia*. These elements are just as present in Caesar's case, although there has been much debate as to whether the dictatorships following his first one were *rei publicae constituendae* or *rei gerundae causa*.

9.3.4 Temporal mobility

The dictatorship's duration increased from six months—considered, with very few exceptions, to be the traditional limit—to a year and more under Sulla (who also abdicated spontaneously). Caesar, finally, deprived the dictatorship of any limit in temporal extension. In the case of Sulla, a particularly authoritative voice of ancient historiography maintains that it was conceived as indefinite (Appian, *BC* 1,461), while critics—who, with one exception

(Hinard, 1999), consider it much longer than six months—are unable to reconstruct its actual duration, between the appointment (probably dating back to December 82) and the abdication (generally placed between the end of 81 and the summer of 79). On the other hand, Caesar's five dictatorships went in the direction of broadening the institution's time horizon. When he was still in Spain, in the midst of the civil war, he learned that he had been appointed dictator for the first time, a position he held for only eleven days, in Rome, in December 49, to preside over the elections of the higher magistrates (while most of the senate and both 'legitimate' consuls were in Thessalonica); in September–November 48—when he was in Egypt—he was appointed dictator for one year (to rewrite the laws and, perhaps, to reorganise the *res publica*, as had already been done by Sulla); in April 46, when he was still in Africa, he was offered an annual dictatorship for ten consecutive years; in 45, when he was already on his way to Spain, the office was renewed as a fourth dictatorship; in January or February 44, finally—in a decisive move—Caesar was appointed dictator for life. Sulla's dictatorship, despite its destabilising effects, could be considered a parenthesis, whereas Caesar's could not.

9.3.5 Spatial mobility

Sulla seemed to 'freeze' space, enlarging it. This is true both for the right to enlarge the *pomerium*—the sacred perimeter delimiting the *Urbs*—and for the definitive settlement of the northern border of *terra Italia* at the Arno–Rubicon line, within which he forbade the entry of armies in arms without senatorial consent (a spatiality that was later broken by Caesar, in the early days of 49 BCE, with his well-known gesture of disobedience). In Caesar's case, on the other hand, the dictatorship exited with him from *terra Italia*, where it had previously been almost constantly confined. His appointment to the first three dictatorships came while he was still in Spain, in Egypt (and this time he held office without returning to Rome), and again in Africa. However, it was Caesar himself, during his fourth dictatorship, who brought the office out of *terra Italia*; the question of the fifth dictatorship is different, linked to a series of other problems, including the imminent expedition against the Parthians. As dictator, Caesar also produced important spatial changes, such as the organisation of *Africa nova* in the form of a *provincia* (46 BCE) or changes in *status*, such as the granting of Roman citizenship to Cisalpine (49 BCE) and *ius Latii* to Sicily (46 BCE), not to mention, of course, his extensive building activity in the *Urbs*, much more ambitious than that of Sulla.

9.3.6 Mobility as a result

Among the aims of both the *popularis* Caesar and the 'reactionary' Sulla was the creation of a new institutional system and a new ruling class, which would inevitably increase social mobility, at least in the immediate future. This for Sulla was achieved by reforming the *cursus honorum*, some magistracies, the priestly colleges (albeit in the restrictive sense of co-optation) and the senate, devising for the latter a system of co-optation of former magistrates that should have been self-sustaining (thanks to a broader point of departure and a supposed suppression of censorship). A particular mobility was that of the proscribed, the Roman citizens outlawed by decree, who ended up fleeing to the entire Mediterranean basin, and that of the colonists, the loyal veterans who were the object of allocations of lands that were often expropriated. The interruption of the *frumentationes*—which took place only in Rome— finally reduced the mobility of citizens from the *terra Italia* to Rome. Caesar followed Sulla's example, albeit with a *popularis* twist: he did so by further increasing the number of magistrates and senators, by recalling exiles, by reintegrating the children of proscribed Sullans, by allocating land to veterans and colonists, and by reducing the number of beneficiaries of *frumentationes* that had been reintroduced in the meantime (although balanced by various measures aimed at improving the conditions of the urban plebs).

9.3.7 The end of the dictatorship

Caesar died a violent death on the Ides of March 44 BCE; the dictatorship— which was already on the verge of becoming a monarchy—had its last flicker of mobility and its last gasps in the Curia of Pompey, along with its last holder, hunted down by assassins. Caesar, as far as we know, was the first Roman to die as a dictator. This seems an interesting fact, in relation to which the scarce attention of historiography is surprising. Immediately after Caesar's death, the Senate abolished the office of dictator. In vain, the people of the *Urbs*, bent by a famine, in 22 BCE asked Augustus—who was Caesar's heir but who had come to power through a long civil war and the gradual construction of the *principatus*, a new institutional organisation—to revive dictatorship, perhaps remembering how Caesar, through it, had solved many of their subsistence problems.

Note

1 Flavio Raviola wrote the part on Greek tyranny, Francesca Cavaggioni the one on early and mid-republican Rome, and Luca Fezzi the one on late republican dictatorship.

Bibliographical note

We have limited ourselves to essential references for the sake of conciseness.

Anderson (2005), Luraghi (2013), Mitchell (2013) and Kõiv (2016) should be mentioned at the very least for the latest innovative reinterpretations of the tyrannical phenomenon. See Catenacci (2012) for a review of the possible etymologies of *tyrannos*. For the chronology of the tyranny in Corinth (and consequently of other archaic tyrannies) Lapini (1996) is fundamental. The works of Finley (1953) and Lewis (1973) on land ownership in classical Athens are always essential. On the cleisthenic reforms, an important recent review in Anderson (2003). Works exemplifying the dynamism and versatility of the tyrants: Angiolillo (1997); Sancisi-Weerdenburg (2000); Arvanitis (2008); Carry (2015).

Among the general works on dictatorship in the Early and Mid-Republican periods, from which a casuistry can also be drawn, see at least: Hartfield 1982; Meloni 1983; Hinard 1988; Nicolet 2004; Wilson 2017; Garofalo 2017-2018. More recent perspectives include an attempt to deny dictatorship an originally emergent profile: Cornell 2015; Easton 2010. With regard to the problematic reconstruction of the early-republican structures mentioned in Section 1, the dictatorial hypothesis is supported, among others, with different nuances, by Mazzarino 1945, De Martino 1972², Valditara 1989; for the etymological question, see Cipriano 1984. On the passage of Dion. Hal 5.73–74 (Section 2), Gabba 1984 remains fundamental. On the *adfectatores regni* Sp. Cassio, Sp. Melio and Capitolino, see Chassignet 2001 for a general overview. On the historical context that forms the background to the IVth -century cases examined in Section 6, suffice it to refer to Cornell 1995. The thesis of a republican sequence is in Flower 2010.

On Sulla's dictatorship, it is enough to cite the contributions of Carcopino (1931), Laffi (1967), Hinard (1988), Hurlet (1993), Keaveney (2005) and David (2017); On Sulla's dictatorship in relation to mobility, see Santangelo (2007); on the same topic in relation to previous dictatorships, see Mazzotta (2019); On Caesar's dictatorship and Caesarism suffice it to cite Meier (1982), Yavetz (1983), Jehne (1987), Canfora (1999), Gabba (2000), Sordi (2000), Zecchini (2001) and Ferrary (2010); on the ties between the two dictatorships and the debates between the IInd and Ist centuries BC, one need only cite Ferrary (1988) and Giardina (2010).

Bibliography

Anderson G (2003) *The Athenian experiment. Building an imagined political community in ancient Attica, 508–490 B.C.* Ann Arbor: The University of Michigan Press.

Anderson G (2005) Before *turannoi* were tyrants: rethinking a chapter of early Greek history. *Classical Antiquity* 24: 173–222.

Angiolillo A (1997) *Arte e cultura nell'Atene di Pisistrato e dei Pisistratidi.* Bari: Edipuglia.

Arvanitis N (2008) *I tiranni e le acque. Infrastrutture idrauliche e potere nella Grecia del tardo arcaismo*, trad. ital. Bologna: Dupress.

Canfora L (1999) *Cesare. Il dittatore democratico.* Roma-Bari: Laterza.

Carcopino J (1931) *Sylla ou la monarchie manquée.* Paris: L'artisan du livre.

Carry A (2015) *Polycrates, tyrant of Samos.* Stuttgart: Franz Steiner Verlag.

Catenacci C (2012) *Il tiranno e l'eroe.* Roma: Carocci.

Chassignet M (2001) La 'construction' des aspirants à la tyrannie: Sp. Cassius, Sp. Maelius et Manlius Capitolinus. In: Coudry M and Späth T (eds) *L'invention des grands hommes de la Rome antique. Actes du Colloque du Collegium Beatus Rhenanus, August 16–18 september 1999.* Paris: De Boccard, pp. 83–96.

Cipriano P (1984) L'etimologia di *dictator* presso gli antichi. In: *Studi latini e romanzi in memoria di A. Pagliaro.* Roma: Università La Sapienza, Dipartimento di studi glotto-antropologici, pp. 167–174.

Cornell TJ (1995) *The beginnings of Rome*. London: Routledge.
Cornell TJ (2015) Crisis and deformation in the Roman republic: the example of the dictatorship. In: Gouschin V and Rhodes PJ (eds) *Deformations and crises of ancient civil communities*. Stuttgart: Franz Steiner Verlag, pp. 101–125.
David JM (2017) Sylla nomothète. In: Schettino MT and Zecchini G (eds) *L'età di Silla. Atti del convegno, Istituto italiano per la storia antica, Roma, 23–24 marzo 2017*. Roma: L'*Erma' di Bretschneider, pp. 91–104.
De Martino F (1972) *Storia della costituzione romana*. I. Napoli: Jovene.
Easton JA (2010) *A new perspective on the early Roman dictatorship, 501–300 B.C.*, a dissertation submitted to the graduate degree program in Classics and the Graduate Faculty of the University of Kansas.
Ferrary JL (1988) Cicéron et la dictature. In: Hinard F (ed) *Dictatures. Actes de la table ronde réunie à Paris les 27 et 28 février 1984*. Paris: De Boccard, pp. 97–105.
Ferrary JL (2010) À propos des pouvoirs et des honneurs décernés à César entre 48 et 44. In: Urso G (ed) *Cesare: precursore o visionario? Atti del convegno internazionale, Cividale del Friuli, 17–19 settembre 2009*. Pisa: ETS, pp. 9–30.
Finley MI (1953) Land, debt, and the man of property in classical Athens. *Political Science Quarterly* 68: 249–268.
Flower H (2010) *Roman republics*. Princeton NJ: Princeton University Press.
Gabba E (1983) Dionigi e la dittatura a Roma. In: Gabba E (ed) *Tria corda. Scritti in onore di Arnaldo Momigliano*. Como: New Press, pp. 215–228.
Gabba E (2000) Le riforme di Cesare. In: Urso G (ed) *L'ultimo Cesare: scritti, riforme, poteri, progetti, congiure*. Roma: L'*Erma' di Bretschneider, pp. 143–149.
Garofalo L (ed) (2017–2018) *La dittatura romana*. I-II. Napoli: Jovene.
Giardina A (2010) Cesare vs Silla. In: Urso G (ed) *Cesare: precursore o visionario? Atti del convegno internazionale, Cividale del Friuli, 17–19 settembre 2009*. Pisa: ETS, pp. 31–46.
Hartfield ME (1982) *The Roman dictatorship: its character and its evolution*. Berkeley: University of California.
Hinard F (ed) (1988a) *Dictatures. Actes de la table ronde réunie à Paris les 27 et 28 février 1984*. Paris: De Boccard.
Hinard F (1988b) De la dictature à la tyrannie. Réflexions sur la dictature de Sylla. In: Hinard F (ed) (1988), pp. 87–96.
Hinard F (1999) Dion Cassius et l'abdication de Sylla. *REA* 101: 427–432.
Hurlet (1993) *La dictature de Sylla: monarchie ou magistrature républicaine? Essai d'histoire constitutionnelle*. Bruxelles-Rome: Institut Historique Belge de Rome.
Jehne M (1987) *Der Staat des Dictators Caesar*. Cologne-Vienna: Böhlau.
Keaveney A (2005) *Sulla. The last republican*. London: Routledge.
Kõiv M (2016) Basileus, Tyrannos and Polis. The dynamics of monarchy in early Greece. *Klio* 98: 1–89.
Laffi U (1967) Il mito di Silla. *Athenaeum* 45: 177–213; 255–277.
Lapini W (1996) *Il POxy. 664 di Eraclide Pontico e la cronologia dei Cipselidi*. Firenze: Olschki.
Lewis DM (1973) Rationes centesimarum. In: Finley MI (ed) *Problèmes de la terre en Grèce ancienne*. Paris-La Haye: Mouton, pp. 187–212.
Luraghi N (2013) Ruling alone: monarchy in Greek politics and thought. In: Luraghi N (ed) *The splendors and miseries of ruling alone*. Stuttgart: Franz Steiner Verlag, pp. 11–24.

Mazzarino S (1945) *Dalla monarchia allo stato repubblicano: ricerche di storia romana arcaica*. Catania: G. Agnini Editore.

Mazzotta MC (2019) L'influenza del dibattito politico postsillano sull'immagine della dittatura nella prima età repubblicana. In: Schettino MT and Zecchini G (ed) *La generazione postsillana. Il patrimonio memoriale. Atti del convegno, Istituto italiano per la storia antica, Roma, 22 febbraio 2019*. Roma: L''Erma' di Bretschneider, pp. 77–95.

Meier C (1982) *Caesar*. Berlin: Severin & Siedler.

Meloni G (ed) (1983) *Dittatura degli antichi e dei moderni*. Roma: Editori Riuniti.

Mitchell L (2013) *The heroic rulers of archaic and classical Greece*. London–New York: Bloomsbury.

Nicolet C (1964) Le 'de republica' (VI, 12) et la dictature de Scipion. *REL* 42: 212–230.

Nicolet C (2004) Dictatorship in Rome. In: Baehr P and Richter M (ed) *Dictatorship in history and theory*. Cambridge: Cambridge University Press, pp. 263–278.

Sancisi-Weerdenburg H (ed) (2000) *Peisistratos and the tyranny: a reappraisal of the evidence*. Amsterdam: Hakkert.

Santangelo F (2007) *Sulla, the elites and the empire: a study of Roman policies in Italy and the Greek east*. Leiden: Brill.

Sordi M (2000) I poteri dell'ultimo Cesare. In: Urso G (ed) *L'ultimo Cesare: scritti, riforme, poteri, progetti, congiure*. Roma: L''Erma' di Bretschneider, pp. 305–316.

Valditara G (1989) *Studi sul* magister populi*: dagli ausiliari militari del* rex *ai primi magistrati repubblicani*. Milano: Giuffré.

Wilson MB (2017) *The needed man: the evolution, abandonment, and the resurrection of the Roman dictatorship*. A dissertation submitted to the Graduate Faculty in History in partial fulfillment of the requirements for the degree of Doctor of Philosophy, CUNY, New York.

Yavetz Z (1983) *Julius Caesar and his public image*. Ithaca NY: Cornell University Press.

Zecchini G (2001) *Cesare e il 'mos maiorum'*. Stuttgart: Franz Steiner Verlag.

10 The Anglo-Venetian moment

Political and legal representations between the Republic of Venice and England in the early modern age

Michele Basso, Mario Piccinini and Alfredo Viggiano

The relationship between the Republic of Venice and England has always been the subject of several studies within the humanities. Our aim is to investigate the still neglected aspect of legal culture and political thought. The challenge is to demonstrate that in the early modern age between 1550 and 1650 there was an Anglo-Venetian moment of the history of legal and political thought. This article represents a first step of a collective work in progress.

To what extent is it possible to speak of an Anglo-Venetian moment in the early modern age? First, we must acknowledge our indebtedness to the Italian scholar Enrico De Mas (De Mas, 1975). In his *Sovranità politica e unità Cristiana nel Seicento-Anglo Veneto*, retrieving a suggestion of Francis Yates, De Mas underlined a specific connection between Venice and England in their common resistance against the politics of Rome, focussing on the irenical and latitudinarian character of this Anglo-Venetian alignment. His stance raised a debate and has been criticised several times since then, often not without reasons, but without denying the fundamental strength of his contribution. For us, the seminal work of De Mas represents an important starting point.

Within this framework, the topic will be developed in the following issues:

- the Venetian and English legal differences from the other countries where the *Ius Commune* was at its height, i.e. when the *Rezeption* of the Roman laws occurred within the German territories of the Empire;
- the mobility of people, ideas, and legal cultures between the Venetian *Dominio* and England, with reference to the role of the Paduan *Studium*; and
- the mobility of notions, propositions, legal and political discourses all the way down to the retrieval of analogies and common concepts between the two areas. We will briefly focus here on the vicissitudes of a notion of the *divine right of kings* in a text by Paolo Sarpi, as a case study.

DOI: 10.4324/9781003278665-14

10.1 Ius commune at borders. Venice and England

When we investigate the intellectual relationships between the Republic of Venice and the Kingdom of England in a crucial period of the early modern age we notice that, whereas in natural sciences there has been a constant and detailed research (Ongaro, Rippa Bonati and Thiene, 2006), the same is not the case for the legal cultures and the political and institutional issues.

Both Venice and England consider their legal mainstream tradition as independent from the Roman canonical tradition connected to the historical experience of the Empire that scholars are used to label as "ius commune". This claim for independence can be partially disputed if we consider the following arguments.

During its territorial expansion within the Terraferma, Venice defeated and incorporated the city of Padua, and the legal traditions of its university. As is widely known, Padua's *Studium* is one of the most important European centres for the dissemination of the legal tradition of *ius commune*. In 1405 the Venetian siege of Padua put an end to the *Signoria Carrarese*. Venice accepted the request, made by a delegation of Paduan citizens, to keep the university seat in Padua, without moving it to Venice ("che'l Studio fusse cunfermado a Padova", Canzian, 2007). From this moment, the *Dominante* established a close and privileged relationship with the university. When the Paduan representatives went to Venice the following year for the "atto di dedizione" in order to deliver the symbols of the city to Venice and to recognise in this way their being subjected to the *Dominante*, the pact was endorsed by an official sermon of the canonist, Francesco Zabarella, the most prominent scholar of the *Studium*, who later became Venice representative ("legato veneziano") at the Council of Pisa (Valsecchi and Piovan, 2020; Valsecchi, 2021). Thus, the *Studium* of Padua became *the* university of the Venetian dominion. No other university was present or allowed and no academic title, except one acquired in Padua, could be considered valid, both for medical arts and *scientia iuris*.

The *Studium* was mostly autonomous, although the Republic carefully supervised its development and, sometimes, made decisions. In 1528, the *Riformatori allo Studio*, a specific magistrature for the university, was set up. This magistrature, for example, created a specific *natio scota iuristarum*, separating the Scottish students from the traditional *natio anglica*, in order to balance the presence of cismontane and ultramontane students' corporate *nationes* (Piovan, 2013). On the one hand, the dualism between the Republic Venetian law and the university Roman canonical law ensured and strengthened the cosmopolitical character of the *Studium*. On the other hand, the *Studium* opened the possibility to deal with and to balance, when necessary, the juridical pluralism of the *Dominio*. Venice never incorporated the *Terraferma* within its civil law, allowing the cities to maintain their own statutory traditions and their *ius commune*, and limited the Republic jurisdictional power to specific interventions through the creation of dedicated magistratures. This was consistent with the Venetian attitude towards its own civil law: the reflection on its sources always aimed to enhance the organisation of juridical and administrative practices, independently from the mainstream of the 16th century legal culture.

Venetian law developed independently from *ius commune*, and therefore also independently from the humanistic and post-humanistic debate on Roman law. Scholars have drawn attention to the so-called "insularity" of Venetian law (Mazzacane, 1984) and it is worth underlining that, in the last century, the term has been widely discussed within English historiography, with reference to the *common law* (Kelley, 1974; Brooks and Sharpe, 1976; Baker, 1985). Nevertheless, we should not think of this idea of "insularity" as an absolute dogma. The relationship between the Paduan jurists and the *Dominante* is certainly not organic and rarely goes beyond the necessity of recognising the Venetian *potestas*. But if we consider the complexity and the stratification of the legal lexica, the relationship with other forms of law is fundamental. This is true, not only for the *ius commune*, but also for the statutory laws of the cities of *Terraferma* (Viggiano, 1993), as well as for the feudal law, which is an important element in the Friulian territories conquered by Venice. All the issues related to intricate relationships with the canonical jurisdiction must also be considered. The University of Padua not only provided the teaching and the transmission of *scientia iuris*, but represented a remarkable workshop of a consulting jurisprudence, which was essential to grant the legal reproduction of the *Dominio*. Moreover, the literary genre of the *Consilia* had a crucial role in ensuring the prestige of Paduan doctors, equally or so more than academic treatises like the *Commentarii*.

Similarly, in England, the claim for full independence was supported by the self-declared autonomy of common law, which excluded all influence from the external legal world. In intertwining politics and law, i.e. customs and statutes, the jurisdictional dimension played a dominant role, and the same parliament was seen as a court of justice. Only during the 17th century did a different perspective arise. Not all English courts, however, were common law courts.

Arthur Duck, in his *De sensu et authoritate juris civilis Romanorum per dominia principum christianorum* (1653), displays an admirable recognition of the Roman legacy within the Christian world. After recording the Venetian legal exception in the Italian peninsula, the author gives a precise framework of the English situation at his time. The dating is important, as it enables us to trace back the relevant social and institutional transformation which occurred in the last decades. There is no mention, for example, of the Star Chamber or of the Court of High Commission, which were both abolished by the Long Parliament in 1541. The frequent use of the expression "until now" is a signal of the disorder of the age, and the closing lines of the chapter that foreshadows the disappearance of Roman law in England, rather than a long-run prognosis, must be read as a hint of the radical crisis of the Reign of Charles Stuart.

"Britain, as it is separated from the ocean", represents somehow an exception. The usage of civil law in England is different from that in the other European countries and it does not have the same authority, having no mention in English books. However, if we consider the courts, the Roman presence is evident. Even in a context where common law is dominant, the Court of Chivalry and the Military Court derive from the so-called *Civil Law*, or simply *Roman Law*. After the separation from the Roman Church, the Ecclesiastical Courts are no longer subjected to the Roman canonical law, although they maintain a profile and a legal culture connected to it, guaranteeing the due observance of the statutes of the Reign and the refusal of any present and prior interference by the Bishop of Rome. In these courts, redefined by statute (37 Henry VIII, c. 17), doctors are admitted as judges and thus civilians gain an important role; in contrast to the canonical law, they can be lay or married people. F. W. Maitland used his irony on this issue, labelling this decision as Henry VIII's *Unam Sanctam* (Maitland, 1898). The Court of Admiralty itself, initially a penal court for issues connected to piracy, grew in importance along with the maritime expansion of the country. This court resorted to civil law together with sea customs, as for example the Rolls of Oberon, enforced in England as law since the reign of King Edward III.

The most important court is certainly the High Court of Chancery, named first by Duck. Even though it is not a court of civil law, its position goes beyond common law, with the aim of giving other remedies besides those of common law. We may refer to equity and good conscience. The Lord Chancellor, traditionally called "the Keeper of King's Conscience", was for a long time a bishop with legal training and the series of Chancellor-Bishops was interrupted only by Thomas More, who was a lawyer. The Chancery used inquisitorial procedures based on witnesses, as in *ius commune*, and therefore its staff (Assessors or Masters of the Rolls) consisted almost exclusively of civilians, who had a degree in Roman Law or in *utroque iure*. Their legal training was provided either by the two English universities, where the teaching of Roman law was by the King's initiative, or from abroad. The same occurred for the Court of Requests and for the other minor courts of equity, and for the courts of Oxford and Cambridge Universities. What is more, civilians were present in many activities related to the *Curia Regis*, from the Privy Council to diplomacy. The role of doctors was endangered during the parliamentarian crisis but had an afterlife during the Restoration. The figure of *consilium* was contextually relevant and was performed by the doctors in *ius commune*, even beyond the kingdom boundaries.

The pluralism of legal languages and of the courts was a hallmark of the English situation for more than a century. After the Act of Supremacy, the dualism of secular and canonical jurisdiction was destined to be substituted by a different reality. The dualism between common law courts and courts of equity and of royal prerogative determined an increasing conflict of competences which was, at the same time, a process of politicisation questioning royal *potestas*. The discussion around the existence of only one legal system raised the issue of the source of law.

Although we should not overlap the cases of Venice and England, there are some similarities such as the predominance of a country law, opposing other sources of law and other legal cultures, and the presence of *ius commune*, granted and favoured at different levels by the political magistrate. In the background, there was a fight against the Roman Church which in England continued even after the Schism and which in Venice worsened in the first decade of the 17th century. Finally, we should take into consideration the "imperial" dimension of the two political realities and their maritime features, emerging in England and declining in Venice.

10.2 Mobility of people, ideas and legal cultures between Venice and England

The presence of English students within the University of Padua is suitably represented by two well-known witnesses: Thomas Coryat (1611), the traveller who popularised the idea of the Grand Tour, and John Evelyn, who enrolled in 1645–46 and wrote in his *Memoirs* about the close connection between the university and Venice. The issue of English students in Padua was treated in the seminal volume by Jonathan Woolfson (Woolfson, 1998), a detailed prosopographic research which analyses the Tudor age (1485–1603). Woolfson's book clearly underlines how the Paduan experience of English students influenced the thought and the social life both of Venice and England, especially in the second half of the 16th century. The author poses two questions: first, how the educational training in Padua found practical application in legal and medical professions; second, how important such mobility of students and scholars in English and Venice history was. This book represents a further confirmation of Padua being, in Shakespearean terms, the "cradle of the arts". Although Woolfson's study is crucial, further research for the period not analysed by the author would be necessary. More recently, the topic of the English presence in Padua has been treated by different contributors, whose studies appeared in an issue of *Renaissance Studies* (Rundle and Petrina, 2013).

The *Studium* of Padua, as mentioned above, was the only university within the Venice Dominion between 1406 and 1797, and under the direct control of the *Dominante*. In history, statistical surveys are not an easy matter, but it is reasonable to say that, in the 16th century, the *Studium* hosted an average of more than one thousand students *per annum*, i.e. 33% of the total population of the town, and a large part of them were students of law. Among them, there were also students from Scotland and England (Gallo, 2021). In 1637 John Donne Jr., the son of the poet, was the first student who earned a degree *in utroque iure*, followed shortly afterwards by two other Englishmen.

Whereas the number of English students with a degree was quite limited (officially only nine students between 1637 and 1657), much larger was the number of students without a degree who attended the university for a short or long period. The Roman legal tradition and an enduring connection with the continent encouraged Scottish students to choose Padua. After the 15th century, the English and Scottish students represented two different national groups, both referred to within the university statutes (Gallo, 2021).

The relationship between Padua and England was relevant. Of great importance was the group of Englishmen who gathered around Reginald Pole, the cousin of Henry VIII and cardinal of the Catholic church, who later almost became Pope. The group had both humanistic and religious interests, and the so-called "*Spirituali*" movement stems from it. Overell (2019) defines Padua as the "nursery of Nicodemism". Many members of this group had a legal training as well, and they made use of it after the group separated. Among them were Thomas Starkey and Richard Morrison. Starkey, who had studied law in Pavia with Giovanni Ripa, a jurist aligned with Zabarella's ideas, moved to Padua to complete his studies and his teacher, Marco Mantova Benavides, was also connected to Zabarella's intellectual legacy (Mayer, 1986). As soon they went back to England, they put themselves at the service of the King, between whom and Pole Starkey sought to mediate (Mayer, 1989 and Elton, 1990). With this aim in mind, Starkey wrote *A Dialogue between Pole and Lupset*, a fictional text with real people, Pole and the humanist Thomas Lupset, Erasmus' and Thomas More's friend, who had died some years before and who had studied in Padua as well. The text, which was published only in the 19th century, pleads the cause of *ius commune*, hoping that it will, sooner or later, be a substitute for the barbarism of common law. Although the text was known by very few, if any, contemporaries, the issue at stake was not isolated. However, the role of Starkey was significant within the Tudor administration and some of his reform proposals deserve attention (Elton, 1974). Morrison followed an analogous path and once in England he entered the King's diplomacy (Sowerby, 2010). His knowledge of Roman law supported his reformist views, but as he considered it too rigid, he always preferred the more flexible common law of England. The humanist Thomas Smith received his legal education in Padua as well, after being appointed first Regius Professor of Civil Law at Cambridge. The author of an important historical study of English institutions, *De Republica Anglorum: the Maner of Gournement or Policie of the Realme of England*, he was State Secretary in Edwardian and Elizabethan times (Dewar, 1964). When Maitland claimed that during the 16th century there was a real menace for common law (Maitland, 1901), his position was criticised and probably misunderstood. When referring to the menace, however, it is remarkable that he mentioned jurists whose legal training had taken place in the Paduan *Studium*.

Another section of the archival research is marked by the collection of memorialist sources, ambassadors' speeches, observers and travellers' rundowns concerning legal experience. Among the numerous rich sources, an important starting one is, of course, the *Calendar of state papers and manuscripts, Relating to English Affairs* (Brown and Cavendish Bentinck, 2013), in the archives and collections of Venice and in other libraries of northern Italy. Furthermore, particular attention should be drawn to the iconographic representation of justice, as well as to the figure of the magistrate and the penal issues.

The communication between Venice and England was made through different media, not only news and reports. It included a circulation of reciprocal knowledge on institutional mechanisms. A key text is *De magistratibus et republica venetorum* published in 1543 by Gasparo Contarini, a Venetian diplomat and member of the Senate, a layman whom Pope Paul III made a Catholic cardinal, because he was very close to Reginald Pole and to the *Spirituali* and therefore reputed to be able to deal with the evangelical world (Gleason, 1993). The book by Gasparo Contarini, circulated in all European countries, was translated into many languages, and offered a "constitutional" image of Venice which in a short time became standard. An English translation by Lewes Lewknor, which appeared in 1599, supplemented Contarini's text with other sources, for instance passages from Donato Giannotti's *Della Repubblica de' Viniziani* (1526–1533). The book was prominent in the making of a Venetian imagery in Jacobean England (McPherson, 1988; Peltonen, 2002).

Equally renowned is the correspondence of Henry Wotton as the English ambassador in Venice and the so called *Relazioni* that the Venetian ambassadors in England presented at the end of their mandate to the Venetian *Senato* veneziano. This material is only a part of the complex relationship between Venice and England but is definitely relevant for the period we are considering.

Our research on this topic ranges from analysis of the rhetorical devices supporting certain legal procedures, to the investigation of the legal figures involved in the trial, to the study on pressure groups, power relations and relations of patronage. In this context two major thinkers emerge, Paolo Sarpi and Edward Coke. Even though their profiles and stances are radically different, in fact opposite, a comparison between the two could be useful. It may be productive to investigate the so-called *inventing tradition* of an indigenous legal background, both in Venice and in England, with the aim of strengthening political legitimation. In his *Intellectual Origins of English Revolution*, Christopher Hill (1965) spoke of Coke as a mythmaker, a term which could also be said of Sarpi. With his collections of *Institutes* and the *Reports,* the English lawyer – a leading figure in the fight of Parliament against Crown – offers the legal basis of the clash against the King. The Venetian prelate was the representative of the defence of the Repubblica in the Interdict war.

In England, Coke's work sought to legitimise the common law, providing several examples and quotations, standing at one point against the ideological and doctrinal background of the King's power. Institutes and Reports reached the point of calling into question the authority of the royal prerogative courts, and for this reason they were banned or destroyed. Through the research on meaningful court cases, Coke was trying to support the legality of procedures based on customs, and to oppose the "tyranny" represented by the King's authority in those cases where he would tend to ignore such legality. As soon as he wrote his *Consulti* during the Interdetto, Sarpi raised a pre-emptive strike against the Pope's role, and provided useful arguments on the fight against the Pope's stance, both from a theological-political and from a diplomatic point of view. The *Istoria dell'Interdetto*, published between 1606 and 1607, aimed at illustrating the reasons that generated the "guerra delle scritture" between Venice and Rome. The case of two ecclesiastics on the Venetian *Terraferma*, charged with common crimes and therefore processed by secular tribunals, was the motive for an attack on the entire control system of Pope Paolo V within the Republic's boundaries.

The political fortune of the two authors can be measured by their opponents' will to prevent the dissemination of their works. James I and the Privy Council tried, without success, to erase Coke's Reports, since they include, according to King James, "many exorbitant and extravagant opinions". When Coke was arrested and imprisoned in the Tower, his manuscripts were confiscated. The rumour that he was working on an essay regarding the Magna Carta was blocked (Hill, 1965). The possibility to intervene and to exert influence by means of the printing press is a strategy with which Coke went beyond his activity in parliament and involved significant strata of what could be defined as an embryonic form of public opinion. Similarly, Sarpi and his followers' work aimed at involving the *Senato*'s elite and readers within and outside Venice. This raised a set of communication strategies aiming at consent and constructing an intermediate space between the public and secret spheres, intertwining technical arguments and moral suasions, legal issues and emotional narratives.

Reading Coke's *Reports* and Sarpi's *Consulti* shows a possible common ground which would be worthwhile to investigate. Relevant issues are oath as a bond of conscience, the leave to appeal and the right of complaint granted to the subjects, the relationship between ordinary and extraordinary courts of justice, the system of legal proofs.

Both authors, sometimes explicitly and sometimes in a more implicit way, constantly underline the fundamental role of customs and of the law which lies in the precedents, in the courts' decisions or within the "nature of things". Of great interest, on this point, is the so-called issue of the *commons*, i.e. the heritage of the land, the archaic right of communities on the usage of waters, pastures, woods, as a way of creating an indigenous law, as a means to protect the subjects' reasons, or as an occasion to evoke a "mystic" of common law as a space of liberty.

10.3 Venice and England. Divine right of kings and divine right of the Republic

In the intellectual scenario of the early modern age, the theory of the divine right of kings plays an outstanding role. The theory has its roots in an ancient idea of sacred royalty and in its Christian interpretation. It is however difficult to connect these roots with the doctrinal construction that, between the 16th and 17th centuries, retrieves the sacred roots as a way of legitimation and no longer as an acquired, traditional legitimacy. What some scholars have labelled a "strange autumnal flowering" (Oakley, 2012 and Oakley, 2015) seems, on the contrary, a doctrinal strategy whose aim is to achieve an "immunisation" of the *potestas*. The theory is destined to implode because of its internal contradictions, opening space to new configurations of legal and political order.

Divine right of kings, as such, is not an expression one finds easily in 17th century texts. It is rather a historiographic category introduced by an English historian, John Neville Figgis, in his book with this title (Figgis, 1896). An Anglican monk, a student of F. W. Maitland – an unbeliever – and of the Catholic Lord Acton, Figgis is a figure of lasting importance within the 20th century studies on political theology. He had formulated the theory of the divine right of kings by overlapping four arguments, each one present in different authors. First, monarchy is ordered directly by God, and second, the inheritance law of a legitimate king is imprescriptible, whatever vicissitudes he has gone through. Third, the kings can be held accountable for their actions only by God, who confers them power. Fourth, even if they are corrupt and act against God's will, no resistance is allowed to their subjects. An active resistance would be considered a sin and it is the duty of the subjects, as good Christians, to react only with a passive obedience; otherwise they are eternally damned. In Figgis, these arguments have a paradigmatic character, covering a doctrinal historical period ranging from the French royalists supporting Henry of Navarra to the last Jacobites and beyond. Although Figgis' text is still an essential reference, somewhat paradoxically, his contribution misses the precise comprehension of James I's stance, even though he states that James gave a formulation of the divine right of the king "in its strictest form". If so, James would have presented traditional theories in a more coherent and partly radicalised form. Three decisive elements seem to have been neglected. First, certainly known by Figgis, is the role assumed by James I as opposed to the contractarianism of George Buchanan, who had been his tutor when he was still only a very young Scottish king. In Buchanan's *De Jure Regni apud Scotos* (1579) the politicisation of Calvinism has one of its utmost expressions. The royal power in James I is ordered just because it is not constituted; therefore it does not derive from the community. The reasoning of *The Trve Lawe of free Monarchies* (1598) stems from this argument, which eventually claims the *apostolic* nature of the King, thus overcoming the Act of Supremacy. Once he becomes King of England, James will insist on this argument, which will be reformulated from time to time, but never abandoned. The second element is connected, even if not directly, to the first. As the position of James I is set as an opponent to a contractarian and presbyterian stance, it needs to be projected in a public space. Hence the constant intertwining of authority and authorship that can be defined as the real innovative feature of James I's viewpoint (Rickard, 2007). What is in the speeches of the subjects – the making explicit of something that the subjects think a common view – becomes here the King's claim, constantly re-iterated through writings or in oral speeches, that immediately reach the press. The political theology of James I is the King's discourse. As food sustains the body – King James said – reminiscence feeds and sustains memory. Third, the King's words and deeds must be communicated, made public. Yet when someone speaks in public, even if endowed with authority, he is no longer the only master of his words. They can be discussed, analysed, interpreted. Therefore, the mastery of the words must be continuously renewed. This is James' contribution in an age when the battle of the books and writings becomes a fundamental feature of modernity, and at the same time conveys an image of sovereignty beyond its definition entering the communicative dimension. James' performance and its paradigm of the "divine right of kings" is not so much connected to an harmonical cosmic order, as some scholars argue. The order needs to be constantly confirmed, which means that the old legitimacy constantly needs the support of legitimation.

If the bond between Venice and England is complex, as mentioned earlier, and intertwines political, diplomatic and religious levels, even more complex is the relationship between King James and Paolo Sarpi, which gave its iconic image to the resistance of the Republic against the Pope. Eager in conferring with the Calvinists, attentive to the reasons of Gallicans and above all to their legal devices, Sarpi remained always true to the self-coined metaphor of the chameleon. He expressed his opinion, but not to all, keeping to himself how deep his consent was, so far as to be accused of hypocrisy and transformism (Lord Acton, 1867; Wootton, 2002). The same attitude was maintained with the Anglicans, even if this was multifaceted. We may consider, for instance, the already mentioned direct or indirect exchanges between Sarpi and Micanzio with Henry Wotton and the relationship with Dudley Carleton, both English ambassadors in Venice during the years of Interdetto and immediately after. The connection between Sarpi and Edwin Sandys is also worth mentioning. A student and friend of Richard Hooker, for a period he was close to the King's project of recomposing the Christian world in opposition to the Roman Church. After his training as a lawyer at Middle Temple, he lived in Italy for many years and enrolled at the University of Padua in 1597. Prompted by the English ambassador, Sarpi added some notes on the Catholic church in Italy to the chapters of Sandys' *A Relation of the State of Religion in Europe*, published anonymously and against the author's will in 1605 (Cozzi, 1967). Sarpi's notes have a more radical anti-Roman tone, and they seem not so consistent with the overall ecumenical goal of the work. Translated into French by the Calvinist Diodati with Sarpi's annotations, Sandys' text enjoyed great fortune in continental Europe. Moreover, it is worth recalling the events that led to the publication in London of the *Istoria del Concilio Tridentino*, and the odd story with the Dalmatian archbishop Marco Antonio de Dominis. The latter is another major figure we need to consider in the development of the Anglo-Venetian moment (Malcolm, 1984; Belligni, 2003). The relationship between Sarpi and the English world is a real one, and at the same time it is elusive and difficult to frame. It depended on the changes of the European religious and political wars. Sarpi's statement on James I was sometimes very hard, as he argued that it would be better for James to concentrate on being the King than the theologian. To be fair, we know that it is very difficult with James I to separate the political from the theological, i.e. cut the theological-political knot. Sarpi's remarks however need to be read from a less contingent perspective. He always refused doctrinal constructions, and his writings were directed to concrete cases, as in anti-Roman writings and in his activity as a *Consultore in iure* for the Venetian Republic.

There are, indeed, some exceptions, and the most striking one is *Della potestà de' prencipi*. Fulgenzio Micanzio is the first to mention its early draft in his *Vita del padre Paolo*. After many vicissitudes, the text was discovered as a transcription in the Beinecke Library at Yale University and is now available thanks to the editorial ability of Nina Cannizzaro and Corrado Pin. The text is incomplete and raises questions on its composition and circulation. Nevertheless, it offers us the opportunity to draw a connecting line with our issue. The content is not particularly original as we can find similar arguments in other writings (*Consulti* 42, 44, 50–51, 84), but its thetic and somehow "systematic" formulations open up new perspectives.

The text deals with the divine right of kings. It is interesting that, when defining a *prencipato* as a political order that in human society is instituted by God, Sarpi unconditionally includes the Republic. We now analyse some lines. One title reads "That the way of governing, in any time, derives from God not only in general, but also as regards either of a person or persons who govern *as an individual*, and that any person who governs does it *iure divino*".

Here there is something more than the Bodinian theory on the forms of sovereignty which undermined the traditional tripartition of the forms of government. An element of individualisation is introduced.

> The King or the Prince, whom I am speaking of, must hold the Majesty, and there is no difference whether he is a single man, or an assembly of few or many people as in the case of aristocracy or democracy. Whoever holds the Majesty rules over all the others, and no one can rule over him; he is neither subject to anyone, yet he rules over all laws, nor can he obligate himself towards any of his subjects [...] The King who is sovereign does not rule according to laws, but he rules over laws, and is obliged only towards his conscience and God.

The theory of a constituted power, even in the case of a prior transfer from the people, is roundly criticised. If the supremacy of the people makes the person of the King a true King, the people keep a superior authority. Sarpi has a different view:

The truth is that [...] the King is a minister of God in his person, and he draws the authority to rule and govern as a sovereign from the source of divine power; therefore, the Prince is not subject to the means by which he was made Prince, but he is subject only to God, the only source of authority.

The element of the dynastic transmission, albeit legitimate, is integrated within this framework. Here is evident the critical stance against the legitimacy argument, so important for James, which is not directly denied but placed on a different level. Sarpi reinterprets the old theory that *Regnum* and *Sacerdotium* are not in the order of flesh and blood, and from this theological statement he brings out a fully political stance. Here is the crucial issue. Bellarmino claims that the Doge receives his title from the elections according to the laws of the Republic; therefore, the Doge may be a leader, but not a sovereign Prince. Bellarmino draws here from the usual vision of comparing Venice with European monarchies, and he uses it against Sarpi, whom he accused of supporting a conciliarist view, putting on the same level Catholic church and Republic, Pope and Doge. Yet, according to Sarpi, Bellarmino misses the point. The Doge "being fully representative of the whole Republic, makes laws; and when he says *Leonardus Donatus Venetiarum Dux*, it is like saying *Respublica Venetiarum*; the Republic doesn't have a Governor by election, but, as laws confirm, *sola Dei gratia*", i.e. *de iure divino*. The divine right regards the power of the Republic, not the person of the Doge. The above-mentioned element of individualisation relates to the former. We maintain that, by considering the Republic an institution governed by *iure divino*, Sarpi refers to James.

Another thinker who offers a different approach to the theory of the divine right of the king is William Barclay, a Scottish Catholic who studied at Bourges and taught, in voluntary exile, in France and in Pont-à-Mousson, in Lorraine (Collot, 1965). In 1600 Barclay published *De Regno et Regali Potestate*, dedicated to Henry IV, a book which criticised all together the supporters of political Calvinism – primarily the Scottish Buchanan and the author of *Vindiciae contra Tyrannos* – and the *ligueurs* theorists such as Jean Boucher, following an approach similar to Bodin's. Barclay coined the term "Monarchomachs", which was destined to have great fortune. In a posthumous text, *De Potestate Papæ: an, et quatenus, in Reges et Principes seculares jus et imperium habeat*, edited by his son John (the author of *Argenis*), he disputed the Pope's claim to exercise power over the King on temporal issues. Published in 1609, the book had such a strong echo in Europe that the Roman church was forced to ask Bellarmino to reply. Although Sarpi appreciated Barclay, his argument is clearly different. In a letter to the Gallican Jacques Guillot, dated September 1609 (Ulianich, 1961), Sarpi stated that Barclay intended to save the dualism between the ecclesiastic and secular power within a Christian State by means of a severe separation of non-interfering competences, such as chancellor and constable. The former is the Pope, the latter is the prince, and God, being over both, is the real King. "Non est quod mihi Barclaius ad divinam maiestatem veluti in comoedia ad Deum ex machina recurrat, tum quia oportet maiestatem esse reiplublicae partem, non externum aliquod, tum quia omnes mundi reipublicae una essent, nempe subiectae Deo...". If both powers affect the Christian State, one, the other or both must be subjected to only one human *summa potestas*, otherwise the State will appear as a two-headed monster. "Sine maiestate humana nulla respublica vel consistet, vel stare poterit". The perspective Sarpi is conferring with is, undoubtedly – even when he does not quote him – King James', and it is also radically redefined. Sarpi keeps the distinction between kingdoms and republics at that time irreversible and retrieves the ancient uniformity of the several human communities, once denoted by the common term *respublica*, within an inclusive theory of the *Summa Maiestas*. According to King James, the potestas is a necessity *de ratione peccati* – a thought he shared with Buchanan – and the King's role is apostolical. There is none of this in Sarpi. What remains is the essential individualisation of an enacted *potestas*, defined in James by the intertwining of authority and authorship. Sarpi shows us how, at the heart of the divine right of kings, lies a theory of the non-deductibility of power. Nothing to do with a justification of *de facto* power, connected to the need to legitimise the resolution of a critical conjuncture, as it was in Oliver Cromwell's England. In the intellectual biography of Father Paolo, some scholars were struck by his choice of keeping himself apart in the position of *giuriconsultore in iure*, acting beyond the usual matters of his engagement during the *Interdetto* and more and more involved in the daily life of the Venetian administration, as if he were moving away from the visible role played before. In fact, his choice proves rigour and coherence. Sarpi's is not a consulting jurisprudence, and never was so (Pin, 2008). It is a governing jurisprudence contributing to and identifying with the discourse of the Republic.

When dealing with the divine right of kings, the Sarpian redetermination is a conceptual breaking point and at the same time a depletion. It does not foresee a different way of thinking about a larger idea of sovereignty and legitimation. Instead, it opens space in its direction and, due to this, reintegrates some elements. Some scholars refer to a chapter "Sarpi and Hobbes". This chapter does not exist; instead, one entitled "Hobbes and Sarpi" does. To deal with it is in the agenda of our project on the Anglo-Venetian moment.

Bibliography

Andrich GL (1892) *Glosse di Antonio Porcellino ai nomi di alcuni giureconsulti iscritti nel s. Collegio De' Giuristi di Padova, da un manoscritto dell'archivio universitario.* Padova: Tipografia all'Università dei Fratelli Gallina.
Baker J (1985) English law and the Renaissance. *The Cambridge Law Journal* 44(1): 46–61.
Belligni E (2003) Auctoritas *e* potestas. *Marcantonio De Dominis fra l'inquisizione e Giacomo I*. Milano: Franco Angeli.

Brooks C, Sharpe K (1976) History, English law and the Renaissance. *Past and Present* 72: 133–142.

Brown R and Cavendish Bentinck G eds (2013) *Calendar of state papers and manuscripts, relating to English affairs: existing in the archives and collections of Venice, and in other libraries of Northern Italy*. Cambridge: Cambridge University Press.

Canzian D (2007) L'assedio di Padova del 1405. *Reti medievali, VIII*. Available at: www.retimedievali.it (accessed 12 May 2022).

Collot C (1965) *L'école doctrinale de droit public de Pont-à-Mousson (Pierre Grégoire de Toulouse et Guillaume Barclay) à la fin du XVI siècle*. Paris: Librairie générale de droit et de jurisprudence.

Cozzi G (1967) Sir Edwin Sandys e la "Relazione dello stato della religione". *Rivista storica italiana* 79(4): 1096–1121.

Cozzi G (1979) *Paolo Sarpi tra Venezia e l'Europa*. Torino: Einaudi.

De Mas E (1975) *Sovranità politica e unità cristiana nel Seicento anglo-veneto*. Ravenna: Longo.

De Vivo F (2007) *Information and communication in Venice: rethinking early modern politics*. Oxford: Oxford University Press.

Dewar M (1964) *Sir Thomas Smith: A Tudor intellectual in office*. University of London: Athlone Press.

Elton GR (1974) *Reform by statute: Thomas Starkey's dialogue and Thomas Cromwell's policy*. In: Elton GR, Studies in Tudor and Stuart Politics and Government, vol. 2. Cambridge: Cambridge University Press.

Elton GR (1990) Review of T. Mayer, Thomas Starkey and the Commonwealth. *The Historical Journal* 33(1): 243–246.

Figgis N (1896) *The divine right of Kings*. Cambridge: Cambridge University Press.

Gallo D (2021) Circulation of legal culture: professor and students. In: *International Seminar Ius Commune At Borders: Borders of Ius Commune*. Padova, 18th March 2021, www.facebook.com/dissgea.unipd/, video section.

Gleason EG (1993) *Gasparo Contarini: Venice, Rome, and reform*. Berkeley: University of California Press.

Helmholz RH (1990) *Roman canon law in reformation England*. Cambridge: Cambridge University Press.

Hill C (1965) *Intellectual origins of the English Revolution*. Oxford: Clarendon Press.

Kelley DR (1974) History, English law, and the Renaissance. *Past and Present* 65: 24–51.

Klinck DR (2010) *Conscience, equity, and the court of Chancery in Early Modern England*. Farnham: Ashgate.

Levack B (1973) *The civil lawyers in England 1603–1641. A political study*. Oxford: Clarendon.

Lord Acton (1867) Fra Paolo Sarpi. *Chronicle*, I (March 30, 1).

McPherson D (1988) Lewkenor's Venice and its sources. *Renaissance Quarterly*, 41(3): 459–466.

Maitland FW (1898) *Roman canon law in the Church of England. Six Essays*. London: Methuen & Co.

Maitland FW (1901) *English law and the Renaissance*. Cambridge: Cambridge University Press.

Malcolm N (1984) *De Dominis, 1560–1624: Venetian, anglican, ecumenist and relapsed heretic*. London: Strickland & Scott Academic Publications.

Mayer T (1986) Marco Mantova and the Paduan religious crisis of the early 16th century. *Cristianesimo nella storia* 7: 41–61.

Mayer T (1989) *Thomas Starkey and the Commonwealth: humanist politics and religion in the reign of Henry VIII.* Cambridge: Cambridge University Press.

Mazzacane A (1984) Lo Stato e il Dominio nei giuristi veneti durante il "secolo della Terraferma". *Storia della cultura veneta* 3(1): 577–650.

Oakley F (2012) *The mortgage of the past: reshaping the ancient political inheritance (1050–1300).* New Haven and London: Yale University Press.

Oakley F (2015) *The watershed of modern politics: law, virtue, kingship, and consent (1300–1650).* New Haven and London: Yale University Press.

Ongaro G, Rippa Bonati M and Thiene G (2006) *Harvey e Padova. Atti del convegno celebrativo del quarto centenario della laurea di William Harvey (Padova 21–22 novembre 2002).* Padova, Centro per la storia dell'università di Padova: Antilia.

Overell MA (2019) *Nicodemites: faith and concealment between Italy and Tudor England.* Leiden and Boston: Brill.

Patterson WB (2000) *King James VI and I and the reunion of Christendom.* Cambridge: Cambridge University Press.

Peltonen M (2002) Citizenship and Republicanism in Elizabethan England. In: Van Gelderen M and Skinner Q (eds) *Republicanism. A shared European heritage* vol 1. Cambridge: Cambridge University Press.

Petrolini C (2021) The Anglo-Venetian moment: from the divine right of Kings to the divine right of the Republic. In: *International Seminar Ius Commune at borders: borders of Ius Commune.* Padova, 3rd June 2021, www.facebook.com/dissgea.unipd/, video section.

Pin C (2008) Paolo Sarpi consultore in iure e i giuristi dell'Università di Padova. *Studi veneziani* 56.

Piovan F (2013) Autonomy by imposition. The birth of the *natio Scota* in the law faculty of the University of Padova (1534). *Renaissance Studies. Journal of the Society for Renaissance Studies* 27(4): 549–559.

Rickard J (2007) *Authorship and authority: the writings of James VI and I.* Manchester: Manchester University Press.

Rundle D and Petrina A (eds) (2013) *Renaissance studies, special issue: The Italian university in the Renaissance* 27(4).

Sarpi P (1969) *Opere.* Milano-Napoli: Ricciardi.

Sarpi P (2001) *I consulti dell'Interdetto 1606-1607.* Pisa-Roma: Istituti editoriali e poligrafici internazionali.

Sarpi P (2006) *Della podestà de prencipi.* Venezia: Marsilio.

Sommerville JP (2014) *Royalists and patriots: politics and ideology in England, 1603–1640.* London: Routledge.

Sowerby TA (2010) *Renaissance and reform in Tudor England: The careers of Sir Richard Morison.* Oxford: Oxford University Press.

Ulianich B (1961) *Paolo Sarpi, lettere ai gallicani.* Wiesbaden: Franz Steiner Verlag.

Valsecchi C and Piovan F (2020) *Diritto, Chiesa e cultura nell'opera di Francesco Zabarella.* 1360–1417. Milano: Franco Angeli.

Valsecchi C (2021) *Francesco Zabarella. Da Padova all'Europa per salvare la Chiesa.* Milano: Franco Angeli.

Viggiano (1993) *Governanti e governati. Legittimità del potere ed esercizio dell'autorità sovrana nello stato veneto della prima età moderna.* Treviso: Canova-Fondazione Benetton Studi e Ricerche.

Woolfson J (1998) *Padua and the Tudors: English students in Italy, 1485–1603.* Toronto: University of Toronto Press.

Woolfson J (2013) Padua and English students revisited. *Renaissance Studies. Journal of the Society for Renaissance Studies* 27(4): 572–587.

Wootton D (2002) *Paolo Sarpi: between Renaissance and Enlightenment.* Cambridge: Cambridge University Press.

11 Mechanics, scholars and objects

The spread of Aristotle's philosophy and its exponents in early modern Europe

Ferdinando Fava and Andrea Savio[1]

This essay discusses the issues surrounding scholar mobility and the use of vernacular Italian in "Le Mecchaniche", Filippo Pigafetta's translation of "Mechanicorum Liber" by Guidobaldo del Monte. The first part of this essay describes the circles within which Mechanics were discussed. The members of these circles were Greek-language enthusiasts, including students, teachers, technicians and military engineers, who frequented the University of Padua's circles and the city's private libraries in the second half of the 16th century. They were Catholic and anti-Ottoman, held philosophical, practical-empirical and rationalist beliefs, and were open to the international mobility of French, Dutch and Iberian scholars. Their hallmark, however, was their determination to disseminate ancient and contemporary scientific studies, especially those concerning everyday issues, which today would be covered by Mechanical Engineering and its related subjects, e.g. Mathematics, Physics and Ballistics. The second part focuses on several key features of the "Mobility Turn", taking a brief look at the free movement of scholars and ideas. It also covers how the concept of motion within "Mechanicorum Liber" and its drawings intertwines with Pigafetta's life, multilingualism, travels to the farthest reaches of Renaissance Europe, and the reasons for these travels. The third part of this essay specifically examines the Mobility Turn and illustrates the initial results of a heuristic intuition that will require further investigation.

11.1 Circles

A plethora of studies has been written on the mobility of university students and academics, particularly on the relationships they established during courses and related research into knowledge transmission and book mobility (on scholar mobility, De Ridder-Symoens, 1996: 444–445; Schwinges, 2018 and, on the mobility of books, Bellingradt, Nelles, and Salman, 2017).

More recently, investigations were conducted into postgraduate circles comprising graduates, academics and artisans-cum-engineers affiliated with major private libraries. In this regard, the city of Padua, with its ancient Studio, and Venice, which was open to the peoples of central and northern

Europe and the Mediterranean, have provided keen insight into the incomplete dynamics of these relationships (on the *Studio di Padova*, see "Quaderni per la storia dell'Università di Padova"; Piovan and Rea, 2001; Blass-Simmen and Weppelmann, 2017).

One of the main scholarly meeting places in the Republic of Venice was the "Studio di Padova", a library owned by Gian Vincenzo Pinelli that was considered "perhaps the greatest private library in mid-to-late XVIth-century Italy" (Barzazi, 2017: 16). Justus Lipsius and Jacques-Auguste de Thou spent time there, but its most famous visitor was Galileo, with Gian Vincenzo Pinelli helping "to bring him to the Studio di Padova, and Galileo stayed in Pinelli's house while he prepared his first lectures" (Grendler, 1981: 144; Nuovo, 2007; Callegari, 2015).

Equally important was a library in San Samuele, Venice, which had similar cultural interests and was owned by the Venetian scholar Giacomo Contarini. "It was one of the best-stocked scientific libraries in Renaissance Italy and boasted texts on mathematics, geometry and calculus. [...] Like Pinelli's library, it was essentially a meeting place where academics struck up friendships" (Savio, 2020: 45). Lesser-known circles included one in Osoppo, modern-day Friuli, run by Giulio Savorgnan, and another in Padua run by brothers Giacomo Alvise and Marcantonio Corner, who founded another prolific scientific family library.

Pinelli had amassed a collection of rare ancient Greek scientific works in his library; Contarini was interested in scales; and Savorgnan in the related subject of lifting heavy weights (on the role of Greek mathematical science manuscripts in the Republic of Venice, see: Irigoin, 1977; Grendler, 1980; Nuovo, 2008: 60–61. On Venice's sale of Greek codices to the Spanish court, see the various references in the *Archivo General de Simancas*, e.g. AGS, *Estado*, Legajo 1509, c. 248. On Giacomo Contarini: Favaro, 1900; Lawrence, 1976. On Giulio Savorgnan, Panciera, 2005: 203). Marcantonio Corner, however, specialised in the motion of catapults designed to hurl burning objects. These scholars wanted to hone the Aristotelian philosophy, or rather its pseudo-Aristotelian version, that pervaded contemporary Padua. They were particularly interested in the mechanical arts and wanted to gain an understanding of the subject's operation through observation-based experience (Garin, 1983; Van Dyck, 2006). Although the mechanical arts entry in Gregor Reisch's "Margarita philosophica" encyclopaedia (1503) opined that mechanics was a dishonourable craft that did not belong to the seven Liberal Arts, the first Venetian edition of Alessandro Piccolomini's "De la istitutione di tutta la vita de l'homo nato nobile e in città libera" (1542) elevated it to a mid-level scientific theory that studied how machinery functioned (Rovida, 2013: 31–70). Subsequently, the mechanical arts were said to be a mixed science, or subordinate to mathematics, with the profession of mechanic being raised to nobility: "a Mechanic, and thus an Engineer, by the example of so many worthy men, is the occupation of a worthy and noble person; and *Mechanica* is a Greek word meaning 'something made with artifice to move, as if miraculously and outside human power, the heaviest weights with little force'" (Pigafetta, 1581: "l'essere Mechanico dunque, e Ingegniero con l'esempio di tanti valent'huomini, è officio da persona degna, e signorile: e Mechanica è voce Greca significante cosa fatta con artificio da movere, come per miracolo, e fuori dell'humana possanza grandissimi pesi con piccola forza". On engineers in the Republic of Venice, see Mazzi and Zaggia (2004).

The study of mechanics spread throughout Italy as a result of the discovery of a Greek treatise in Cardinal Basilio Bessarione's Venice library. Humanistic, philological and economic interest in the trade and the printing of Greek manuscripts had made Venice one of the Mediterranean's leading markets. The treatise, which at the time was attributed to Aristotle, was titled "Mechanical Problems" (Μηχανικά). It was first translated into Latin in 1517 in Paris by the Venetian Fausto Vettor, and again in 1525 in Venice by Leonico Tomeo (Helbing, 2008: 573–575; van Leeuwen, 2016). The preservation of Greek scientific manuscripts in the libraries of the Republic of Venice led to a surge of interest in this field, with research being conducted in both Venice and Padua (see the chapter by Margherita Losacco herein). Despite an extensive network of Spanish, French and German scholars springing up in its wake, research into the subject was conducted principally by Italians.

Although the theory of mechanics was based on ancient cases, 16th-century studies were considered to be cutting-edge science, and all Republic of Venice circles shared an interest in applied mechanics. Galileo was invited to teach in Padua as a result of Pinelli and Contarini's recommendations, and it was they who enabled Galileo to conduct his early research into this field, with Galileo's first extant letter from his Paduan period discussing "the practical problem of the motion of a ship (not the motion of theoretical bodies through theoretical media as in the *De motu*)" (Schmitt, 1969: 134). In the latter half of the 16th century, scholarly debate revolved around inclined planes, falling bodies, the upward motion of light bodies and the motion of projectiles, which later scholars would call the "compensatory principle" and the "proto-inertial principle", which dealt with dynamics and kinematics.

11.2 Moving objects and languages

Padua and Venice, along with Urbino, were Europe's capitals for the study of mechanics. During the 16th century, courses in mechanics were taught by a number of scholars, including Pietro Catena, Giuseppe Moleti and Galileo in Padua, or by the Venetian Giovan Battista Benedetti in Turin, as well as by intellectuals such as Daniele Barbaro. "[O]ut of this fruitful Paduan ambience came two important works dealing directly with the Mechanica, written by visitors to Padua in the early 1540s – Alessandro Piccolomini and Diego Hurtado de Mendoza [ambassador to Venice from 1539 to 1546]" (Rose and Drake, 1971: 82; Laird, 1986).

The scientific and historiographical fortunes of mechanics are intricately tied to the history of language. Ancient Greek manuscripts were translated into Latin, but translations also began to appear in national languages. In 1545, Diego Hurtado de Mendoza translated "The Aristotelian Mechanics" from Greek into Castilian (Iommi Echeverría, 2011), and in 1581, Filippo Pigafetta translated the Latin work "Mechanicorum Liber" into vernacular Italian (Keller, 1976; Rossi, 1997). These publications were the culmination of much debate in Paduan circles about whether vernacular tongues should be used as languages of science to achieve greater practical and professional developments within society.

Filippo Pigafetta was a multi-faceted professional, being a translator, engineer, informer, spy and tireless traveller. His political network was well-defined: to ensure rapid mobility and security, he needed the support of the Venetian consular and mercantile organisations. His career as an informer overrode his fiduciary relationships and specifically his local allegiances (Keblusek and Noldus, 2011). His political connections were founded on client–patron relationships (he secured connections with certain Venetian patricians), peer friendships (fellow university students or soldiers with whom he had fought) and geographical loyalties (the network of Venetians and Vicentines, which proved especially important when Pigafetta was living in London and Paris); the latter group, in particular, were certainly not Spanish supporters. According to the terminology of the time, rather than a real spy Pigafetta was

> an informer and agent, mostly under the cover of a curious traveller or engineer, or even at times a pilgrim: a "friend" was the term adopted in spying circles to denote the most trustworthy informers, and without doubt, he was considered as such.
>
> (Savio, 2020: 51)

He also frequented all of the Republic of Venice circles that studied mechanical matters, becoming one of Italy's greatest experts in the field. Pigafetta was skilled in Mediterranean languages, as well as some northern European ones, and believed that communicating in vernacular Italian, rather than in Latin, was a more practical way of bringing mechanics to a wider audience. He "also faced the problems of translating technical Latin terms into common vernacular ones and of reorienting the entire work to a new audience" (Henninger-Voss, 2000: 235). As a translator, Pigafetta retained those vernacular translations from Latin needed to meet certain criteria if they were to be understood properly because "learned technical terms may make a text inaccessible to readers lacking sufficient knowledge of Greek and Latin mathematics. In this struggle over language, Pigafetta sided with the non-specialists, as is also demonstrated by a brief anecdote he wrote about the elitism of the learned" (Castagné and Frank, 2013: "termini tecnici dotti possono dunque rendere il testo inaccessibile a lettori che non possiedono una cultura matematica greca e latina sufficiente. In questa lotta per la lingua, Pigafetta si schierò dalla parte dei non specialisti, come dimostra anche un suo breve aneddoto sull'elitarismo dei dotti"), of which there were very few (Biblioteca Ambrosiana di Milano, *R 121 sup.*, f. 15r, 5 *novembre* 1580, letter by Filippo Pigafetta to Guidobaldo del Monte; on Galileo and Guidobaldo del Monte, see Frank and Napolitani, 2015).

As humanism became more widespread, Italy's scholars became increasingly convinced that knowledge had to be practice-based, with language being the easiest means of transmitting it to the widest possible audience, a method that became known as "vernacular epistemology" (Long, 2001; Smith, 2004). A recent research project, "Aristotle in the Italian Vernacular: Rethinking Renaissance and Early-Modern Intellectual History (c. 1400-c. 1650)", documented both the importance of Aristotelianism in the vernacular and the democratisation of scientific knowledge in the Renaissance (Sgarbi, 2016: 75). Engineers possessed a thorough empirical understanding of technical matters, but few of them read Latin or Greek, thus making vernacular translations essential.

To complete the discussion, it would be useful to summarise the pseudo-Aristotelian thought-shaping mechanics discussed in the circles of Pinelli and Contarini. This feat can only partly be achieved, however, as the search for additional correspondence between their members continues. As knowledge of mechanics advanced within the Republic of Venice, so did the mobility of military matters among both Italian and European scholars, with early practical knowledge garnered from studies being applied to new maritime or land warfare technology in a bid to bolster Europe's anti-Ottoman defences. Correspondence between Filippo Pigafetta and Giulio Savorgnan reveals an obsession with constructing new offensive and defensive weapons. One of Galileo's few surviving documents from his time in Padua is a letter from Giacomo Contarini, then Superintendent at the Arsenal of Venice (1593), asking a question about the motion of war galley oars (Concina, 1984: 127). And it is the most recent investigations into mechanics in the Republic of Venice that might explain Galileo's "Short Instruction on Military Architecture" and "Treatise on Fortification", as well as his relations with military engineers during his time in Padua (on Galileo the mechanics expert, see Howard, 2022).

The word "science" occurs five times in Pigafetta's ten-page preface to his translation of del Monte's "Mechanicorum Liber", when he writes about the "true motion" of weights. Pigafetta's aim undoubtedly differed from his successors in later centuries, yet his preface contains brief accounts of kinematic concepts such as motion, e.g. "any motion contrary to nature", and the movement and velocity of machines.

11.3 Mechanics and the Mobility Turn

Two factors triggered the tentative emergence of ideas that would eventually lead to a clear mathematical and kinematic concept of movement: Guidobaldo del Monte's "Mechanicorum Liber" and the erudite discussions in Padua's private libraries about winches, inclined planes, levers and projectiles among soldiers, artisans, philosophers and humanists. In the introduction to his Italian translation of "Mechanicorum Liber", Filippo Pigafetta wrote about the movement, motion and speed of machinery, ideas that not only appear throughout del Monte's text, but are also illustrated in his copious plates (see Figures 11.1 and 11.2).

These plates, however, were not designed merely to be accompanying drawings, as they played a central role in illustrating the theory behind "Mechanicorum Liber", which would later contribute to Galileo's concept of motion. They reproduce everyday items of machinery that were well-known to the craftsmen and soldiers, including Pigafetta, who frequented Padua's private libraries. The plates contained pragmatic knowledge of machines found in the workplace, and in the personal and collective lives of Italy's contemporary social fabric. At the same time, however, they also contained capital letters that pointed to adjacent plates, where the machines were broken down into geometric lines, points and shapes. This was how del Monte and his contemporary polymaths illustrated the theory behind these machines, in the belief that they were doing so in the dominant Aristotelian tradition. By translating a machine into abstract form, they could see beyond its pragmatic purpose to reveal its underlying theory. Doing so transformed these machines into conceptual objects. "Frontier objects" and "epistemic objects", categories which knowledge anthropology and science philosophy use to analyse the ever-evolving construction of scientific knowledge and interdisciplinarity, enable us to establish (and this is our heuristic interpretation) what these plates contributed to the development of the concept of movement that emerges from "Mechanicorum Liber" (Cresswell, 1997; Massumi, 2002; Cunningham and Heyman, 2004; Damerow, Freudenthal, McLaughlin, and Renn, 2004; Bertoloni Meli, 2006; Sheller and Urry, 2006; Salazar and Jayaram, 2016). The concept of "frontier objects" arose in the late 20th century in a bid to acknowledge that different communities of practice attribute their own meanings and purposes to the same object (Star and Griesemer, 1989). The term was first coined to differentiate between the meanings that birdwatchers and professional biologists gave to the specimens of birds on display at Berkeley's Museum of Vertebrate Zoology (Star and Griesemer, 1989). Something is deemed to be a "frontier object" when it is found in exactly the same form in a number of communities of practice, but fulfils the different information requirements of each community (Trompette and Vinck, 2009). In other words, these objects have different meanings in different social worlds, but their form is common enough to more than one world to make them recognisable, with them functioning as a means of transposition, or a bridge, between these worlds. They can be interpreted in a variety of ways (Star, 2010). We propose that winches and inclined planes, alongside the other machines depicted in the plates of "Mechanicorum Liber", be considered "frontier objects" because the members of the private library circles, the soldiers, builders and philosophers, had their own uses for them in their own

Dell'Asse nella Rota.

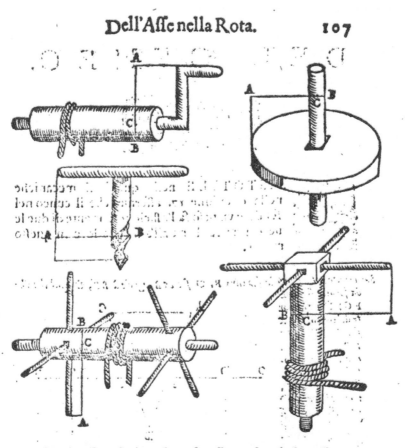

L'Autore hà qui messo queste cinque figure, lequali rappresentano cinque istrumenti da mouer pesi, iquali si riducono sotto questa facultà, accioche si vegga essi esser vna cosa medesima con l'istrumento dell'asse nella rota già dichiarato; & vi hà posto le lettere A B C con le sue linee, per dar ad intendere, che il peso hà la proportione medesima alla possanza, che lo sostiene, che hà A C à C B, & se sarà mosso il peso da vna possanza mouente, lo spatio della possanza sarà similmente allo spatio del peso, come A C à C B; laqual possanza deuesi intendere posta in cima de' manichi delle stanghette discosto dal centro tanto quanto è C A. Il peso hassi poi da intendere legato ad vna corda, che sia auolta d'intorno all'asse, ilquale sia lontano dal centro tanto quanto è C B: & cosi per le cose dotte, in questo Trattato, la possanza che sostien haurà quella proportione al peso, che hà C B à C A. Con simile modo s'ha da intendere la figura, che hà il timpano, considerando che se la forza fosse nella stremità del timpano, & il peso sarebbe auolto d'intorno all'asse. Quanto alla triuella, ò succhiello che si nomi, per essere vn'istrumento fatto non per sostenere, ma per mouere, egli è bisogno, che la possanza habbia proportione maggiore al peso di quel che hà C B à C A per la vndecima propositione di questo nella leua.

IL FINE DELL'ASSE NELLA ROTA.

Figure 11.1 Filippo Pigafetta, *Le meccaniche*, detail. Courtesy of the Biblioteca Civica Bertoliana, Vicenza.

Della Taglia

Sia il peso *A* ilquale si habbia ad alzare in sù ad angoli retti al piano dell'orizonte: & come si costuma di fare: sia attaccata di sopra vna taglia, che habbia due girelle, gli assetti dellequali siano in B C: & sia anche legata vn'altra taglia al peso, laquale similmente habbia due girelle, gli assetti delle quali siano in D E: & per tutte le girelle d'ambedue le taglie sia condotta intorno la corda, laquale in vno de i capi, come in F deue essere legata. Pongasi ancora la possanza che moue in G, laquale mentre discende, il peso *A* per lo contrario sarà leuato in suso, si come afferma Papo nell'ottauo libro delle raccolte matematiche, & Vitruuio nel decimo dell'architettura, & altri.

Hor in che modo questo instrumento della taglia si riduca alla leua, & perche vn peso grande si moua da piccola forza, & in qual modo, & in quanto tempo; & perche la corda debba essere legata da vn capo: & quale debba essere l'officio della taglia, che è posta di sotto, & quale di quella, che stà di sopra, & in che modo si possa trouare ogni proportione data ne i numeri tra la possanza, & il peso, diciamo.

Siano

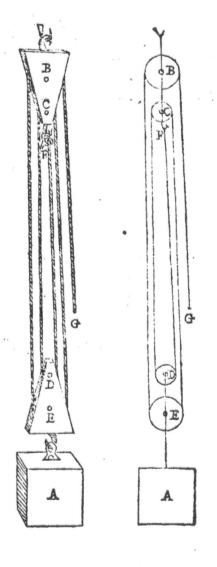

Figure 11.2 Filippo Pigafetta, *Le meccaniche*, detail. Courtesy of the Biblioteca Civica Bertoliana, Vicenza.

distinct fields of expertise. Machines were thus a medium, a bridge crossing the frontier between social universes with their own practices and discourse. The machines in these plates, however, should be considered both as "frontier objects" and "epistemic objects" (Rheinberger, 1997).

"Epistemic objects", another category from late-20th-century science history and philosophy used to analyse the development of scientific knowledge, are objects of analysis whose hallmark is that they are still "open", i.e. they raise questions continually, and only by observing them does their complexity progressively emerge. These objects are part of knowledge-discovery processes geared towards the gradual construction of particular knowledge. Although they belong to consolidated, widespread practices from a distinct time in history, they paved the way for subsequent concepts, steering scholars towards knowledge that would be recognised as such only later. The machines and plates in "Mechanicorum Liber" are epistemic objects, as the science behind them laid a pathway towards a future concept of motion that was a far cry from the dominant concept of their time, i.e. its kinematic reduction and later its mathematisation. Furthermore, del Monte's lever becomes a set of interrelated lines and no longer looks as though it has the force to move bodies. His battlefield projectile is a harmless dot moving through an isotropic void.

The plates that illustrate del Monte's text are hologram-like in appearance, as their images seem to be projected in a range of perspectives depending on the viewer's position. Within them, a host of ideas and distinct representations of movement coexist, each one emphasised differently according to the viewer's vantage point, but never completely distinct. This was to happen at a later stage. These machines are objects from the contemporary social and historical world, intertwined as they were with the practices and customs of daily life, yet they coexist alongside the abstract concept of model machines, a display of theory that completely dismantles their reality. The correspondence between Pigafetta and del Monte on the Italian vernacular words to be used to translate Latin is evidence of both the real and abstract worlds that exist within the same form, each mapped out by the viewer's perspective: the ex-soldier and translator on the one hand, and the erudite humanist theorist on the other. Motion seems to be an integral part of social relationships and places, as well as abstract, as it does not belong to the physical world. Its reduction to the kinematics of a point, in a space void of quality and content, an "isotrope", where mobility and immobility become equivalents, was only to be achieved decades later: a concept on a distant horizon drafted by the machines and plates of "Mechanicorum Liber". If the relational paradigm of the Mobility Turn is founded upon fresh analysis of social phenomena, the distinction between movement that was "contentless, seemingly natural and devoid of meaning, history, ideology" (Cresswell, 2006: 3), and mobility-movement as a social and political construction, then this distinction was heralded by the text of "Le Mecchaniche" and introduced by its plates. This paradigm strives to restore meaning, history and ideas to the analysis of movement, and to re-establish continuity with the other world that exists within the very same machine; movement is no longer reduced to a kinematic change of position outside of bodies, but is an inextricable part of the social fabric and its spatiality. Whether this concept can be considered a contemporary revival of certain elements of Aristotle's concept of motion, the dismantling of which began with "Le Meccaniche", is a subject for further study.

Note

1 Andrea Savio wrote the first and second sections, Ferdinando Fava the third.

References

Barzazi A (2017) *Collezioni librarie in una capitale d'antico regime. Venezia secoli XVI-XVIII.* Roma: Storia e Letteratura.

Bellingradt D, Nelles P and Salman J (eds) (2017) *Books in motion in early modern Europe beyond production, circulation and consumption.* London: Palgrave Macmillan.

Bertoloni Meli D (2006) *Thinking with objects. The transformation of mechanics in the seventeenth century.* Baltimore: The Johns Hopkins University Press.

Blass-Simmen B and Weppelmann S (eds) (2017) *Padua and Venice: transcultural exchange in the early Modern Age.* Berlin-Boston: de Gruyter.

Callegari M (2015) Gian Vincenzo Pinelli. In *Dizionario Biografico degli Italiani.* Roma: Treccani, 83: 405–407.

Castagné N and Frank M (2013) *Definizione dell'italiano scientifico nel tardo Cinquecento: la traduzione del Mechanicorum Liber di Guidobaldo dal Monte.* Laboratoire italien, 13 Available at: http://journals.openedition.org/laboratoireitalien/737 (accessed 16 February 2022).

Concina E (1984) *L'arsenale della Repubblica di Venezia. Tecniche e istituzioni dal Medioevo all'età moderna.* Milano: Electa.

Cresswell T (1997) Imagining the nomad: Mobility and the postmodern primitive. In: Strohmeyer U and Benk G (eds) *Space and social theory: interpreting modernity and postmodernity.* Oxford: Blackwell, pp. 360–379.

Cresswell T (2006) *On the move: mobility in the modern Western world.* New York: Routledge.

Cunningham H and Heyman J (2004) Introduction: Mobilities and enclosures at borders. *Identities: Global Studies in Culture and Power*, 11(3): 289–302.

Damerow P, Freudenthal G, McLaughlin P and Renn, J (2004) *Exploring the limits of preclassical mechanics: a study of conceptual development in early modern science: free fall and compounded motion in the work of Descartes, Galileo, and Beeckman.* New York: Springer.

de Ridder-Symoens H (1996) Mobility. In de Ridder-Symoens H (ed) *A history of the university in Europe*: Volume II: *Universities in early modern Europe (1500–1800).* Cambridge: Cambridge University Press, pp. 416–448.

Echeverría VI (2011) El movimiento de proyectiles en la mecánica de Diego Hurtado de Mendoza y la nueva dinámica renacentista. *Asclepio. Revista de Historia de la Medicina y de la Ciencia*, 63(1): 179–192.

Favaro A (1899–1900) Due lettere inedite di Guidobaldo del Monte a Giacomo Contarini. *Atti dell'Istituto Veneto di scienze lettere arti* 69: 303–312.
Frank M and Napolitani PD (2015) Il giovane Galileo e Guidobaldo dal Monte: discepolo e maestro?. In *Scienze e rappresentazioni: saggi in onore di Pierre Souffrin: atti del convegno internazionale, Vinci, Biblioteca Leonardiana, 26–29 settembre 2012*. Firenze: L.S. Olschki, pp. 173–197.
Garin E (1983) Aristotelismo veneto e scienza moderna. In Olivieri L (ed) *Aristotelismo veneto e scienza moderna. Atti del 250 anno accademico del Centro per la storia della tradizione aristotelica nel Veneto*. Padova: Antenore, pp. VIII–38.
Grendler M (1980) A Greek collection in Padua: The library of Gian Vincenzo Pinelli (1535–1601). *Renaissance Quarterly*, 33: 386–416.
Grendler M (1981) Book collecting in counter-Reformation Italy: the library of Gian Vincenzo Pinelli (1535–1601). *The Journal of Library History*, 16(1): 143–151.
Helbing MO (2008) La scienza della meccanica nel Cinquecento. In: Clericuzio A and Ernst G (eds) *Il Rinascimento italiano e l'Europa. Le scienze*. Treviso-Vicenza: Angelo Colla, pp. 573–592.
Henninger-Voss M (2000) Working machines and noble mechanics. Guidobaldo del Monte and the translation of knowledge. *Isis*, 2: 233–259.
Howard D (2022) Invenzione e realtà: Domande di brevetto presentate al Senato veneziano. In: Howard D (ed) *L'architettura proto-industriale del Veneto nell'età di Palladio*. Roma: Officina Editore per il CISA Palladio, in press.
Irigoin J (1977) Les ambassadeurs à Venise et le commerce des manuscrits grecs dans les années 1540–1550. In: Beck HG, Manoussacas M and Pertusi A (eds) *Centro di mediazione tra Oriente e Occidente (secoli XV–XVI). Aspetti e problemi*. Firenze: Olschki, pp. 399–415.
Keblusek M and Noldus BV (eds) (2011) *Double agents: cultural and political brokerage in early modern Europe*. Leiden: Brill.
Keller AG (1976) Mathematicians, mechanics, and experimental machines in northern Italy in the sixteenth century. In: Crosland M (ed) *The emergence of science in Western Europe*. New York: Science History Publications, pp. 15–34.
Laird WR (1986) The scope of renaissance mechanics. *Osiris* 2: 43–68.
Long PO (2001) *Artisan/practitioners and the rise of the new sciences, 1400–1600*. Corvallis; Oregon State University Press.
Massumi B (2002) *Parables for the virtual: movement, affect, sensation*. Durham, NC: Duke University Press.
Mazzi G and Zaggia S (eds) (2004) *"Architetto sia l'ingegniero che discorre". Ingegneri, architetti e proti nell'età della Repubblica*. Marsilio: Venezia.
Nuovo A (2007) The creation and dispersal of the library of G.V.P. In: Myers R and Harris M (eds) *Books on the move. Tracking copies through collections and the book trade*. Newcastle–London: Giles Mandelbrote, pp. 39–68.
Nuovo A (2008) La struttura bibliografica della biblioteca di Gian Vincenzo Pinelli (1535–1601). In: Sabba F (ed) *Le biblioteche private come paradigma bibliografico*. Roma: Bulzoni, pp. 57–68.
Panciera W (2005) *Il governo delle artiglierie. Tecnologia bellica e istituzioni veneziane nel secondo Cinquecento*. Milano: Franco Angeli.
Pigafetta F (1581) Prefazione "Ai Lettori de Le Mecaniche dell'Illustrissimo sig. Guido Ubaldo de Marchesi del Monte". In: *Le mecaniche dell'illustrissimo signor Guido Ubaldo de' marchesi del Monte, tradotte in volgare dal signor Filippo Pigafetta, nelle quali si contiene la vera dottrina di tutti gli istrumenti principali da mover pesi*

grandissimi con picciola forza, a beneficio di chi si diletta di questa nobilissima scienza, e massimamente di capitani di guerra, ingegneri, architetti e d'ogni artefice che intenda per via di machine far opre maravigliose e quasi sopra naturali. Venetia: appresso Francesco di Franceschi Senese, unnumbered page.

Piovan F and Sitran Rea L (eds) (2001) *Studenti, università, città nella storia Padovana*. Padova: Centro per la storia dell'università.

Raugei AM (2018) *Gian Vincenzo Pinelli e la sua biblioteca*. Genève: Droz.

Rheinberger HJ (1997) *Toward a history of epistemic things. Synthesizing proteins in the test tube*. Stanford: Stanford University Press.

Rose PR (1976) Iacomo Contarini. *Physics*, 18: 117–129.

Rose PL and Drake S (1971) The Pseudo-Aristotelian questions of mechanics in Renaissance culture. *Studies in the Renaissance*, 18: 65–104.

Rossi P (1997) *La nascita della scienza moderna in Europa*. Roma-Bari: Laterza.

Rovida E (2013) *Machines and signs: a history of the drawing of machines*. New York–London: Springer.

Salazar NB and Jayaram K (eds) (2016) *Keywords of mobility critical engagements*. Oxford: Berghahn.

Savio A (2020) *Tra spezie e spie. Filippo Pigafetta nel Mediterraneo del Cinquecento*. Roma: Viella.

Schmitt CB (1969) Experience and experiment: a comparison of Zabarella's view with Galileo's in *De Motu*. *Studies in the Renaissance*, 16: 80–138.

Schwinges RC (2018) Akademische Mobilität in der älteren Vormoderne (1350–1550). In: Crousaz K, Gillabert M and Rathmann-Lutz A (eds) *Attraktive Orte: Zur Aufnahme ausländischer StudentInnen/Accueillir l'étudiante étrangerère*. Zurich: Chronos, pp. 27–40.

Sgarbi M (2016) Aristotele per artigiani, ingegneri e architetti. *Philosophical Readings*, 8: 67–78.

Sheller M and Urry J (2006) The new mobilities paradigm. *Environment and Planning A*, 38(2): 207–226.

Smith PH (2004) *The body of the artisan: art and experience in the scientific revolution*. Chicago: University of Chicago Press.

Star SL and Griesemer JR (1989) Institutional ecology, "Translations", and boundary objects: amateurs and professionals on Berkeley's Museum of Vertebrate Zoologie, 1907–1939. *Social Studies of Science*, 19: 387–420.

Star SL (2010) Ceci n'est pas un objet-frontière. Réflexions sur l'origine d'un concept. *Revue d'anthropologie des connaissances*, 4(1): 18–35.

Trompette P and Vinck D (2009) Retour sur la notion d'objet-frontière. *Revue d'anthropologie des connaissances*, 3(1): 5–27.

Van Dyck M (2006) Gravitating towards stability: Guidobaldo's Aristotelian-Archimedean synthesis. *History of Science*, 44: 373–407.

Van Leeuwen J (2016) *The Aristotelian mechanics: text and diagrams*. Berlin, Springer.

Archives

Archivo General de Simancas, e.g. AGS, *Estado*, Legajo 1509, c. 248.

Biblioteca Ambrosiana di Milano, *R 121 sup.*, f. 15r, 5 novembre 1580, letter by Filippo Pigafetta to Guidobaldo del Monte.

12 Synchronic development or diffusion? The temporal mobility of violent practices before and after WWI[1]

Giulia Albanese and Matteo Millan

12.1 Introduction

In 1908, a major agricultural strike erupted in the province of Parma, in Italy. Famous for its renowned *prosciutto* and cheese, the province of Parma was one of the richest and most developed agricultural areas, not just in Italy but in the whole world. The clashes immediately became very intense because of the determination and deep hatred between the parties involved: on the one side, the workers' trade unions led by Alceste De Ambris, on the other, the association of agricultural owners and large tenants led by Lino Carrara. Determined to go for broke and to avoid a workers' victory at all costs, Carrara adopted a broad range of measures, the most radical of which was undoubtedly the establishment of a sort of private police force, the *Volontari Lavoratori*, consisting of agricultural entrepreneurs, nationalist students and ex-military personnel, with the task of opposing the workers and protecting private properties. Faced with the hesitancy of the traditional police forces, Carrara made no bones about the fact that the *Volontari Lavoratori* represented "the public force of the private state", and aimed therefore to be the forerunners of a new political power (Adorno, 2008; Millan, 2019). Three years after the end of the strike of Parma, the French anarcho-syndacalist, Antoinette Cauvin (*nom de guerre* Madame Sorgue), stated during a union meeting:

> I see there is a volunteer police force being organised [in England]. That is the most serious blunder. I knew these volunteer police. I have seen them at work in Parma. There they deliberately pursued a policy of exasperation. It will lead to civil war.

Madame Sorgue's reference to a "volunteer police force" was neither casual nor generic. It was a reference to a body of voluntary citizens of the same name founded in London in 1911 during the tense months of the Great Unrest.

(Saluppo, 2021: 231)

DOI: 10.4324/9781003278665-16

In November 1922, Adolf Hitler had stated:

> They call us German fascists. I do not want to discuss at this moment to what extent this comparison is right. But what we have in common with the fascists is unconditional love for our country, the will to snatch the working class from the claws of the International and the fresh spirit of camaraderie from the front line.
>
> (Goeschel, 2020: 2–3)

Not so very differently, on the 21st of November 1923, Benito Mussolini and Miguel Primo de Rivera met at Palazzo Venezia, during an important state visit by Alfonso XIII to the King of Italy. On that occasion, in which, rhetorically, the link between the *primoderrivista* and the Fascist experience emerged on a number of occasions, the Spanish dictator made reference to a proximity between the Spanish Somatén and the Italian Militia as institutions both aimed at the "secular institution of civilisation and order" (Quiroga, 2007: 146). In both cases, these similarities would have had at least partial second thoughts and retractions, depending on the moment and the season. It is nonetheless evident that these two references were a sign of the fact that the experience of *squadrismo* and its role in the ascent of Fascist power had left their mark on public opinion, including beyond the borders of Italy, notwithstanding that this was not the only example of paramilitarism in Europe of the early post-war period.

These episodes tell us different things about the circulation of the practices and political ideas in Europe in the early part of the 20th century. On the one hand, the example of the strike of 1908 is exceptional and, at the same time, emblematic of cultures and practices that were very widespread throughout pre-war Europe. Exceptional because it connects two phenomena which are, in reality, different, and, in the sources of the period, it is indeed rare to find testimony of transnational links or simple equivalence between the various armed associations operating in different European states. It is also emblematic because, without imitating or influencing each other, armed associations, usually with a markedly bourgeois social composition and operating outside strict state control, were a common presence in Europe during what is known as the Belle Époque (Millan, 2021a).

On the other hand, less unique, but the importance of which was perhaps not fully accepted by historiography, the recognition at European level of the March on Rome is a sign of early European acknowledgment of the exceptional nature of the Italian Fascist enterprise and its role, starting from the March on Rome, as a point of reference and as a European, and probably also global, model. The experience of *squadrismo* had a role in this European and international interest, as well as – although the two experiences are not immediately comparable – the institutionalisation of this body into the Voluntary Militia for National Security.

Since the 90s, historiography has strongly identified the First World War as the midwife of political violence and of the paramilitarism which developed in subsequent years.[2] Following the signing of the armistices, central and eastern Europe was in fact afflicted by civil wars, revolutionary movements and ethnic cleansing. From the massacres in Asia Minor to the proxy war in the Baltic regions to the daily brutality of the Russian civil war, the wars after the War left millions of dead on the ground, very many of which were civilians, and led to the birth and, frequently to the sudden fall, of new political regimes (Gerwarth, 2016; Gerwarth and Horne, 2012). Contemporaneously, Mediterranean Europe was witnessing unprecedented levels of political violence and social unrest which would lead in just a few years to the establishment of dictatorial regimes in Spain, Italy and Portugal (Albanese, 2016). In both cases, armed groups of civilians, militarily organised, were a disruptive organisational and political novelty, causing the emergence of a profound crisis in which old and new political regimes fell. Among the major powers, only France and the United Kingdom seemed immune to the wave of profound political and social upheaval following the arrival on the scene of the paramilitary movements. In reality, the clashes in Ireland were evidence that armed paramilitary groups were also a common presence in the victor countries where social and political conflicts and tensions, often long-lasting, resurfaced without a solution being found (Eichenberg, 2010).

In post-war Europe, the spread of paramilitary groups was a new phenomenon on account of the extent and intensity of the violence deployed, even if armed civilian movements had been a constant presence in European and world history. The emergence of this transnational phenomenon has inevitably attracted the attention of historians, also as a heuristic tool for analysing the emergence of fascist and authoritarian movements and regimes. George Mosse, referring above all to Germany, traced the causes back to a so-called brutalisation, that is to say, the transposition into civilian life of warlike practices, of a visceral hatred for the enemy and of a substantial indifference to the value of human life, experienced by millions of men in the trenches of the World War (Mosse, 1990). More recently, after a wide discussion of Mosse's theory over the years, Robert Gerwarth and John Horne offered a wide rethink of Mosse's interpretation, and have emphatically defined a "war in peace" the crises of statehood in the defeated countries: the focus was thus shifted from the experience of war to the post-war crisis (Gerwarth, 2016; Gerwarth and Horne, 2012). These studies have, in some ways, identified a series of causes – different from each other, but not the result of imitation – rooted in the experiences and economic, social and institutional effects of the war, to explain the emergence of the paramilitary violence of these years and of the spreading of violent and authoritarian practices. In these principal interpretations, however, the First World War acted as a watershed: either directly (brutalisation) or indirectly (collapse of statehood in the post-war period). The implicit assumption derived from this was that, in the models of behaviour, in the repertoire of practices but also in the motivations that spurred them into action, the post-war paramilitary groups were influenced in various ways by the recent experience of war. At the same time, the importance of the outcome of the war in defining the framework of conflict after the war became a discriminating factor. These points are obviously difficult to deny and are almost obvious in their immediacy. Above all, for post-war historians, the period preceding the conflict was marked by substantial peace, not only international but also internal, following significant social conquests, the establishment of wider democratic participation and rapid technological developments in a broad range of sectors and fields, from technology to medicine. In this context, the presence of paramilitary groups before the World War hit the wrong note.

This chapter is organised in two sections – devoted, respectively, to the practices and political cultures of the armed civilian deployment in the period pre-1914 and in the early post-war years – and attempts to reflect, albeit briefly, on two different phenomena. On the one hand, the chapter reflects on the circulation of practices and political ideas linked to the use of violence and to the emergence of paramilitary movements during two different periods, before and after the war, and observes some of the structural differences in them. On the other hand, adopting a long-term diachronic perspective, it evaluates the presence and impact of processes of cultural transfer of the idea of paramilitarism, as a social decision to use organised non-state violence to resolve problems of a social, political and ethnic nature. This enables consideration of two different models of circulation of ideas and practices, one based on the coexistence of transnational phenomena and specific national variations, and another on explicit processes of imitation and transfer.

This obviously highlights a significant methodological issue because, if the historiography that researched the mobility in recent years has largely focused on transfers, the synchronic emergence of similar phenomena caused by social, economic and political transformations should not be underestimated, or applied to a single model of imitation. It should be fully taken on and implemented, even when – as in the case reported in the opening – it initiates dialogue between different parallel experiences, which should not be read, however, in terms of action/reaction, nor only thought of in terms of a comparison that does not take account of broader contexts than those national.[3]

12.2 The mushrooming of armed associations in pre-1914 Europe

In pre-war Europe, groups of armed civilians were a common presence. From the big industrial cities to the country villages, armed associations were a very widespread and legal phenomenon which enjoyed broad social acceptance. As members of shooting clubs, civic militias, paramilitary groups and private police forces, hundreds of thousands of European male citizens attended armed associations on a daily basis. From the end of the last decade of the 19th century, the growth of these armed associations accelerated in an unprecedented way. It was certainly not a new phenomenon; nevertheless, mainly following the revolutionary wave of 1848–49 and certainly after the Franco-Prussian war, groups such as civic militias and city watch groups had become increasingly rare and were considered to be a manifestation of backwardness, the residue from bygone times. The contextual reinforcement of modern police forces paid for out of collective taxation and of permanent armed forces based on general conscription had supplanted, at least in continental Europe, the majority of voluntary armed groups. And yet the two decades between the end of the 19th century and the beginning of the 20th century saw a revival of these groups. This phenomenon was not only characterised by its European scope but by the – in some ways amazing – simultaneity with which it happened without, however, many of these groups having any connection with each other. In many cases, these were groups that had, for decades, experienced a difficult existence or had even fallen into oblivion. In 1890–91, a new regulation transformed the ancient Catalan militia of the Somatén into a hybrid organisation, composed of civilians but supervised by the army, the explicit objective of which was to protect social peace and to combat socialism. At the beginning of the 20th century, the Citizen patrols, a sort of civic guard charged with patrolling the streets of the Italian city of Bologna, were re-established – in this case, also with the support of the local authorities – to assist law enforcement in the repression of crime and in the fight against strikes. After years of inactivity, the Belgian Civic Guard – a real fossil of the past that had its origins in 1848 – was mobilised to fight certain big strikes, like those that broke out in Brussels and Leuven in 1902. From 1907 to 1908, at the same time as the large mass demonstrations organised by the Austrian social democrats requesting that universal suffrage be granted, ancient civic organisations like the Bürgercorps experienced a real renaissance which was accompanied by a new social legitimacy: from old-fashioned and somewhat bizarre groups of uniformed house-owners they became, even in the smallest villages of Cisleithania, the bulwark of bourgeois reaction to the activism of the working masses.

Other times, in contrast, rather than the re-founding of old organisations, new groups were created out of nowhere. In 1891, the Prussian government founded the Zechenwehren, an auxiliary police corps composed of supervisors and managers of the large mines of the Ruhr, tasked with supporting law enforcement in case of strikes. In 1911, in the midst of that wave of strikes that became known as The Great Unrest, the Civil Defence League was established in Liverpool and it soon gathered 2,500 members in order to "assist the Authorities in preserving the health, safety and well-being of the City in time of need". In the same year, the Volunteer Police Force was created, a sort of private police force that aimed to combat strikes and to protect the internal security of the kingdom. It enjoyed the political and financial support of some of the great peers of England. Some years earlier, Italian farmers had also decided to mobilise themselves into militias to protect their properties and livestock during some major strikes, openly challenging – as we shall see – not just the socialist unions but also the State authorities.[4]

What these groups had in common was the patriotic and bourgeois counter-mobilisation to the profound political and social changes that were taking place, certainly at different times but following substantial consistency, throughout the continent. The use of armed mobilisation of private individuals was not, in fact, a legacy of the past and the consequence of policies that were still weak or in the process of consolidation, but the exact opposite. Sometimes, this armed mobilisation was supported and encouraged by the state authorities themselves, determined to balance the widening of rights and political participation, with a realignment of the so-called loyal classes. This is the case, for example, with the German Zechenwehren and the Catalan Somatén mentioned earlier. In other cases, the bourgeois mobilisation took place, not just without state support, but against it: in fact, the authorities were judged to be hopelessly weak, disorganised and tolerant. In these latter cases in particular, underpinning the bourgeois self-mobilisation, were confused, rudimentary, popularised and re-adapted doctrines of social contract.

The bourgeois armed mobilisation between the 19th and 20th centuries was not however limited to the sphere of social conflicts. In other words, not only did it assume defensive tendencies on the occasion of big strikes or mass demonstrations to broaden the suffrage, but it also took on the form of a realignment and consolidation of patriotic ideals. At the end of the day, obstructing internal disorder and consolidation on the home front had to go hand in hand, above all in a global context in which social conflicts and military preparation were not two separate worlds but two sides of the same coin. With even greater clarity than the bourgeois anti-worker mobilisation, all over the continent there was a double impetus towards the organisation of groups of armed civilians. On the one hand, governments and authorities invested money and forces, pushed through specific legislation and supported politically the creation of scholastic battalions and youth organisations, bodies of armed volunteers with auxiliary functions, shooting clubs; on the other hand, many of these institutional initiatives did nothing but sanction and formally recognise independent initiatives from civil society. This was the case, to name but a few examples, of the French Bataillones Scolaires, founded in 1882 to prepare the young French militarily for the next war; or else the Italian Corpo Nazionale Volontari Ciclisti e Automobilisti (National Corps of Volunteer Cyclists and Motorists), created in 1904 out of the principal cycling associations of the country and officially recognised in 1908; or the groups of volunteer motor boatmen in Germany and in the Austro-Hungarian Empire; and also thousands of shooting groups throughout the whole of Europe. If, in the Germanic area, these groups were an expression of bourgeois respectability and manifestation of the loyal classes, in other countries they were instead a school of patriotism and militarism (like in France and partly in Italy and Spain) (Bourzac, 2004; Papa, 2013; Camilleri, 2022).

The binding link between the bourgeois mobilisation in arms on the eve of the First World War was the desire to reaffirm an articulated idea of order at a moment when, because of wide social transformations, the traditional institutional structures, from civilian powers to the army and police forces, from associations to work relationships, seemed in a state of crisis and unable to give satisfactory responses.

The protection of public order, the fight against crime, opposing and halting the advance of rival political parties, but also the preparation for war, the reaffirmation of morally challenged gender identity principles – these were the different meanings of a concept of order that, in many different variations, seemed to involve wide sections of the bourgeois classes throughout Europe. And for many of these men, these ideals were so strong as to justify, not just a simple mobilisation in the field of associations or politics, but a mobilisation in arms. Sometimes, this only took place in a performative capacity to demonstrate the cohesion and compactness of the loyal classes, but other times, it took place concretely and was translated into forms of political violence.

12.3 Becoming a model: the case of Italy

In March 1919, when Benito Mussolini founded the *Fasci di Combattimento* (the Fascist squads), groups of men who would be merged into the Fascist fighting squadrons had already begun, some months earlier, to stand out for their actions in Italy, especially in Milan. By the end of 1918, and more clearly in 1919, it was already possible to observe the action of squads of ex combatants or of those too young to have had the experience of war, who were mobilised – after the end of the war – to defend the reasons for intervention and the nationalist positions (Gentile, 1989; Franzinelli, 2003; Fabbri, 2009).

It is worth noting, for example, the booing and violence against Leonida Bissolati at La Scala Theatre in Milan in January 1919. Bissolati was considered guilty of having reiterated his democratic positions on the geopolitical structure of the eastern border in the post-war period. On that occasion, groups of special forces, nationalists and future Fascists came together. The activity of these men devoted to the exercise of violence against political opponents was rather lively in the first months of 1919. These groups had been able to count on a fairly decisive presence of ex combatants and special forces, who were reclaiming their place in the post-war society and deploying their warrior virtues and abilities in the use of arms. In 1919, the organisation of the Fascist squads, despite an ambiguous political agenda, also aimed – if not mainly – at the organisation of these men and the capitalisation of their capacity to use violence in a society deeply marked by the war. However, this was also a way of capitalising the experience of interventionism and other experiences of armed volunteering in the period before the war, experiences that had reared their ugly head in Italy and in Europe to defend private property, to respond to the social and political action of left-wing groups and to restore order. In Milan, at least from the middle of 1919, both in industrial and commercial areas and among the authorities themselves, initiatives were put in place to create bodies of armed civilian volunteers with the task of supporting law enforcement, taking as explicit model of reference the citizens

Corpo delle Pattuglie Cittadine (Citizens' Patrols) that had been operating for decades in Bologna (Millan, 2021b: 248).

Italy was not an exceptional case of the use of violence in the public and political space and nor was the presence of paramilitary groups in the public scene exceptional, as we have seen. Throughout Europe during those months, masses of demobilised men were pressing for recognition of their role in the post-war societies. This presence was much stronger and more significant in the situations in which – as has been amply demonstrated by Robert Gerwarth – defeat in war and the collapse of imperial institutions, often combined with revolutionary attempts, had determined phases of interregnum and sometimes also of civil war. In the cases of imperial collapse and revolution, the presence of paramilitary groups and their role in the respective societies was far more pervasive than it was in Italy. This was the case in Russia and the entire ex-Tsarist Empire, especially the Baltic States and Ukraine where, starting with the revolution, paramilitary groups were more active during the civil wars that followed, but also of all the successor states of the Tsarist and Habsburg Empire. The motivations behind these paramilitary formations were in the rejection of the new political configuration of the successor states, in the attempt to build homogeneous political areas in terms of nationality or religion and in the defence of the economic and social order against the revolution. The violence in these cases began decisively as early as 1917 in the case of Russia and the ex-Tsarist Empire territories. The determining factor in giving rise to these scenarios was undoubtedly defeat in the First World War (Gerwarth, 2016).

These were not the only contexts in which an increase in violence by private groups and armed squadrons could be observed, as there were countries where, in common with Italy, they had won the war or else had not participated in it. Between 1918 and the beginning of 1919, Portugal had experienced a civil war that had pitted republicans against monarchists and also, to a degree, lay people and extremist Catholics. The return to a republican order would not however have resolved definitively the use of paramilitary violence. Also in Spain, which had remained neutral, it was already possible to witness an escalation of violence against social unrest and union organisation of the workers' world from 1917. This was also combined with conflicts between regionalists and centralists, where different national and regional perspectives clashed (Albanese, 2016). In this context, there were even some, like Antonio Gramsci, who predicted that the spread of violence in Spain might constitute a transitional phase that would cross all the European states and would lead to the "armament of the middle classes and [to the] introduction, in the class struggle, of military methods and surprise attacks" (Gramsci, 1921).

The Italian case was thus presented, in the first months of 1919, as not necessarily or especially original, if looked at from a European perspective, despite the fact that, already in 1919, two significant deviations could be observed: on the one hand, the choice of the squadrist movement – fairly unprecedented in the European paramilitary context – and, in particular, of its leader and organiser, to participate in political elections with its own list and, therefore, to open a more institutional channel of communication with the traditional political forces; on the other hand, the start of the Fiume adventure by Gabriele d'Annunzio, in September 1919, which undoubtedly constituted a significant and anomalous political experiment in the European political panorama and was regarded as such by intellectuals, artists and activists from all over Europe who were watching with interest Fiume and the invention of "dannunzian" politics.[5] If it was not for these two anomalies, however, the Italian paramilitary experience up until the end of 1920 or the beginning of 1921 might appear as an epiphenomenon of something that, with partly different forms, was also happening elsewhere.

However, things were more complex than that: first of all, because already by 1919 and then with more intensity in the Fascist renaissance in the autumn of 1920 and the first few months of 1921, in addition to the conquest of public spaces occupied by the socialists (at territorial and institutional level), the invention of new forms of politics would be encompassed within the Fascist movement, thanks to the reuse of formulae coined by D'Annunzio and to the mythical reconstruction and to the narrative and rhetorical talent of Mussolini.[6] A series of codes of recognition, identification and sharing that passed through symbols, key phrases, shared gestures and codification of the objectives, which the violence contributed to cementing. If they could be assimilated in part to the symbols of construction of institutional military bodies, were rarely codified so effectively in other contemporary (or preceding) paramilitary contexts. This was in part because Fascism was not characterised only by the presence of armed squadrons. It also had a leader who was even more political than military, Benito Mussolini, and a newspaper, "Il popolo d'Italia". This meant that, during the months from the foundation congress of the National Fascist Party to the March on Rome, squadrismo was a fundamental part of the party, aimed at broadening its power over the country and to its conquest, but it was not the only element of construction of a Fascist alternative to the liberal State. The role of Mussolini's newspaper and of the diplomatic and political activity of its leader (and of some others around him) was fundamental for the efficacy of Fascist political action and for making it a model worthy of interest in the rest of Europe (Albanese, 2017).

12.4 Conclusion. Different systems of diffusion

The (re-)flourishing of armed associations in pre-war Europe was, in large measure, a response to the processes of political, social and institutional reconfiguration that involved the entire continent. This contributed to an explanation of how large sectors of private citizens, almost simultaneously, came to believe that forming armed associations could be one of the answers to the crisis which they were experiencing. Interestingly, however, the institutional frameworks and history of each country played a pivotal role in defining the characteristics of the armed associationism. For example, defeat in the Franco-Prussian war of 1870–71 sharpened the appetite for *revanche* in the French population and authorities, which was translated into a myriad of associations of military preparation and in heavy investment by republican governments in the paramilitary training of the younger generations. At the same time, the foundation of the Ulster Volunteer Force would simply not have happened if the liberal British government had not decided to embark forcefully on the road of Home Rule for Ireland.

In a certain sense, the same could also be said for the development of the armed associations and paramilitary groups of the early post-war period. Because of the war and the defeat and collapse of empires and states, the paramilitary groups of the post-war period could be formed, widely in many cases, outside of any institutional framework, thanks to the absence of fully legitimate actors to be in control of the force. It was also thanks sometimes to the continuity between these associations and informal military groups and military bodies in which these men were placed during the war (it is the case, for example, of the Italian special forces, but also the Freikorps, formed by ex-combatants of the imperial German army). This provoked an exponential development of these groups – both in numerical terms and in respect of the practices of violence used, which abandoned the civic character of the pre-war period to assume a clear military connotation, aimed at annihilating the enemy. Against this background, explicit, direct continuity with pre-war armed associations was often not possible, except in specific cases, such as in Spain, where the reconfiguration of the Somatèn also came about because of Spain's absence of experience of the First World War. At the same time, however, pre-war experience provided a script for designing similar initiatives, such as the above-mentioned citizen patrols, or the early post-war Austrian and Bohemian civic guards, heirs to the Bürgercorps of the Habsburg period (Morelon, 2020: 217–218).

Nevertheless, both in the pre- and post-war period, the tendency emerged, although in very different contexts, from groups that were paramilitary or militarised, but private, to become bearers of political projects outside or alongside political institutions. This happened both in the case of Italy, Spain and Portugal, where armed, as well as paramilitary mobilisation, was not the result of institutional collapse provoked by the global conflict, and in the defeated countries of central and eastern Europe and the states that came after them. This phenomenon shows how the paramilitary groups of the post-war period also resulted from the affirmation of practices of self-organisation and of volunteers of order, developed in the decades preceding the war – a possibility which also concerned and concerns the contexts of the successor states of the post-war period, where such experiences had been developed and had a bearing. Throughout Europe, as we have seen, armed groups had origins which were in reality much older and were aiming to be a response to the enlargement and reconfiguration of the public sphere and of the democratic mechanisms. In post-war Europe, therefore, the presence of multiple causes may be assumed (some of ancient origin, others more recent; some local and national, others continental in scope) that interacted with each other to create specific and yet similar paramilitary phenomena and armed associations.

The birth (or re-birth) of paramilitary phenomena was therefore a continental phenomenon characterised by a marked synchronicity, as much before as after the war: it was the epiphenomenon and tangible expression, on an institutional, associative and political level, of ideas broadly shared by European social sectors faced with the effects of common democratisation processes and social upheaval in the period preceding the First World War, and of institutional crisis, revolutionary fear and authoritarian dreams in the subsequent period. These immense social and political transformations, because they happened in a synchronic manner, could only be the result of transfer processes which had been going on for decades, as well as, obviously, the impact of the war and its geopolitical consequences. At the same time, both before and after the war, the national legislative framework and the different attitude of the institutions and historic traditions played a fundamental role in shaping the specific characteristics of each individual association, limiting direct imitation, and making each of the associations specifically national, or even local or regional. In general, though, imitation and reciprocal transnational influence between the various institutions were limited, whereas the political cultures, fears and expectations which had produced the flourishing of the individual associations were very strong and shared. This marked synchronicity is, however, articulated in different ways according to the contexts.

As has been recently highlighted, nationalism and globalisation are not two mutually exclusive phenomena. On the contrary, one is the product of the other. Introducing the concept of *geteilte Geschichten*, Sebastian Conrad and Shalina Randeria emphasised how the term combines the two opposing connotations of "shared" and "divided", to indicate the presence, in a global context, of common elements and profound local differences. In this way, especially at a time of profound global changes, the making of social and political phenomena was the result of "diachronic 'stages of development'" that interacted with "synchronic 'staging of the world'". This ambivalence emerges clearly in the genesis of pre- and post-war armed associations (Conrad, 2010: 6–8; Conrad and Randeria, 2002).

At the same time, we can also observe that the emergence of an exceptional experience such as that of Fascism in Italy in the early 1920s led to a change of pace in relation to the circulation of political ideas and practices, transforming Italy from one of the actors of a phenomenon that was also occurring synchronically elsewhere – both before and after the war – into a reference model for the whole of Europe. This model undoubtedly concerned the ideological *koiné* that Fascism represented, the ability of a movement with those characteristics to take power, as well as the specific nature of a paramilitary movement that knew how to transform itself into a militia-party, thanks to a series of special circumstances. Among these, we should list Italy's particular role in the early post-war period in the continental geopolitical context, Mussolini's political skills in taking the lead of this paramilitary movement and of federating a series of armed defence groups, organised at local level, and his ability to act simultaneously at national and parliamentary level. It is significant that precisely the model of paramilitary and armed organisation and of militia-party, and its ambiguous relationship with the political system, would be the most important lesson that Fascism would give to Hitler and to the National Socialist Movement, thus marking the history of Europe in the decades to come.[7] Unlike other paramilitary groups, both in the pre- and post-war period, on the one hand, Italian Fascism was not exclusively related to a paramilitary dimension, but on the other – and perhaps because of this – it was a movement (a militia party, in fact, to take up the famous definition of Emilio Gentile) that had succeeded in gaining political power, immediately demonstrating that it was a viable alternative to the contradictions and inefficiencies of liberal democracies. By doing this, it realised the dreams of many throughout Europe who had already taken to the streets, armed, in the pre-war period but it was also to feed the authoritarian fantasies of many contemporary movements.

These case studies lead us to reflect on the importance of the process of dialogue among these experiences and on the importance of looking at the forms of transfer, ideological mobility and political practices. We can certainly assume that the impact of Fascism in Europe during the 1920s and also on Nazism itself has been partially neglected, both from the point of view of the mobility of ideas and political practices and of the impact of both these aspects on other political contexts. Nevertheless, it appears evident that the success of this political movement was partly the fruit of the emergence in the decades before the First World War of reactions to ongoing democratisation processes and of the emergence, in the new social, economic and political framework that they determined, of organisational practices and ideological perspectives which Fascism itself heralded. In this fertile ideological and political context, the Italian experience was able to have a significant impact.

Notes

1 Although the essay is the fruit of collaborative reflection, Matteo Millan is the principal author of the first section, Giulia Albanese of the second. The introduction and conclusion have been written by four hands. Please take into consideration that the bibliographical references are limited to the barest minimum for space reasons.
2 For a broad, general definition of paramilitarism, focused on links between state and armed groups, see Üngör (2020: 6–13).
3 For a reflection on these issues, see at least Kocka and Haupt (2009); Saunier (2013). The theme of the emergence of contemporary phenomena had already been raised by Marc Bloch in his fundamental article on comparative history (Bloch, 1928). Particularly interesting for the systematisation of these themes in the perspective of mobility studies is a series of studies on policy transfers with regard to which we remember at least Benson and Jordan (2011).
4 For a summary, see Millan (2021a).

5 For the international dimension of the events at Fiume, see in particular Salaris (2002).
6 See on this in particular the seminal study of Ledeen (1977).
7 On the relationship between Fascism and Nazism, see at least Goeschel (2020), which also reconstructs the historiography on the subject, and Schieder (2017). For more in general on the impact of Italian Fascism, see at least the fundamental Woller (2001), which, however, underestimates the impact of the 1920s.

References

Adorno S (2008) *Gli agrari a Parma. Politica, interessi e conflitti di una borghesia padana in età giolittiana.* Parma: Diabasis.

Albanese G (2016) *Dittature mediterranee: sovversioni fasciste e colpi di Stato in Italia, Spagna e Portogallo.* Roma: Laterza.

Albanese G (2017) Una marcia, tante marce. In: Giardina A (ed.) *Storia mondiale dell'Italia.* Roma-Bari: Laterza, pp. 602–605.

Benson D and Jordan A (2011) What have we learned from policy transfer research? Dolowitz and Marsh revisited. *Political Studies Review* 9(3): 366–378.

Bloch M (1928) Pour une histoire comparée des sociétés européennes. *Revue de synthèse historique* 46: 15–50.

Bourzac A (2004) *Les bataillons scolaires: 1880–1891 – L'éducation militaire à l'école de la République.* Paris: Editions L'Harmattan.

Camilleri N (2022) Gunshots, sociability, and community defense. Shooting associations in Imperial Germany and its colonies. *Journal of Modern European History* 20(2): 236–257.

Conrad S (2010) *Globalisation and the nation in Imperial Germany.* Cambridge: Cambridge University Press.

Conrad S and Randeria S (2002) Geteilte Geschichten: Europa in einer postkolonialen Welt. In: Conrad S and Randeria S (eds) *Jenseits des Eurozentrismus: Postkoloniale Perspektiven in Den Geschichts- Und Kulturwissenschaften.* Frankfurt: Campus Verlag.

Eichenberg J (2010) The dark side of independence: paramilitary violence in Ireland and Poland after the First World War. *Contemporary European History* 19(3): 231–248.

Fabbri F (2009) *Le origini della guerra civile: l'Italia dalla Grande Guerra al Fascismo (1918–1921).* Torino: Utet.

Franzinelli M (2003) *Squadristi: protagonisti e tecniche della violenza fascista, 1919–1922.* Milano: Mondadori.

Gentile E (1989) *Storia del partito fascista 1919–1922: movimento e milizia.* Roma-Bari: Laterza.

Gerwarth R (2016) *The vanquished: why the First World War failed to end, 1917–1923.* London: Allen Lane.

Gerwarth R and Horne J (eds) (2012) *War in peace: paramilitary violence in Europe after the Great War.* Oxford: Oxford University Press.

Goeschel C (2020) *Mussolini and Hitler: the forging of the Fascist alliance.* New Haven, CT–London: Yale University Press.

Gramsci A (1921) Italia e Spagna. *Ordine Nuovo*, 11 March. Torino.

Kocka J and Haupt HG (eds) (2009) *Comparative and transnational history: Central European approaches and new perspectives.* New York–Oxford: Berghahn Books.

Ledeen MA (1977) *D'Annunzio: The first Duce*. Baltimore, MD: The Johns Hopkins University Press.
Millan M (2019) "The public force of the private state" – strikebreaking and visions of subversion in liberal Italy (1880s to 1914). *European History Quarterly* 49(4): 625–649.
Millan M (2021a) Belle Époque in arms? Armed associations and processes of democratization in pre-1914 Europe. *Journal of Modern History* 93(3): 599–635.
Millan M (2021b) From "State protection" to "private defence": strikebreaking, civilian armed mobilisation and the rise of Italian Fascism. In: Millan M and Saluppo A (eds) *Corporate policing, yellow unionism, and strikebreaking, 1890–1930: in defence of freedom*. Abingdon: Routledge.
Morelon C (2020) Respectable citizens: civic militias, local patriotism, and social order in late Habsburg Austria (1890–1920). *Austrian History Yearbook*: 193–219.
Mosse GL (1990) *Fallen soldiers: reshaping the memory of the World Wars*. New York–Oxford: Oxford University Press.
Papa C (2013) *L'Italia giovane dall'Unità al Fascismo*. Roma: Laterza.
Quiroga A (2007) *Making Spaniards: Primo de Rivera and the nationalization of the masses, 1923–30*. Basingstoke: Palgrave Macmillan.
Salaris C (2002) *Alla festa della rivoluzione: artisti e libertari con D'Annunzio a Fiume*. Bologna: il Mulino.
Saluppo A (2021) Vigilant citizens: the case of the volunteer police force, 1911–1914. In: Millan M and Saluppo A (eds) *Corporate policing, yellow unionism, and strikebreaking, 1890–1930: in defence of freedom*. Abingdon: Routledge.
Saunier P-Y (2013) *Transnational history: theory and history*. Basingstoke: Palgrave Macmillan.
Schieder W (2017) *Adolf Hitler: Politischer Zauberlehrling Mussolinis*. Berlin–Boston: De Gruyter.
Üngör UÜ (2020) *Paramilitarism: mass violence in the shadow of the State*. Oxford: Oxford University Press.
Woller H (2001) *Roma, 28 Ottobre 1922: l'Europa e la sfida dei fascismi*. Bologna: il Mulino.

Afterword

Aristotle Kallis
KEELE UNIVERSITY

From encounter to friction: mobilities of ideas in (their) context

The new mobilities paradigm challenged convincingly and productively the overwhelming "sedentarist bias" of the mainstream of social sciences and humanities (Malkki, 1992), in favour of a "nomadic metaphysics" (Cresswell, 2006, 26–27). But, at the same time, it opened itself up to criticisms regarding a 'presentist' focus that deprived mobility of its complex historical genealogies and contextually signified patterns of cultural production (Inglis, 2014). If the mobilities paradigm offers unique opportunities to analyse a wide range of mobile practices in spatial and power relations, then humanities have a unique and critical role to play in "vibrant interdisciplinary discussions on the phenomena, technologies, and infrastructures of mobility" by adding temporal depth to them (Lee and Shin, 2002, 1–5). In this respect, the set of contributions to the 'Ideas' section of this interdisciplinary volume on mobilities – wide-ranging in chronological coverage and studied expressions of ideational mobility alike – make a compelling case both for the analytical benefits of the mobilities paradigm in the historical study of mobile practices and for the unique perspectives that historical scholarship can bring to the field of mobilities studies.

The field of ideas remains the perennial child prodigy in the field of mobilities studies. Full of potential yet young and disobliging, it remains somewhat ill-fitting and thus peripheral to the mainstream of mobilities research (Cresswell, 2011, 251). This is largely because ideational mobilities integrate a much wider spectrum of mobile practices beyond abstract, elusive pieces of information, knowledge or practices flowing across space. For ideas to 'move' across space and over time, to move in particular directions at differential pace, to move purposefully in one sense but not in another, the unpredictable intermediation and interaction of a series of agencies and structures needs to be accounted for. Mobilities of ideas are often driven by personal mobilities; or they are enabled and facilitated through movement of textual artefacts, such as written records; or they may be shaped through particular – facilitating or blocking – infrastructures that favour certain kinds of flow and particular kinds of interaction, in some places and directions, at some points in time. To understand why, how, when, and where ideas move, as well as to appreciate the variable effects of their mobilities in/across space and time, we often need to mobilise the full apparatus of mobilities studies – and then align it with a host of other methodologies and tools that interrogate the local, the particular, the contingent, and the unpredictable.

Both space and time, individually and in their interactions, matter enormously when analysing mobilities (Cresswell, 2006, 4). As produced and constantly reproduced categories, space and time also produce and shape uniquely each instance of mobility within and across them. We know only too well by now that mobility is one thing and motility, the capacity or potential for movement, is another (Kaufman, 2000). Technologies and infrastructures of movement have changed dramatically over time and asymmetrically across space. If, in earlier historical periods, mobility and motility were seriously constrained both by the gravity of (spatial) distance and by limitations in the operation of networks of movement (network/cognitive/cultural/ distance) (Hall, 2008, 22), then innovations from printing to wireless communication to logistics and transformations such as increased literacy, urbanisation or mass travel dramatically increased the speed and range of the flow of information. Whereas ideas used to travel exclusively or mostly through physical contact and their diffusion required co-presence (of people and textual material artefacts), as we move to the modern period it became increasingly possible for them to move independently of human interaction and even, in the last hundred and fifty years, without a material trace at all (Pooley, 2017, 65–70 and Cresswell, 2006, 15–21).

Still, enhanced motility does not automatically or neatly translate into equivalent mobility. Even if ideas could somehow 'travel' from a geographic A to a more or less distant B, even if they could overcome gravity and friction caused by spatial distance, even if they circumvent obstacles and dead-ends, this did not mean that, once found in another context, they could continue to move in different directions (Cresswell, 2010 and Cliff, Martin, Ord, 1974). This is because the physical availability of information in a new distant context (be that via speech, written record, book etc.) did not guarantee by itself (i) broader access to the information; and (ii) the active interest (at-traction) necessary to produce a deeper contact and engagement between local agents and the new idea. Depending on the historical period, factors such as education and literacy, linguistic and cultural difference, as well as the availability of the record providing access to a specific idea/information, were key factors that could restrict ideational mobilities. For example, contributions to this volume have underlined the role of translation in enhancing access to knowledge coming from distant sources and coded in unfamiliar languages. Even the decision to render a text into vernacular idioms or to extrapolate a more impactful visual record (Fava and Savio, this volume) could make a huge difference in terms of the further access to, and diffusion of, written records as well as their associated ideas and knowledges.

Bruno Latour has underlined the significance of recording knowledge in ways that made it accessible, reproducible, permanent, and relatable to other pieces of knowledge through what he called 'inscriptions' (Latour, 1986). Intriguingly Latour called these inscriptions 'immutable mobiles' – seemingly a contradiction but in fact capturing the particular dynamics of inscription (writing, recording, translating, popularising etc.) as one of those all-important 'moorings' that, while seemingly static, actually serve to facilitate, catalyse, and supercharge movement (Hannam, Sheller, Urry, 2006). Translation has always been a crucial aspect of this inscription process – not only literally, as a rendition of a text into another language, but also in metaphorical terms, indicating a move from medium to medium, culture to culture, period to period, audience to audience, as well as from temporality to permanence (Draude, 2017). By serving as a powerful technique of recontextualisation/localisation of ideas and knowledge, translation in any of these senses is an immutable mobile par excellence – stable yet generative of different possibilities and momentum for mobility (Greenall and Løfaldli, 2019).

As highlighted by Latour, inscriptions are also implicated in one further important process of mobility. It is their local accumulation and organisation as accessible pieces of knowledge that create a framework for *contact* and *productive engagement* as precondition for further ideational mobilities. The example of Padova as a centre of such an accumulation, codification, and cross-linking of knowledge is eloquently highlighted in multiple contributions to this section (Fava and Savio and Basso, Piccinini, and Viggiano). Functioning as a 'contact zone' – a space "where cultures meet, clash, and grapple with each other" (Pratt, 1991, 34) – for the circulation of ideas and encouraging the formation of local and international knowledge exchange communities and networks, the university and the wider learning infrastructures established around it (libraries, knowledge groups and liaisons, networks of contact) fostered further opportunities for exchange that supercharged mobilities across people, communities, places, cultures, and cognitive fields. Movement here served both as the precondition and consequence of further ideational mobilities: knowledge that had already been inscribed, translated, and organised could be accessed and processed by itinerant humans present in Padova before becoming circulated in a variety of mediated forms to new, distant, and/or different networks and audiences through diverse media like correspondence, translation, and so on. Contact zones provided the wherewithal of knowledge and unique opportunities for circulation by acting as both magnets (of people, ideas and knowledge, exchange) and laboratories of production and circulation of ideas.

The importance of contact zones as a place of accumulation/organisation of differential knowledge and meeting point was pronounced in earlier historical periods, when the friction of distance rendered movement difficult and the capacity for inscription, translation, and access to knowledge was constrained. In more recent times, however, both the circulatory potential of information/knowledge and the ease of inscription were dramatically expanded. The gradual decoupling of ideational mobilities from the physical movement of people or artefacts as a precondition for the diffusion of knowledge progressively freed ideas from gravity and distance decay, generating in the process new, sweeping geographies of circulation and contact (Waters and Leung, 2017, 271). At the same time, the easier recording and reproducibility of information, as well as its systematic organisation, facilitated its transmission across different contexts. This dramatically expanded field of inscription and circulation, however, led to two paradoxes. The first paradox was that, as the bandwidth of ideational mobilities and the facilitating mechanisms for accessing it exploded, so did the volume of inscribed knowledge. *Contact* was thus transformed from a problem of limited movement and restricted access to knowledge to a challenge of singling out knowledge from a surfeit of potentially available resources. If earlier contact zones served as places of aggregation of information, of enabling access to it, and of archiving, their modern equivalents have functioned primarily as curation devices against the backdrop of a dizzying profusion of available knowledge. In the latter case contact is less the outcome of the encounter with mobile information and more the product of a significantly more active, actor-driven process of *selective, affective engagement*. Therefore, understanding modern ideational mobilities has become less and less a problem of mapping physical routes or tracking the itineraries of people and artefacts; instead, it concerns primarily accounting for the 'stickiness' of particular ideas over many other alternatives in a given context. The second paradox of ideational mobilities in the modern world is that, in seeking to account for these mobilities, we resort to a vocabulary of slowness and resistance, by definition suggestive of reduced or impeded, not enhanced, mobility. And yet, as Anna Lowenhaupt Tsing (2005, 14–19) has shown, the "grip of encounter" is precisely what underpins productive engagement with ideas. In a world that is deluged with inscriptions and behaves like a slippery plateau of incessant superfluidity, we have become understandably fascinated by those occurrences of creative contact as an adhesive, not just mobile event.

Tsing's book is aptly entitled *Friction*. This 'friction' is the strangest of mobility beasts. A metaphor borrowed from physics, it describes a force that is at the same time resistant to, and generative of, movement; it is a variable of mobility that translates one set of forces into another upon contact between two discrete surfaces. The concept of friction has steadily gained purchase in the field of mobilities studies (Cresswell, 2014, 2010; for an overview of approaches see Rabbiosi 2022, 144) but still remains a relatively niche tool of analysis, not least because of its semantic ambiguity and counter-intuitiveness. Yet this is precisely what makes it so relevant to the study of ideational mobilities in particular. Friction draws attention to the contextual (spatial, cultural, temporal) factors that generate the proverbial heat of meaningful contact between the local and the itinerant, effecting unpredictable changes to both in the process. This heat, evidenced in the travelling momentum of tyranny as signifier and signified in the ancient Greek and Roman worlds (Cavaggioni, Fezzi, and Raviola) to the 16th/17th-century 'Anglo-Venetian moment' (Basso, Piccinini, and Viggiano) to the diffusion of f(F)ascism as a source of political inspiration in the 1920s (Albanese and Millan), was what underwrote, shaped, and changed mobile practices and outcomes. Friction does not necessarily stop or impede movement but rather it transforms it into a fascinating dialectical process involving interaction between the surface of two entities that have come into contact. Contact here indicates not just a mere encounter (an access event, important though this is) but also engagement that disrupts the original autonomous flow of each of the two objects caused by this initial encounter. What makes this contact fascinating is *difference*: each surface has its own unique fractal morphology, not to mention special history, and therefore the fit between the two can never be perfect; but the all-important grip results from enough adhesion between the two surfaces – what Tsing (2005, 16) described as "encounters (and connections) across difference". What happens after friction has been generated is fascinating because it constitutes an exception amidst so many other incessant fleeting encounters that generate little or no contact, little or no heat, little or no stickiness, in the end limited or no change. Once two entities engage 'across difference', the creative result is unpredictable in form, direction or duration – but change in each of the two objects' shape and trajectory is inevitable.

How useful is this scientific analogy for the study of ideational mobilities? The intricate histories of the word 'mobility' over time (Biasiori) highlight the volatility inherent in translating concepts from the scientific to the social world. With few objects to observe in interaction and often no mobile people or artefacts to track down, the mobilities of ideas challenge the orthodoxies not only of the mobilities paradigm but also of the physics behind the friction metaphor. Ideas may move – but they do so with their unique heavy contextual baggage in each case, moving along discrete trajectories prior to contact. This whole drama of mobility also involves further capricious variables – especially human agency and a range of unique contextual factors that may increase or reduce its potential to transform the encounter into an active engagement and meaningful interface between the two entities coming into contact. Above all, however, in the domain of ideational mobilities, ideas and knowledges encounter each other and their audience *in* and *through context*. The inscription of, and access to, an idea does not guarantee meaningful contact with local knowledges. They also do not suffice to explain why new ideas 'stick' or not in particular spatiotemporal settings, if they engage or otherwise with local knowledges, if they become localised and "made particular" or retain their alterity (Cresswell, 2015, 83–85 and Cresswell, 2014, 114). Context, in space and in time, matters enormously – first, as a snapshot, a temporal and spatial-cultural record of past mobilities and their sedimented effects; and second, as laboratory of dynamic unique interactions that facilitate, impede, refract, and shape patterns of mobilities in the present and, in the process, alter the context itself. Context is not simply the receptacle of the encounter here and now but a unique palimpsest of numerous inscriptions and sedimentations over a long period of time; the scene of multiple intersecting translocal and diachronic encounters. Using the friction analogy, we can think of context as the fractal local surface of the encounter between ideas and people across difference. The surface belies a stratigraphy made up of layers of sedimented history and renders the encounter itself and its effects unpredictable at the time, even as they may seem observable, ex post facto, under the long-term privileged gaze of the historian.

How do we get from encounter to engaged contact and friction? 'Stickiness' relies both on at-tention (literally to stretch *towards*) and at-traction (to draw *together*) of human agents inside the local context to the idea – in that order. Attention is the essential precondition of attraction but, even then, engaged contact – not to mention stickiness and friction – are far from guaranteed. When a new idea does encounter and engage with existing trends in a different context, it actually becomes intertwined in a unique, unpredictable chemistry that may be exclusive to its particular place and time but whose components often come a very long way. To take an example that features across different contributions to this section, the reasons behind the centrality of Padova in the mobilities of knowledge about mechanics in the early modern period (Fava and Savio) had to do with its accumulated reputation as centre of knowledge and debate, particularly accessible by people outside the Venetian territories but also as a privileged repository of inscriptions of knowledge; and yet it also took the rediscovery and translation of a cherished ancient manuscript to supercharge the process further. Scholars were attracted to Padova because of this reputation but they also interacted with the accumulated knowledge selectively and with significant prior bias. Every encounter and interaction across difference in the university halls and the city's numerous libraries or meeting places used by various learned communities left an imprint locally, just as it produced effects that travelled further afield, following the routes of people or objects or inscriptions.

We are thus back to the importance of the context as a receptacle of people and their ideas, a record of the indentations of history. When accounting for the striking transnational diffusion of interwar fascism (Albanese and Millan), we are presented with a challenge of explaining the patterns of its asymmetrical momentum across a wide range of local contexts (Weyland, 2021, 10 and Kallis, 2021). This is a challenge that may not be possible to address simply by tracing the mobilities of fascist ideas and practices in the post-WW1 period and by analysing the dynamics of their local encounters. The success of fascism in countries like Italy and Germany, as well as its mixed fortunes in other European countries at the time, highlights the need to study the interaction between fascist ideas and local contexts synchronically; but it also demands that we go much deeper into the historical registers that shaped each of these contexts diachronically. Diffusion, as we know only too well by now, is far from a neat one-way process of transmission from a privileged source to a passive audience largely deprived of agency. No idea, no matter how successful in one place and time, is guaranteed to succeed in others. The productive engagement of people and groups (carrying their own individual and collective predispositions) with different ideas depends on the mobilities that make the contact possible in the first place; yet it also involves a different order and scale of mobilities: at-tention, at-traction, friction/traction. All these instances tend to get juxtaposed to movement but they are in fact translations, conversions or shifts thereof; therefore, mobile practices par excellence.

The chemistry involved in attention, attraction, and friction makes full sense only when analysed as part of its particular spatio-temporal context. The longer-term register of paramilitary activism in many European countries that stretched back to the late 19th century may help explain the strength of the allure of fascism there in the immediate post-WW1 period. At the same time, however, 'fascism' did not circulate without its contextual baggage – initially as a novel Italian political technology of mobilising activism, later as a strategic regime template for replacing the liberal-parliamentary system, while also effectively crushing the left. These fascist political and ideological innovations circulated freely across different contexts by virtue of modern communication and information systems, amidst an incessant stream of other bits of information; but the ways in which, and the degree to which, they came to be seen by local actors as resonant with their expectations made all the difference between attraction and engagement, on the one hand, and disinterest and lack of attention, on the other.

Context cuts in many ways then. It is the locus of ideational encounters and the unique prism that refracts them. It is also where the condensed mobilities that shaped a local past diachronically meet and interact with mobilities in the present (Merriman and Pearce, 2017). Like friction, context is tantalisingly protean: at once solid (as a record of history) and dynamic (as an agent of friction in past and present alike); and even as a record or inscription it may appear im-mobile but is actually forged through past mobilities and encounters (Osborne, 2021, 71). Particularly in the modern world of massively augmented noise and superfluid information/knowledges, context is essential for understanding the miracle of engaged contact across difference and productive friction when it actually occurs. Appreciating this diachronic-synchronic significance of the context in ideational and other mobilities may just be the most compelling argument in favour of the productive 'friction' between humanities and mobilities studies.

References

Cliff AD, Martin RL, and Ord JK (1974) Evaluating the friction of distance parameter in gravity models. *Regional studies* 8, pp. 218–86.
Cresswell T (2006) *On the move: mobility in the modern Western world.* New York and London: Routledge.
Cresswell T (2010) Towards a politics of mobility. *Environment and planning D: society and space* 28(1), pp. 17–31.
Cresswell T (2011) Mobilities II. *Progress in human geography* 36(5), pp. 645–53.
Cresswell T (2014) Friction. In: *The Routledge handbook of mobilities*, edited by Peter Adey, David Bissell, Kevin Hannam, Peter Merriman, and Mimi Sheller, pp. 107–15. London and New York: Routledge.

Cresswell T (2015) *Place: an introduction*. Chichester, Malden MA, and Oxford: John Wiley & Sons.
Draude A (2017) Translation in motion: a concept's journey towards norm diffusion studies. *Third World thematics: A TWQ Journal* 2(5), pp. 588–605.
Greenall AK and Løfaldli E (2019) Translation and adaptation as recontextualization: the case of the Snowman. *Adaptation* 12(3), pp. 240–56.
Hall MC (2008) Of time and space and other things: laws of tourism and the geographies of contemporary mobilities. In: *Tourism and mobilities: local-global connections*, edited by Peter M Burns, and Marina Novelli, pp. 15–32. Wallingford and Cambridge MA: CABI.
Handel A (2018) Distance matters: mobilities and the politics of distance. *Mobilities* 13(4), pp. 473–87.
Hannam K, Sheller M, and Urry J (2006) Editorial: mobilities, immobilities and moorings. *Mobilities* 1, pp. 1–22.
Inglis D (2014) What is worth defending in sociology today? Presentism, historical vision and the uses of sociology. *Cultural sociology* 8(1), pp. 99–118.
Kallis A (2021) The transnational co-production of interwar 'fascism': on the dynamics of ideational mobility and localization. *European History Quarterly* 51/2, pp. 189–213.
Kaufmann V (2000) *Re-thinking mobility: contemporary sociology*. Aldershot: Ashgate.
Latour B (1986) Visualization and cognition: drawing things together. In: *Knowledge and society: studies in the sociology of culture past and present*, edited by H Kuklick, pp. 1–40. London: Jai Press.
Lee J and Shin I (2022) Introduction: the humanities in the age of high mobility. *Special issue: constellation of humanities, technologies and geographies – Mobility humanities* 1(1), pp. 1–5.
Lowenhaupt Tsing A (2005) *Friction: an ethnography of global connection*. Princeton NJ: Princeton University Press.
Malkki L (1992) National geographic: the rooting of peoples and the territorialization of national identity among scholars and refugees. *Cultural anthropology* 7(1), pp. 24–44.
Merriman P and Lynne P (2017) Mobility and the humanities. *Mobilities* 12(4), pp. 493–508.
Meusburger J HP and Heffernan M (eds) (2017) *Mobilities of knowledge*. Cham: Springer International Publishing.
Osborne JF (2021) *The Syro-Anatolian city-states: an Iron Age culture*. Oxford and New York: Oxford University Press.
Pooley CG (2017) *Mobility, migration and transport*. Cham: Springer.
Pratt ML (1991) Arts of the contact zone. *Profession*, pp. 33–40.
Rabbiosi C (2022) The frictional geography of cultural heritage. Grounding the Faro Convention into urban experience in Forlì, Italy. *Social and cultural geography* 23(1), pp. 140–57.
Waters J and Leung M (2017) Trans-knowledge? Geography, mobility, and knowledge in transnational education. In: *Mobilities of knowledge*, edited by Heike Jöns, Peter Meusburger, and Michael Heffernan, pp. 269–85. Cham: Springer International Publishing.
Weyland K (2021) *Assault on democracy: communism, fascism, and authoritarianism during the interwar years*. Cambridge: Cambridge University Press.

Index

Note: Page numbers in *italics* indicate a figure and page numbers in **bold** indicate a table on the corresponding page. Page numbers followed by 'n' indicate a note.

Abrahamsson C 33
Act of Supremacy 162, 167
Acton, Lord 167, 168
Adey P 22, 33, 54, 73, 120
Adorno S 187
Africa nova 154
Agamben G 74
Aguiar M 104, 105
Aitken S 96
Akerman JR 90
Albanese G 189, 194, 195, 198n1
Alpini P 48
Altínbas N 64
Álvarez NC 26, 28, 29, 31
Ameel L 102
American silver 25, 30
Anderson B 96
Anderson G 155, 156
Anderson J 102, 110
Angiolillo A 156
Anglo-Venetian moment 159, 169; issues 159; mobility of people/ideas/legal cultures 163–6; Republic of Venice 159; Venice and England 166–71; Venice and the Kingdom of England 160–3
animations, map-mobilities 94–6
Anstey PR 139n9
Antwerp 14, 31
Appadurai A 93
Aradau C 139n11
Arens EH 45
Arnold D 40
Arrighi G 22
Arru A 63
Arvanitis N 156

Asdal K 9
avvisi 15–17

Baker J 161
Banaji J 22
Barbierato F 65
Barclay W 170
Barzazi A 176
Bateson G 74
Bauman Z 83
Bayly C 7
Beckert S 22
Beckingham D 108
Béguinot A 47, 48
Behringer W 8
Belknap G 47, 49
Bellavitis A 65, 68n4
Belligni E 169
Bellingradt D 10, 176
Belting H 96
Bemong N 108, 109
Benda J 137–8, 139n15
Benigno F 130
Benjamin W 138
Bennett J 118
Benson D 198n3
Benveniste E 138n1
Beretta M 46
Bergson H 136, 137, 138, 139n13; Anglophone reception of 137; *La pensée et le mouvant* 137; *l'évolution créatrice* 137
Bernardi T 60, 61, 62, 65
Bertilorenzi M 22, 25, 30, 33
Bertoloni Meli D 180
Bertoncin M 77, 84n1

Bertrand G 60
Biancani F 61, 62
Bissell D 54, 73, 120, 121
Blackmore R 129
Blair A 11
Blass-Simmen B 176
Bloch M 198n3
Bonato A 48
Borghart P 108, 109
Boschma RA 83
Bourzac A 192
Boym S 66
Braidotti R 52, 53
Braudel F 54, 80
Bray F 41
Bredekamp H 96
Brendecke A 17, 79
Brice J 94
Brighenti AM 80, 81
Broehl WG Jr. 24
Brokaw CJ 18n2, 18n3
Brooks C 161
Brosseau M 107, 110–11
Brown B 91, 120, 121n1
Brown R 165
Brückner M 92, 93
Brunet R 73, 80, 84n1
Brunt L 27
Bruzzi S 57, 62, 64, 67n1
Buchanan G 167, 170–1
Buono A 62
Burke P 9, 18n3
Büscher M 120

Caesar GJ 152–5
Caffiero M 61
Caglioti DL 63
Cairncross F 83
Calabi D 65
Callegari M 176
Camacho-Hübner E 89
Camilleri N 192
Camporesi P 135
Canadelli E 41, 46
Canepari E 64
Canetti E 80
Canfora L 156
Cannon E 27
Canzian D 160
Caquard S 94
Caracausi A 24, 27
Caracciolo M 103, 107, 111
Carcopino J 156

Carruthers M 11
Carry A 156
cartes de visite 46–50
cartography: filmic experiments 94; knowledge 93; space 91; thinking/methodologies, re-mobilisation of 89
Castagné N 178
Castells M 7
Catenacci C 155
Catena P 177
Cavaciocchi S 24
Cavendish Bentinck G 165
Çelik H 11
Cerutti S 55
Chamberlayne E 132
Chambers D 62
Chandler D 95
Chassignet M 156
Chaudhuri KN 30
Chicago Board of Trade 32
Chow K-W 18n3
Cipolla CM 31
Cipriano P 156
circles, within mechanics 175–7
circulations: map-mobilities 92–4; notion of 42–5
civil wars 154, 187, 189, 194; English Civil War (1642–51) 130; in Russia 189
Clancy-Smith J 60–2
Clarsen G 56, 57
Classen A 90
Cliff AD 202
Clifford J 105
Colavizza G 18n10
Cold War 30, 43
Colley L 63
Collot C 170
commodities: chain 23, 28, 32, 34; frontiers 22; mobility, actors of 28–30; synchronicity 25–8; transformation of goods 24
Concina E 179
Connolly DK 90
Conrad S 197
Consulti (Sarpi) 166
Contarini, Gasparo 165
Continental Grain Company 30
Cornell TJ 156
Cornish C 45, 47
Cosgrove D 108
Cossa, F Del 128
Costa P 68n4
Council of Pisa 160

Covid-19 pandemic 94
Cozzi G 168
Craig LA 63
Craine J 96
Cresswell T 7, 8, 44, 46, 53, 56, 73, 76, 86, 107, 120, 139n11, 180, 183, 201, 202, 204, 205
Cromwell O 171
Cunningham H 180

D'Alembert JB 139n8
Dalton C 91
Damerow P 180
Dant T 118
Da Silva JG 31
Daston L 14
David JM 156
De Ambris A 187
De Beauvoir S 53
De Dobbeleer M 108, 109
Defrance S 49
Delbourgo J 41, 42
Della Dora V 89, 90
del Monte G 175, 179–80, 183
De Martino F 156
De Mas E 159
Demoen K 108, 109
De Munck B 8, 60
de Ridder-Symoens H 175
Dervin F 136
De Temmerman K 108, 109
de Thou J-A 176
De Visiani R 48
De Vito CG 25
De Vivo F 10, 17
Dewar M 164
Dewsbury JD 112, 120
Deza E 84n1
Deza MM 84n1
Dialeti A 67n2
dictatorship: connotative/distinctive feature 151; dictatorial mobility 142; dictatorial powers, evolution of 150; dictator's authority 147; perception 153; as product movement 148; on Publius Cornelius Scipio Aemilianus 152; temporal mobility 153
Diderot D 139n8
Dieste M 63
digital cartography 89, 94–5
digital mobile mapping 90, 95
Diodati G 168
Dionysius of Halicarnassus 152

Di Pasquale F 61
distance: absolute 78; actions **76**; active/imposed **76**; gendered mobilities 63–6; handling 77; management 80; managing reciprocal distances 81; power dynamics/relational distance 83; psychological colouring of 82; psychological positional 77; psychological proximity 82; type of power **79**; types of space **77**
Divall C 121
Dodge M 88, 89, 94
Donati S 60
Donato KM 53, 54
Dong W 91
Donne, John, Jr. 163
Dora VD 43, 90
dos Reis F 92
Drake S 177
Draude A 203
Dreyfus L 24, 29
Driver F 45
Duck A 161
Duggan M 91
Dursteler E 63
Dyche T 130, 131

Easton JA 156
Edgerton D 41–2
Edney M 88, 89, 92
Edwards E 47
Eibl-Eibesfeldt I 81
Eichenberg J 189
Elden S 73
Elliott JH 26
Elton GR 164
Engels F 135
England J 165
Erünsal I 18n3
Evans A 120
Evelyn J 163

Fabbri F 193
Fabrikant S 94, 96
Fallopio G 48
Fan F 41
Favaro A 176
Febvre L 127
Federico G 27
Ferraro JM 64, 65
Ferrary JL 156
Fidotta G 95

Index   211

Fielding H 132
Figgis JN 167
Figgis N 167
Filippini NM 65
Fincham B 120
Finch J 102
Finley MI 156
Flower H 156
Flynn DO 23
Fonseca M 53
forced mobility 13, 53, 138
Foucault M 138n1
Frank M 178, 179
Franzinelli M 193
Frenken K 83
Freudenthal G 180
Frøland HO 30
Fugger JJ 12
Fuller G 121
Funkenstein A 130

Gabaccia D 53, 54
Gabaccia DR 54
Gabba E 156
Gallaud D 83
Gallo D 163, 164
Gänger S 42–5
Garberson E 11
García Guerra EM 28
Garin E 176
Garofalo L 156
Gatrell AC 84n1
Gaudin G 79
Gekker A 95
gendered mobilities: approaches 53, 66; challenging history of 53; documenting/controlling 60–3; overview of 53–5; prism 54; representing, in historical records 55–60; spaces/distances/networks 63–6
Gentile E 193, 198
geohumanities 3, 102, 112–14, 121; approaches 3, 121
Gereffi G 34
Gerlach J 91
Gerwarth R 189, 194
Giannotti D 165
Giardina A 156
Gilroy P 105
Ginzburg C 56, 139n13
Giráldez A 23
Gleason EG 165

globalization: global commodities 23–5, 117; grain market 29; knowledge 42; logistics hubs 26; wave of 22
Goeschel C 188, 199n7
Gontarski SE 137
Gramsci A 194
Grangaud I 55
Grappi G 80
Grasland C 84, 84n1
Greefs H 60
Greenall AK 203
Greenblatt S 7
Green NL 53
Green-Simms LB 105
Gregory of Nyssa 14
Grendler M 176
Griesemer JR 180
Griffin C 120
Grinberg I 24
Grogin RC 137
Guerry L 54
Guillot J 170
Gurr JM 102

Hacke D 65
Hacker R 18n4
Hahn B 41
Halegoua GR 91
Hall MC 202
Hancock AM 54, 61
Hanley W 62
Hannam K 2, 54, 73, 203
Hannerz U 65
Hannuna G 62
Harley JB 89, 96
Harrison P 112
Harrower M 94, 96
Hartfield ME 156
Hartig O 12, 13
Harvey D 75, 77, 83
Harzig C 56, 60
Haupt HG 198n3
Hawkins H 112, 113
Heffernan M 44, 46, 47
Heidegger M 118
Helbing MO 177
Henninger-Voss M 178
Herzfeld M 54
Herzog T 62
Heyman J 180
Hilaire-Peréz L 41
Hill C 165
Hill LD 24

Hinard F 154, 156
Hind S 90, 95
Hirschman AO 139n10
Hjorth L 91
Hobbes T 131, 139n11
Hoerder D 56, 60
Hoffman KJ 24
Holdaway J 54
Holloway J 108
Holloway SK 25
Hones S 103, 110
Hooker R 168
Hopkins TK 34
Horne J 189
Howard D 179
Howell P 108
Huang H 91
Hulme A 93
humanities: contribution, to mobility studies 105; creative turn in geography 113; mobilities studies 3; sedentarist bias 201
human mobility 55, 60, 62
Hurlet 156
Hyman MD 41

Iacovetta F 54
immutable mobiles 9, 17, 46, 92, 117, 203
Infelise M 15, 18n10, 18n11, 18n12
Inglis D 201
Ingold T 107, 111
Ingulstad M 30
Irigoin J 176

Jacob C 90
James I (King of England) 166–9
Jameson F 90
Janni P 77, 91
Jayaram K 180
Jehne M 156
Jerusalem 63, 90
Jones O 120, 121n1
Jöns H 44, 46, 47
Jordan A 198n3
Jordanova L 46
Jordheim H 9
Juhlin O 120, 121n1

Kallis A 3, 201, 206
Kaplan F 18n10
Kapoor I 84
Keaveney A 156
Keblusek M 178

Keller AG 178
Kelley DR 161
Kellner S 12
Kelly M 97
Keunen B 108, 109
Kilcher A 43
Kitchin R 89, 95
Kneale J 108
knowledge: discovery processes 183; mobility of 41; politics of 78; transformation 40; transmission 175
Kocka J 198n3
Kõiv M 155
Krajewski M 11
Krämer F 11
Kristeva J 136

Laffi U 156
Lagendijk A 78, 81
Laird WR 177
Lambeck P 14
Lambert D 121
Lammes S 92, 95
Lanaro P 65
Lapini W 156
Larsen J 64, 73
Larsson Heidenblad D 40, 44
late republican dictatorship: end of dictatorship 155; mobility as result 154–5; mobility in judgments 153; mobility in 'models' 152–3; mobility in purpose 153; spatial mobility 154; temporal mobility 153–4
Latham A 107, 109
Latour B 9, 10, 17, 44, 89, 92, 93, 117, 203
Laurier E 91, 120, 121n1
Law J 117
Lawson J 108
Ledeen MA 199n6
Lee B 93
Leech J 134
Lee J 201
Leigh P 134, 135
Leonardi N 47
Leung M 204
Levinson M 25, 79
Lewis DM 156
Liao H 91
Liberman N 78
Licinio-Sextian laws 151
Lipsius J 176
LiPuma E 93

214 *Index*

literary geography 102, 105, 107, 110, 113
literary mobilities 102, 103–5
Lo Basso L 26
Lobo-Guerrero L 92
Locke J 129, 139
Løfaldli E 203
Long PO 179
Lo Presti L 92, 94, 95, 97
Lorentzen A 78, 81
Lorimer H 119, 120, 121n1
Lourdusamy JB 41
Lowenhaupt Tsing A 204
Ludmilla J 46
Luibhéid E 61
Lupton D 118
Luraghi N 155
Lussault M 73–5
Lynne P 207
Lyons G 73

Machiavelli N 129, 138n7
Maenius C 151
Maitland FW 162, 164, 167
Malcolm N 169
Malenbaum W 27
Malkki L 201
Manalansan M 54
Mantova Benavides M 164
map-mobilities 92, 117; animations 94–6; circulations 92–4; navigations 89–91; non-interactive two-dimensional map 94; overview of 88–9; tracing 94
mapping 94, 96–7, 107, 204; in artistic and humanistic fields 97; cognitive 90; crisis-mapping 95; digital 89–90, 95; digital mobile 90; ego-centric 91; map-makers 94; map-mobilities 89–91; mobile 97; mobile mapping practices 88, 91; non-Western maps 89; pre-cartographic forms of 90; real-time 95; of time-in-space 89
Maréchaux B 31
Marichal C 23
Markham B 96
Markovits C 43
Marsilio C 26
Martin AS 32
Martini M 54
Martin RL 202
Massumi B 180
Mathieson C 104, 105, 121
Mattern S 95

Mattirolo O 47
Mayer T 164
May J 84n3
Mazzacane A 161
Mazzamauro A 24
Mazzarino S 156
Mazzi G 177
Mazzotta MC 156
McAvinchey C 97
McCormack D 107, 109
McDermott J 9, 18n3
McGregor M 91
McGuinness M 120
McLaughlin D 110
McLaughlin P 180
McNamara K 107, 109
McNeill D 107, 109
McPherson D 165
mechanics: circles 175–7; and mobility 179–84
Meier C 156
Meloni G 156
Merriman P 1, 3, 54, 73, 91, 103–5, 112, 113, 117, 118, 120, 121, 136, 207
Meusburger P 44, 46, 47
Michael M 118
mid-republican Rome 147; dictatorial action 150–1; dictatorship, connotative feature of 151–2; functions/duties 149–50; models/readings 148–9; onomastic mobility 147; quantitative mobility 149; time/space 150
Millan M 187, 188, 194, 198n1, 198n4
Milone F 27
Milton JR 139
Mioche P 33
Mitchell L 155
Mol A 33, 117
Moleti G 177
Molino P 7, 10, 16, 17, 18n2, 18n9
Montgomery SL 43
Moore JW 22
Morelon C 196
More T 162
Morgan D 30
Morgan K 83
Morokvasic M 53
Morrison R 164
Morton C 47
Mosse GL 189
Moxham N 18n10
Mukherjee S 54

Munich's Ducal Library 12
Muriel García N 63
Murray L 120
Mussolini B 188, 193, 195, 197

Napolitani PD 178, 179
narrative mobilities 102; dynamic provocations 103–5; geographies in motion 102–3; geohumanities 112–14; literary mobilities 103–5; mobile chronotopes, narrative constellations of 108–10; mobile "geocritical" approach 106–12; moving with(in) narratives 110–12
Nash C 119
Natale S 47
navigations: digital 91; experiential dimension 91; mobile devices 91; visual regime of 90
Nelles P 8, 10, 176
Nesbitt M 45
new mobilities paradigm 2, 91, 103, 104, 201
Nicetas Georgius see Gregory of Nyssa
Nicolet C 156
Niess RJ 139n14
Nilsson HA 40, 44
Nirenberg D 61
Noble A 120, 121n1
Nobtaro I 27
Noldus BV 178
Nollet JA 129
non-representational methods 119, 120, 121
Nordberg K 40, 44
North R 131
November V 89
Nuovo A 176

Oakley F 167
Oliver J 93
Ongaro G 160
Ord JK 202
Ortelius A 14
Osborne JF 207
Östling J 40, 44
Overell MA 164

Panciera W 176
Papa C 192
Pase A 77, 84n1, 94
Passi G 55, 57
Patel R 22

Pearce L 91, 102–5, 108, 109, 113, 117, 121, 136
Peltonen M 165
Pereira S 53
Perkins C 89, 92, 95
Perry M 120, 121n1
Pessar P 54
Peterle G 102, 108
Petrina A 163
Petrolini C 11
Philo P 151
Phizacklea A 53
photography 49–50, 57–8, 94; commercial 57–8; reproduction tool 48; "social use" of 47
Pica D 120, 121n1
Piccolomini A 176–7
pictures, mobility of 45–50
Pierce L 1
Pigafetta F 177–83, *181*, *182*
Pin C 169, 171
Pink S 91
Piovan F 160, 176
Pirie GH 84n1
Plakotos G 67n2
Platun J 97
Plebani T 65
political violence 188, 189, 193; armed civilians, in pre-1914 Europe 190–3; historiography 188; Italy, becoming model 193–5; post-war Europe 189; practices and political cultures 190; synchronicity/imitation of 188
Pomeranz K 27
Pompermaier M 60
Pompey G 152, 155
Poni C 24, 27
Pontedera G 48
Poole D 92
Pooley CG 202
post-colonial studies 40, 46, 105
post-war crisis 189
Pouchepadass, Jacques 43
Pratt ML 203
Prieto E 106, 107
Prior A 92
Pullan B 62

Quiroga A 188

Rabbiosi C 204
Raffestin C 75, 78, 80, 81
Raj K 40–4

Rallet A 83
Ramella F 63
Randeria S 197
Rankin W 89
Ravenstein EG 63
Raymond J 17, 18n10
Reddleman C 91
Red Sea 63–4
Renn J 40, 41, 180
Revel J 7
Rey A 130
Rheinberger HJ 183
Ribeiro A 29
Rickard J 167
Riello G 23
Rippa Bonati M 160
Roberts L 40, 41, 42, 45
Rockefeller SA 45
Rodríguez-Pose A 81
Romano A 8, 41
Rose M 112
Rose N 118
Rose PL 177
Rose PR 177
Rossetto T 88, 91, 94, 96, 97
Rossi P 178
Rovida E 176
Rowbotham S 61
Rundle D 163

Saccardo PA 46–9
Sacchi Landriani M 25
Safier, Neil 43
Said E 105
Salaris C 199n5
Salazar NB 180
Salman J 10, 176
Salmela M 102
Salmerón A 128
Saluppo A 187
Salzberg R 8
Sancisi-Weerdenburg H 156
Sandmo E 40, 44
Santangelo F 156
Santos J 24
Sapir I 11
Saraiva T 41
Sarasin P 43
Sargentson C 29
Sarnelli T 66, 67
Sarpi P 159, 165, 166, 168–71
Saunders A 102, 110
Saunier P-Y 198n3
Savio A 176, 178, 184n1

Savorgnan G 179
Scarabello G 64
Schäfer D 38, 43
Schaffer S 41, 42
Schettini L 61
Schieder W 199n7
Schlögl R 8, 9
Schmitt C 74
Schmitt CB 177
Schobesberger N 15
Schröder T 17
Schulze M 43
Schwartz R 91
Schwinges RC 175
Scott JC 76, 83
Scott JW 53
Secord JA 39, 40
sedentarist bias 201
Segal Z 94
Serrano Hernández ST 28
Sezer Y 18n3
Sgarbi M 179
Sharpe K 161
Sharpe P 54, 60
Sheller M 2, 7, 25, 38, 39, 54, 73, 103, 104, 106, 109, 118, 120, 180, 203
Sheringham O 97
Shin I 201
Shoemaker R 132, 139n12
Siebenhüner K 63
Simandan D 78, 84n1
Sinke SM 61
Sitran Rea L 176
Sivasundaram S 40, 41
Slauter W 15
Smith PH 39, 43, 179
social mobility 53, 82, 144, 154
social power dynamics: distances, at stake 78–83; distances, on move 75–7; handling distances 77–8; overview of 73–5
Soja EW 80
Sorbera L 57
Sordi M 156
Sormani P 120, 121n1
Sowerby TA 164
Spadaro B 66
Speake J 91
Spethmann A 12
Spiers EM 121
Spinney J 120
Spooner FC 31
Stabili MR 54
Starkey T 164

Star SL 180
Stehr N 46
Strebel I 120, 121n1
Stuckey JA 28
Suárez Espinosa M 26
Subrahmanyam S 43
Sulla LC 152
Swan L 120, 121n1

Tally RT 89
Tally RT Jr 89, 102, 106
Tandeter E 28
Taraud C 59
Taylor A 11
Taylor AS 120, 121n1
Thatcher J 91
Thébaud F 54
Thiene G 160
Thompson EP 132, 134
Thrift N 84n3, 118–20
Timmerman C 53
Tirabassi M 54
Tomas N 56
Topik S 27
Torre A 83
Tosi A 46
Trompette P 180
Trope Y 78
Tsing, AL 204, 205
Tucker JE 65
tyrannical mobility 142; *Athenaion politeia* 146; case of 142; dictatorial mobility 142; explicit 145; historical phenomenon 142–4; late republican dictatorship *see* late republican dictatorship; mid-republican *see* mid-republican Rome; model/practice of power 144; Solonian text 145
tyranny: archaic tyrannies 145; elective tyrants 148

Ulianich B 170
Üngör UÜ 198n2
urban mobility 63–4, 66, 74
Urry J 2, 7, 46, 54, 83, 104, 106, 109, 118, 120, 180, 203
Uteng TP 53, 56

Valditara G 156
Valenzuela Márquez J 79
Valsecchi C 160
Van Dyck M 176
Van Eck C 96
Van Leeuwen J 177

Van Netten D 90
Vannieuwenhuyze B 94
Vannini P 119
Van Praag L 53
Venice 10, 15, 26, 31, 54, 61, 64–5, 78, 159, 176–8; divine right of kings 166–71; divine right of the Republic 166–71; legal tradition of *ius commune* 160–3; mobility of people, ideas and legal cultures 163–6; Venetian magistracy 56; Venetian territories 206
Vergunst J 120
Verhoeff N 90
Vettor F 177
Viggiano 161
Vila Vilar E 29
Vinck D 180

Wallerstein I 22, 34
Wallet F 83
Walsby M 10
Warde W 130
Waters J 204
Watts L 120, 121n1
Weilenmann A 120, 121n1
Weppelmann S 176
Westphal B 106–8
Weyland K 206
Widmannstetter JA 12
Wigen K 95
Williams JC 24
Wilmott C 91, 95
Wilson MB 156
Wilson MW 95, 96
Winter A 60
Winterer C 95
Witchger K 120
Woller H 198n7
Woolfson J 163
Wootton D 168
Wotton H 165, 168
Wylie J 112

Yavetz Z 156
Yun-Casalilla B 26

Zaggia S 177
Zakharova L 41
Zarzycka M 93, 101
Zecchini G 156
Zedelmaier H 12
Zemon Davis N 56
Zenobi L 7, 8, 18n1
Zucca Micheletto B 53, 54

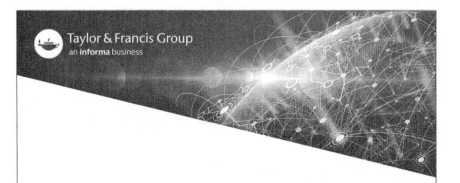